Connected Mathematics™

Samples and Populations

Data and Statistics

Teacher's Guide

Glenda Lappan
James T. Fey
William M. Fitzgerald
Susan N. Friel
Elizabeth Difanis Phillips

PEARSON
Prentice Hall

Needham, Massachusetts
Upper Saddle River, New Jersey

Connected Mathematics™ was developed at Michigan State University with financial support from the Michigan State University Office of the Provost, Computing and Technology, and the College of Natural Science.

This material is based upon work supported by the National Science Foundation under Grant No. MDR 9150217.

This project was supported, in part, by the
National Science Foundation
Opinions expressed are those of the authors
and not necessarily those of the Foundation

The Michigan State University authors and administration have agreed that all MSU royalties arising from this publication will be devoted to purposes supported by the Department of Mathematics and the MSU Mathematics Education Enrichment Fund.

Photo Acknowledgements: 5 © Joseph Nettis/Photo Researchers, Inc.; 11 © Bob Daemmrich/Stock, Boston; 20 © Judy Gelles/Stock, Boston; 22 (both photos) Michael Dwyer/Stock, Boston; 24 © Tony Duffy/Allsport; 33 © Rick Lee/ Superstock; 45 © Doris DeWitt/Tony Stone Images; 49 © UPI/Corbis-Bettmann; 50 © Stuart Struever/Tony Stone Images; 56 © Sue Ogrocki/Reuters/Corbis-Bettmann; 65 © D. LaBelle/The Image Works

Many of the designations used by manufacturers to distinguish their products are claimed as trademarks. Where those designations appear in this book, and the publisher was aware of a trademark claim, the designations have been printed in initial caps or all caps.

PEARSON
Prentice
Hall

ISBN 0-13-180805-2
3 4 5 6 7 8 9 10   07 06 05 04

The Connected Mathematics Project Staff

Project Directors

James T. Fey
University of Maryland

William M. Fitzgerald
Michigan State University

Susan N. Friel
University of North Carolina at Chapel Hill

Glenda Lappan
Michigan State University

Elizabeth Difanis Phillips
Michigan State University

Project Manager

Kathy Burgis
Michigan State University

Technical Coordinator

Judith Martus Miller
Michigan State University

Collaborating Teachers/Writers

Mary K. Bouck
Portland, Michigan

Jacqueline Stewart
Okemos, Michigan

Curriculum Development Consultants

David Ben-Chaim
Weizmann Institute

Alex Friedlander
Weizmann Institute

Eleanor Geiger
University of Maryland

Jane Miller
University of Maryland

Jane Mitchell
University of North Carolina at Chapel Hill

Anthony D. Rickard
Alma College

Evaluation Team

Mark Hoover
Michigan State University

Diane V. Lambdin
Indiana University

Sandra K. Wilcox
Michigan State University

Judith S. Zawojewski
National-Louis University

Graduate Assistants

Scott J. Baldridge
Michigan State University

Angie S. Eshelman
Michigan State University

M. Faaiz Gierdien
Michigan State University

Jane M. Keiser
Indiana University

Angela S. Krebs
Michigan State University

James M. Larson
Michigan State University

Ronald Preston
Indiana University

Tat Ming Sze
Michigan State University

Sarah Theule-Lubienski
Michigan State University

Jeffrey J. Wanko
Michigan State University

Field Test Production Team

Katherine Oesterle
Michigan State University

Stacey L. Otto
University of North Carolina at Chapel Hill

Teacher/Assessment Team

Kathy Booth
Waverly, Michigan

Anita Clark
Marshall, Michigan

Julie Faulkner
Traverse City, Michigan

Theodore Gardella
Bloomfield Hills, Michigan

Yvonne Grant
Portland, Michigan

Linda R. Lobue
Vista, California

Suzanne McGrath
Chula Vista, California

Nancy McIntyre
Troy, Michigan

Mary Beth Schmitt
Traverse City, Michigan

Linda Walker
Tallahassee, Florida

Software Developer

Richard Burgis
East Lansing, Michigan

Development Center Directors

Nicholas Branca
San Diego State University

Dianne Briars
Pittsburgh Public Schools

Frances R. Curcio
New York University

Perry Lanier
Michigan State University

J. Michael Shaughnessy
Portland State University

Charles Vonder Embse
Central Michigan University

Field Test Coordinators

Michelle Bohan
Queens, New York

Melanie Branca
San Diego, California

Alecia Devantier
Shepherd, Michigan

Jenny Jorgensen
Flint, Michigan

Sandra Kralovec
Portland, Oregon

Sonia Marsalis
Flint, Michigan

William Schaeffer
Pittsburgh, Pennsylvania

Karma Vince
Toledo, Ohio

Virginia Wolf
Pittsburgh, Pennsylvania

Shirel Yaloz
Queens, New York

Student Assistants

Laura Hammond
David Roche
Courtney Stoner
Jovan Trpovski
Julie Valicenti
Michigan State University

Patricia Wagner
Holmes Middle School

Greg Williams
Gundry Elementary School

Lansing

Susan Bissonette
Waverly Middle School

Kathy Booth
Waverly East Intermediate School

Carole Campbell
Waverly East Intermediate School

Gary Gillespie
Waverly East Intermediate School

Denise Kehren
Waverly Middle School

Virginia Larson
Waverly East Intermediate School

Kelly Martin
Waverly Middle School

Laurie Metevier
Waverly East Intermediate School

Craig Paksi
Waverly East Intermediate School

Tony Pecoraro
Waverly Middle School

Helene Rewa
Waverly East Intermediate School

Arnold Stiefel
Waverly Middle School

Portland

Bill Carlton
Portland Middle School

Kathy Dole
Portland Middle School

Debby Flate
Portland Middle School

Yvonne Grant
Portland Middle School

Terry Keusch
Portland Middle School

John Manzini
Portland Middle School

Mary Parker
Portland Middle School

Scott Sandborn
Portland Middle School

Shepherd

Steve Brant
Shepherd Middle School

Marty Brock
Shepherd Middle School

Cathy Church
Shepherd Middle School

Ginny Crandall
Shepherd Middle School

Craig Ericksen
Shepherd Middle School

Natalie Hackney
Shepherd Middle School

Bill Hamilton
Shepherd Middle School

Julie Salisbury
Shepherd Middle School

Sturgis

Sandra Allen
Eastwood Elementary School

Margaret Baker
Eastwood Elementary School

Steven Baker
Eastwood Elementary School

Keith Barnes
Sturgis Middle School

Wilodean Beckwith
Eastwood Elementary School

Darcy Bird
Eastwood Elementary School

Bill Dickey
Sturgis Middle School

Ellen Eisele
Sturgis Middle School

James Hoelscher
Sturgis Middle School

Richard Nolan
Sturgis Middle School

J. Hunter Raiford
Sturgis Middle School

Cindy Sprowl
Eastwood Elementary School

Leslie Stewart
Eastwood Elementary School

Connie Sutton
Eastwood Elementary School

Traverse City

Maureen Bauer
Interlochen Elementary School

Ivanka Berskshire
East Junior High School

Sarah Boehm
Courtade Elementary School

Marilyn Conklin
Interlochen Elementary School

Nancy Crandall
Blair Elementary School

Fran Cullen
Courtade Elementary School

Eric Dreier
Old Mission Elementary School

Lisa Dzierwa
Cherry Knoll Elementary School

Ray Fouch
West Junior High School

Ed Hargis
Willow Hill Elementary School

Richard Henry
West Junior High School

Dessie Hughes
Cherry Knoll Elementary School

Ruthanne Kladder
Oak Park Elementary School

Bonnie Knapp
West Junior High School

Sue Laisure
Sabin Elementary School

Stan Malaski
Oak Park Elementary School

Jody Meyers
Sabin Elementary School

Marsha Myles
East Junior High School

Mary Beth O'Neil
Traverse Heights Elementary School

Jan Palkowski
East Junior High School

Karen Richardson
Old Mission Elementary School

Kristin Sak
Bertha Vos Elementary School

Mary Beth Schmitt
East Junior High School

Mike Schrotenboer
Norris Elementary School

Gail Smith
Willow Hill Elementary School

Karrie Tufts
Eastern Elementary School

Mike Wilson
East Junior High School

Tom Wilson
West Junior High School

Minnesota

Minneapolis

Betsy Ford
Northeast Middle School

New York

East Elmhurst

Allison Clark
Louis Armstrong Middle School

Dorothy Hershey
Louis Armstrong Middle School

J. Lewis McNeece
Louis Armstrong Middle School

Rossana Perez
Louis Armstrong Middle School

Merna Porter
Louis Armstrong Middle School

Marie Turini
Louis Armstrong Middle School

North Carolina

Durham

Everly Broadway
Durham Public Schools

Thomas Carson
Duke School for Children

Mary Hebrank
Duke School for Children

Bill O'Connor
Duke School for Children

Ruth Pershing
Duke School for Children

Peter Reichert
Duke School for Children

Elizabeth City

Rita Banks
Elizabeth City Middle School

Beth Chaundry
Elizabeth City Middle School

Amy Cuthbertson
Elizabeth City Middle School

Deni Dennison
Elizabeth City Middle School

Jean Gray
Elizabeth City Middle School

John McMenamin
Elizabeth City Middle School

Nicollette Nixon
Elizabeth City Middle School

Malinda Norfleet
Elizabeth City Middle School

Joyce O'Neal
Elizabeth City Middle School

Clevie Sawyer
Elizabeth City Middle School

Juanita Shannon
Elizabeth City Middle School

Terry Thorne
Elizabeth City Middle School

Rebecca Wardour
Elizabeth City Middle School

Leora Winslow
Elizabeth City Middle School

Franklinton

Susan Haywood
Franklinton Elementary School

Clyde Melton
Franklinton Elementary School

Louisburg

Lisa Anderson
Terrell Lane Middle School

Jackie Frazier
Terrell Lane Middle School

Pam Harris
Terrell Lane Middle School

Ohio

Toledo

Bonnie Bias
Hawkins Elementary School

Marsha Jackish
Hawkins Elementary School

Lee Jagodzinski
DeVeaux Junior High School

Norma J. King
Old Orchard Elementary School

Margaret McCready
Old Orchard Elementary School

Carmella Morton
DeVeaux Junior High School

Karen C. Rohrs
Hawkins Elementary School

Marie Sahloff
DeVeaux Junior High School

L. Michael Vince
McTigue Junior High School

Brenda D. Watkins
Old Orchard Elementary School

Oregon

Canby

Sandra Kralovec
Ackerman Middle School

Portland

Roberta Cohen
Catlin Gabel School

David Ellenberg
Catlin Gabel School

Sara Normington
Catlin Gabel School

Karen Scholte-Arce
Catlin Gabel School

West Linn

Marge Burack
Wood Middle School

Tracy Wygant
Athey Creek Middle School

Pennsylvania

Pittsburgh

Sheryl Adams
Reizenstein Middle School

Sue Barie
Frick International Studies Academy

Suzie Berry
Frick International Studies Academy

Richard Delgrosso
Frick International Studies Academy

Janet Falkowski
Frick International Studies Academy

Joanne George
Reizenstein Middle School

Harriet Hopper
Reizenstein Middle School

Chuck Jessen
Reizenstein Middle School

Ken Labuskes
Reizenstein Middle School

Barbara Lewis
Reizenstein Middle School

Sharon Mihalich
Reizenstein Middle School

Marianne O'Connor
Frick International Studies Academy

Mark Sammartino
Reizenstein Middle School

Washington

Seattle

Chris Johnson
University Preparatory Academy

Rick Purn
University Preparatory Academy

Contents

Probability is a tool for understanding sampling issues in statistics; statistics is a tool for representing and analyzing data that may then be used to draw conclusions about a population. *Samples and Populations* helps students to make connections between probability and statistics.

This unit offers a review of statistics concepts introduced in grade 6 and reinforced in grade 7. Students begin with an introduction to box-and-whiskers plots as a tool for comparing data sets. In the remaining investigations, students explore what samples are and how they are related to populations, ways to select samples, and the use of random samples. Issues of representativeness and bias in data analysis are also addressed.

Statistics is the science that relies on data to answer questions. A statistical investigation typically encompasses four interrelated components[*]:

- *Posing the question* Formulating the key questions to explore and identifying what data to collect in order to address the questions

- *Collecting the data* Deciding how to collect the data as well as collecting the data

- *Analyzing the data* Organizing, representing, summarizing, and describing the data and looking for patterns in the variation of the data

- *Interpreting the results* Predicting, comparing, and identifying relationships and using the results from the analyses to make decisions about the original questions

Students' recognition and use of the process of statistical investigation is important in working with statistics. We continually want to focus their attention on the *process* even as we work with them to develop strategies that are *part* of the process, such as computing measures of center or spread and making graphs.

[*] Graham, A. *Statistical Investigations in the Secondary School.* Cambridge: Cambridge University Press, 1987.

The Mathematics in Samples and Populations

An initial step in the analysis phase of a statistical investigation is to make one or more representations of the data. In doing so, decisions must be made about whether the data will be left ungrouped (as raw data) or grouped in some way (through data reduction). The graphs that students have encountered in previous Connected Mathematics units reflect various levels of data reduction.

Data Representations

Line plots and bar graphs provide representations of tallied data. The *x*-axis displays the values in the data. In bar graphs, the *y*-axis shows the frequency of occurrence, or count, for each data value; these are indicated by the heights of the bars. In line plots, the number of marks above a data value indicates its frequency.

The line plot and the bar graph below represent the same data set.

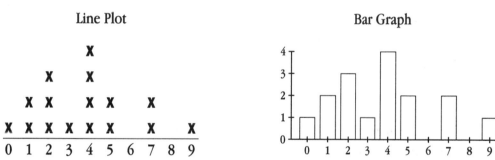

In stem-and-leaf plots (stem plots) and histograms, data are grouped in intervals. In stem plots, the individual data values may still be identified from the graph. Histograms are used to display continuous data (for example, measurements such as height and weight or ratings based on a continuous scale); each bar represents an interval of values. The height of a bar indicates the frequency of values in that interval. Once data are graphed using a histogram, it is not possible to identify individual data items.

The stem plot and the histogram below represent the same data set.

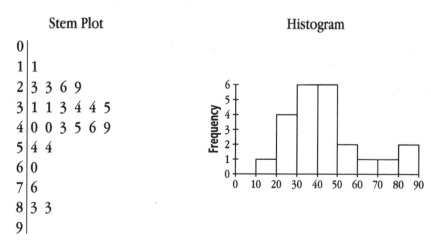

In box-and-whiskers plots (box plots), data are grouped by first being reduced to a five-number summary, consisting of the minimum value, the lower quartile, the median, the upper quartile, and the maximum value. The shape of a box plot and the five-number summary provide benchmarks for dividing the data into quartiles. It is not possible to identify individual data items from a box plot; however, it is easy to see the spread of the data and to identify the median, as it is one of the five summary numbers. In this unit, box plots are used extensively to compare sets of data.

Box Plot

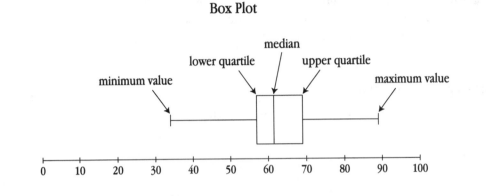

Sampling

The essential idea behind sampling is to gain information about the whole by analyzing only a part of it. A *census* is a sample that consists of the entire population; generally, conducting a census is not possible or reasonable because of such factors as cost and the size of the population. Thus, a primary issue in sampling is choosing a *representative* sample. This includes identifying a sensible general strategy for doing so or at least identifying the conditions that a good sample should meet to be as representative of the population as possible without concern about the effects of variability or size.

One way to ensure representativeness is to select *random* samples. The essential feature of a random sample is that every member of the population has an equally likely chance of being chosen to be part of the sample.

Attention must be given to the various kinds of bias that can enter from faulty sampling plans and to the issue of asking good questions of a chosen sample. Two further points are important. First, even with a good sampling strategy, descriptive statistics such as means and medians of the samples will vary in value. Second, the accuracy of a sample statistic improves with the size of the sample.

Connected Mathematics™ was developed with the belief that calculators should always be available and that students should decide when to use them. Students will need access to graphing calculators for most of their work in this unit. It's best if their calculators have the capacity to display a function as a table and that an overhead display model of their calculator is available.

Samples and Populations involves extensive use of box-and-whiskers plots and histograms, as well as calculations of means and five-number summaries of data sets. Graphing calculators with statistics capabilities handle these operations with varying degrees of sophistication. Use of computer software for statistics and graphs is encouraged but optional.

Several graphing calculators perform statistical operations. If you are deciding which calculators to purchase, you will want to consider each model's capabilities. For example, some graphing calculators (such as the TI-83) show box plots with and without outliers; others (such as the TI-80 and TI-82) show them only without outliers. Whatever graphing calculator students use, you will want to be aware of any modifications you may need to make to help students complete the work in this unit. For example, if students' calculators do not show box plots with outliers, you will need to make sure they can identify outliers using the data in the box plots.

The instructions below are written for the TI-80 graphing calculator. If your students use a different calculator, consult the manual for instructions on these procedures.

Entering Data

Data are entered into the calculator as lists. The TI-80 accepts up to 99 data values in each of six lists, L1 through L6. To enter lists of data, press STAT and the screen will display something similar to that shown below left. Press ENTER to select the Edit mode, and you will see two of the six lists, L1 and L2. Using the arrow keys, you can move to the other lists. To enter data, enter one value per line; the location in which you are currently entering is shown at the bottom of the screen. Once you enter data in L1, use the arrow keys to move to the top of L2. The screen shown below right shows the beginning of two lists of data from Investigation 1 in this unit: L1 contains the quality ratings for natural brands of peanut butter, and L2 contains the quality ratings for regular brands of peanut butter.

```
EDIT CALC
1:EDIT...
2:SORTA(
3:SORTD(
4:CLRLIST
```

L1	L2
71	76
69	60
60	54
60	43
57	40
52	35
L1(1)=71	

To clear a list of all data values, highlight the name of the list (such as L1), press CLEAR, and then press ENTER.

Before making any statistics graphs with the data you have entered into lists, make sure there are no equations in the Y= list (press Y= to access the list); any equations in this list would be graphed along with the plotted data.

Making a Box-and-Whiskers Plot

To make a box plot of the data you have entered, press 2nd Y= to display the STAT PLOT menu, which looks like the screen shown below left. Notice that there are several plots and that you can see which are on and which are off to identify those that are currently active. Make sure all plots are off; if they are not, choose 4 PLOTSOFF. Press ENTER to select PLOT1, which looks like the screen shown below right.

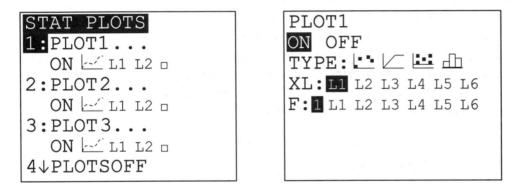

Use the arrow keys and ENTER to move around in the screen and highlight elements as shown above. First, position the cursor over ON and press ENTER. Now you can choose a graph from four choices: scatter plot, line graph, box plot, and histogram. Move the cursor to the box plot and press ENTER. Now you must indicate in which list the data are; move the cursor to L1 and press ENTER.

You now need to set the values for the window that will display the box plot. Press WINDOW, which will display a screen similar to that shown below left. In the box plot shown below right, the values range from 11 to 89; a good setting for the *x*-axis is from 0 to 100 with a scale of 10; enter these values into XMIN, XMAX, and XSCL. There is no frequency in box plots; however, a small scale must be indicated for the *y*-axis. A simple choice is 0 to 1 with a scale of 1; enter these values into YMIN, YMAX, and YSCL. To display the box plot, press GRAPH.

```
WINDOW
  XMIN=0
  XMAX=100
  XSCL=10
  YMIN=0
  YMAX=1
  YSCL=1
```

To display the box plot in L2 as well, display the STAT PLOT menu, activate PLOT 2, select box plot, and select L2. Now two plots are activated; when you press GRAPH, you will see both box plots (see the screen below left). Adjust the window settings if necessary.

Note that box plots displayed on a calculator do not show a number line marked with numbers but only with tick marks, so students need a clear understanding of what is being displayed. The TI-80 does not display outliers, though other graphing calculators (such as the TI-83) and statistics software programs (such as Statistics Workshop) will.

Below are box plots of the same data set made with the TI-80 and Statistics Workshop.

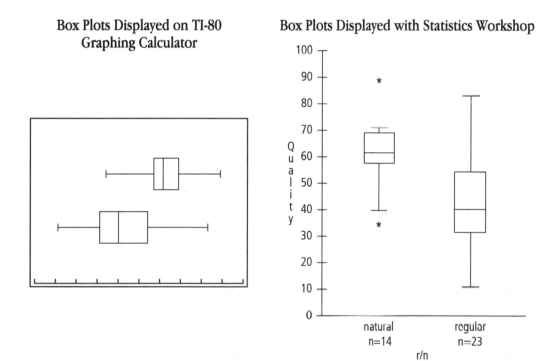

Box Plots Displayed on TI-80 Graphing Calculator

Box Plots Displayed with Statistics Workshop

Displaying the Summary Statistics from a Box Plot

Use the calculator's trace function to identify the five summary numbers on a displayed box plot. Press ⎡TRACE⎤, and the cursor will blink somewhere on the box plot. Use the right and left arrow keys to move the cursor back and forth across the box plot; the values of the five-number summary will be displayed in the lower-left corner of the screen. If a second box plot is displayed, move to it by using the up and down arrow keys.

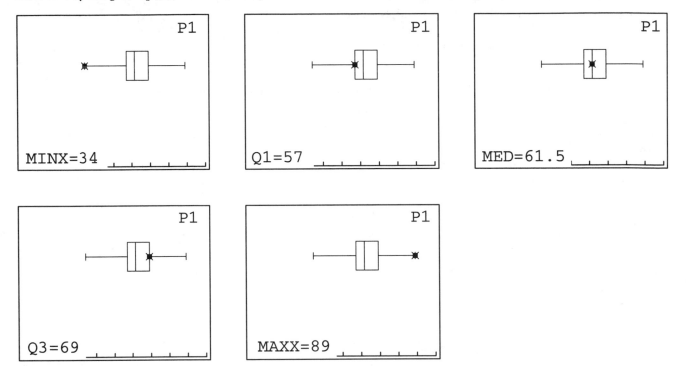

Making a Scatter Plot

Data given as pairs of points can be entered into the calculator and plotted. For example, the screen below shows the beginning of two lists of data from Investigation 1: L1 contains the quality ratings for natural brands of peanut butter, and L2 contains the price per serving for these same brands. This gives two lists of the paired (quality rating, price per serving) data points for the natural brands of peanut butter.

L1	L2
71	27
69	32
60	26
60	26
57	26
52	21

L1(1)=71

To make a scatter plot of the data you have entered, use the commands in the STAT PLOT menu. Display the STAT PLOT menu, which looks like the screen shown below left, by pressing 2nd Y=. Select a plot to use; for example, press ENTER to select PLOT1, which looks like the screen shown below right.

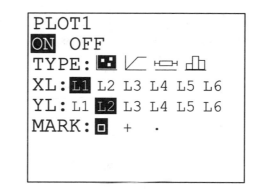

Use the arrow keys and ENTER to move around in the screen and highlight elements as shown above. First, position the cursor over ON and press ENTER. Now you can choose a graph from four choices: scatter plot, line graph, box plot, and histogram. Move the cursor to the scatter plot and press ENTER. Now you must indicate in which lists the data are located. Move the cursor to L1 for the data to be displayed on the x-axis and to L2 for the data to be displayed on the y-axis; press ENTER after each choice. Select the symbol to be used to mark points on the scatter plot.

You now need to set the values for the window that will display the scatter plot. Press WINDOW, which will display a screen similar to that shown below left. In the scatter plot shown below right, the values along the x-axis range from 11 to 89; a good setting for the x-axis is from 0 to 100 with a scale of 10. Enter these values into XMIN, XMAX, and XSCL. The values along the y-axis range from 9 to 34; a good setting for the y-axis is from 0 to 40 with a scale of 10.

Enter these values into YMIN, YMAX, and YSCL. To display the scatter plot, press GRAPH.

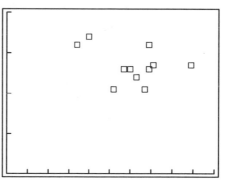

To create a scatter plot that reflects two sets of data on the same graph, enter the paired data points into two sets of lists. For example, the (quality rating, price per serving) data points for the natural brands of peanut butter can be entered into L1 and L2, and the (quality rating, price per serving) data points for the regular brands of peanut butter can be entered into L3 and L4.

Choose PLOT1 to plot the data points in L1 and L2, and select a symbol. Choose PLOT2 and a different symbol to plot the data points in L3 and L4. Press GRAPH, and the scatter plot display will show plotted points using two symbols.

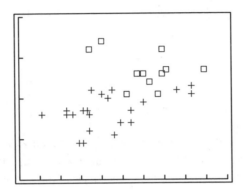

To display more than one type of statistics plot for the same entered data, designate them using different plot numbers in the STAT PLOT menu, from PLOT1 to PLOT3. Shown below is a box plot and a scatter plot of the same data.

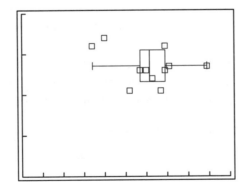

Making a Histogram

To make a histogram of the data you have entered, display the STAT PLOT menu, which looks like the screen shown below left, by pressing 2nd Y=. Make sure all plots are off; if they are not, choose 4 PLOTSOFF. Select a plot to use; for example, press ENTER to select PLOT1, which looks like the screen shown below right.

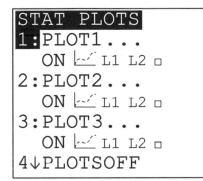

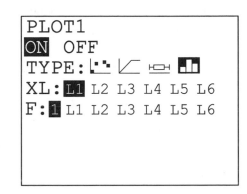

Use the arrow keys and ENTER to move around in the screen and highlight elements as shown above. First, position the cursor over ON and press ENTER. Then choose a graph from the four choices: scatter plot, line graph, box plot, and histogram. Move the cursor to the histogram and press ENTER. Move the cursor to indicate in which list the data are located, such as L1, and press ENTER. Select 1 for the frequency of the data and press ENTER.

Next you need to set the values for the window that will display the histogram. Press WINDOW, which will display a screen similar to that shown below left. In the histogram shown below right, which shows the quality ratings for natural brands of peanut butter from Investigation 1, the values along the x-axis range from 11 to 89; a good setting for the x-axis is from 0 to 100 with a scale of 10. Enter these values into XMIN, XMAX, and XSCL. The frequencies in this graph range from 0 to 7; a good setting for the y-axis is from 0 to 10 with a scale of 1. Enter these values into YMIN, YMAX, and YSCL. To display the histogram, press GRAPH.

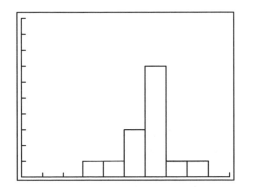

Entering a Formula as a List

It is possible to derive a list using a formula. For example, Additional Practice problems 9–12 for Investigation 1 ask students to compute and graph wingspan-to-length ratios for a set of airplanes. To enter these ratios into a list without calculating each ratio individually, enter the values for body length into L1 and the values for wingspan into L2. Highlight L3 with the cursor, and enter the formula to divide L2 by L1. To do so, press [2nd][2] to indicate L2, press [÷] to indicate division, and press [2nd][1] to indicate L1. Press [ENTER], and L3 will fill with values that reflect the ratios of these two data sets.

L1	L2
46.6	44.4
70.7	59.6
59.5	48.1
57.1	45.2
69.1	73.3
28.6	26.3
L1 (1) = 46.6	

L2	L3
44.4	------
59.6	
48.1	
45.2	
73.3	
26.3	
L3=L2/L1	

L2	L3
44.4	.953
59.6	.843
48.1	.808
45.2	.792
73.3	1.061
26.3	0.920
L3 (1) = .95278969 . .	

Generating Random Numbers

The RAND function generates a random number between 0 and 1. The numbers from 1 to 100, for example, would be represented by the decimal numbers .00 to .99, with .00 representing 100. To use the RAND function, display the MATH PRB menu, which looks like the screen shown below left, by pressing [MATH]. Select PRB (probability), and press [ENTER] to select RAND. Continue to generate random numbers by successively pressing [ENTER].

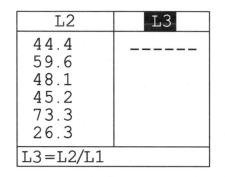

```
MATH  NUM  PRB
1:RAND
2:nPr
3:nCr
4:!
5:RANDINT(
```

```
RAND
                .093
                .126
                .368
                .709
                .011
                .812
```

To change the seed value, which controls the random number sequence, first store an integer in RAND by pressing [STO▶] and an integer. Change the number of decimal places that are displayed by pressing [MODE] to display the mode screen and using the arrow keys to select FLOAT and to choose the number of decimal places.

The RANDINT function generates a random integer within a specified range. To use the RANDINT function, select PRB from the MATH PRB menu (as described above), and press [ENTER]. Enter the upper and lower boundaries of the random integers to be generated; for example, enter RANDINT(1, 7) to generate random integers from 1 to 7.

Calculating Summary Statistics Using a List of Data Values

Summary statistics can be computed directly from a list of values. To compute summary statistics for a list of values you have entered, press $\boxed{\text{STAT}}$ and choose CALC. You will see a list of choices; select 1 for calculating one-variable statistics, and press $\boxed{\text{ENTER}}$. Designate the list containing the values (for example, press $\boxed{\text{2nd}}$ $\boxed{\text{1}}$ to indicate L1), and press $\boxed{\text{ENTER}}$. The screen will display the summary statistics in this order: the mean of the values, the sum of the values, the sum of the squares of the values, the sample standard deviation, the population standard deviation, the median of the values, and the number of values in the list.

Mathematical and Problem-Solving Goals

Samples and Populations was created to help students

- Employ the process of statistical investigation to explore problems

- Analyze data using tables, stem-and-leaf plots, histograms, and box-and-whiskers plots

- Compare data using measures of center (mean, median), measures of spread (range, percentiles), and data displays (stem-and-leaf plots, histograms, box-and-whiskers plots)

- Explore relationships among data using scatter plots

- Distinguish between samples and populations, compare samples, and use information drawn from samples to make conclusions about populations

- Apply selected concepts from probability to understand the concept of randomness and to select random samples

- Explore concepts of representativeness and sample size as they relate to using random and nonrandom samples to draw conclusions about the characteristics of populations

- Design a survey, focusing on how questions are asked

The overall goal of the Connected Mathematics curriculum is to help students develop sound mathematical habits. Through their work in this and other units, students learn important questions to ask themselves about any situation that involves the principles explored in this unit, such as: *What is the question being asked? How have the data been collected? How have the data been analyzed and interpreted? What kinds of comparisons and relationships among the data were explored? How has the original question been answered? Do these conclusions make sense? Can I use these results to make predictions or generalizations about the population? Was the sample from which the data were collected representative in terms of size and the way in which it was chosen? Was there any bias in the ways the data were collected or analyzed? Do I now have new questions that I want to investigate based on the results of this investigation?*

Investigation 1: Comparing Data Sets

Students analyze data from a study on the quality, price, and sodium content of a variety of peanut butters, which are classified by four attributes: natural or regular, creamy or chunky, salted or unsalted, and name brand or store brand. Students review the use of stem-and-leaf plots and measures of center and are introduced to box-and-whiskers plots as tools for comparing data. They also explore relationships among data using scatter plots.

Investigation 2: Conducting Surveys

Students consider the distinction between samples and populations and use results of analyses of data from samples to make estimates about population characteristics or behaviors. First, students consider the implications of making estimates about the entire U.S. population based on a telephone survey involving a few thousand people. The survey raises issues about projecting from data collected about a sample to an entire population. Next, they consider a variety of sampling strategies, analyzing the advantages and disadvantages of each and determining which would produce the sample most representative of the population. Finally, students consider issues that are important in developing surveys as they design a survey and write survey questions.

Investigation 3: Random Samples

Students consider the differences among convenience samples, voluntary-response samples, and random samples. They explore techniques for choosing samples randomly from a population— such as spinners, numbers cubes, and random-number generators on calculators—and think about why random samples are often preferable. They then investigate the idea that sample size affects the accuracy of population estimates. Through sampling and determining statistics, students learn that by taking larger samples one can often reduce the variability in sample distributions and make more accurate predictions.

Investigation 4: Solving Real-World Problems

Students apply what they have learned about samples to engaging real-world situations. First, they analyze measurements of Native American arrowheads found at six different archaeological sites. Scientists know the approximate time periods during which four of the sites were settled; the time periods for two newer sites are unknown. Students explore how data from the known sites may be used to make predictions about the newer sites. Next, they employ a sampling procedure to investigate how many chocolate chips must be added to a batch of cookie dough to ensure that each cookie in the batch will contain at least five chips.

Connections to Other Units

The ideas in *Samples and Populations* build on and connect to several big ideas in other Connected Mathematics units.

Big Idea	Prior Work	Future Work
using the process of statistical investigation to explore problems	beginning to use the process of statistical investigation *(Data About Us)*	continuing to frame exploration of statistical concepts within the process of statistical investigation *(high school)*
composing and decomposing graphs and recognizing the elements of graphs, the interrelationships among graphical elements, and the impact of these elements on the presentation of information in a graph	working with a variety of graphs, including line plots, bar graphs, circle graphs, stem-and-leaf plots, histograms, box-and-whiskers plots, and scatter plots *(elementary grades, Data About Us, Bits and Pieces II)*	reviewing and extending work with graphs to emphasize scatter plots and line graphs that consider such relationships as change over time *(high school)*
describing the shape of the data in a graph, including such elements as clusters, gaps, outliers, symmetry or skew, what is typical, the spread in the data, and single or multiple peaks in the data	working with a variety of data contexts involving problems that are meaningful to students and discussing what is known once data are collected and represented *(elementary grades, Data About Us, Data Around Us)*	reviewing and extending work with graphs, particularly extending measures of spread to include the concept of standard deviation *(high school)*
distinguishing between a sample and a population; raising questions about the representativeness of sample data and sources of bias; and using different ways to generate samples, paying special attention to random sampling	informally exploring concepts as part of the process of statistical investigation in applied situations *(elementary grades, Data About Us, How Likely Is It?, What Do You Expect?)*	placing greater emphasis on using and selecting samples and ways to address representativeness and bias *(high school)*

Materials

For students

- Labsheets
- Graphing calculators (preferably with the capacity to display a function as a table)
- Statistical computer software, such as Statistics Workshop, that performs statistical operations and creates statistical graphs, including box plots (optional; see "Resources" below)
- Transparencies of Labsheet 3.2 (optional; 2 per group)
- Blank transparencies (optional)
- Grid paper (provided as a blackline master)
- Large sheets of paper (optional)
- 10-section spinners (provided as a blackline master)
- 12-section spinners (optional; provided as a blackline master)
- 10-sided number cubes (as many as are available)
- Paper clips or bobby pins (for spinners)

For the teacher

- Transparencies and transparency markers (optional)
- Transparencies of Labsheets 3.2 and 3.3 (optional)
- Overhead display model of students' graphing calculator (optional)
- Two brands of peanut butter, crackers, and two knives for spreading (optional; If possible, choose brands from the table of data in Investigation 1, one with a low quality rating—perhaps a local store brand—and one with a high quality rating.)
- Large sheets of paper (optional)

Resources

Use of computer software for statistics and graphs is encouraged but optional. The following is one of several available programs.

Statistics Workshop (Mac Plus or later). Pleasantville, N.Y.: Sunburst Communications.

Pacing Chart

This pacing chart gives estimates of the class time required for each investigation and assessment piece. Shaded rows indicate opportunities for assessment.

Investigations and Assessments	Class Time
1 Comparing Data Sets	5 days
Check-Up	$\frac{1}{2}$ day
2 Conducting Surveys	4 days
3 Random Samples	4 days
Quiz	1 day
4 Solving Real-World Problems	3 days
Self-Assessment	Take home
Final Assessment (Unit Test or Unit Project)	1 or 2 days

Samples and Populations Vocabulary

The following words and concepts are used in *Samples and Populations*. Concepts in the left column are those essential for student understanding of this and future units. The Descriptive Glossary gives descriptions of many of these terms.

Essential terms developed in this unit	**Terms developed in previous units**	**Nonessential terms**
biased sample	data	database
box-and-whiskers plot, box plot	equally likely	quartile
convenience sample	mean	simulate
distribution	median	
five-number summary	probability	
histogram	random	
population	range	
random sample	statistics	
representative sample	survey	
sample		
scatter plot		
stem-and-leaf plot, stem plot		
systematic sample		
voluntary-response sample		

Embedded Assessment

Opportunities for informal assessment of student progress are embedded throughout *Samples and Populations* in the problems, the ACE questions, and the Mathematical Reflections. Suggestions for observing as students explore and discover mathematical ideas, for probing to guide their progress in developing concepts and skills, and for questioning to determine their level of understanding can be found in the Launch, Explore, and Summarize sections of all investigation problems. Some examples:

- Investigation 2, Problem 2.1 *Launch* (page 36a) suggests general questions you can ask to help guide students in thinking about samples drawn from larger populations.

- Investigation 1, Problem 1.2 *Explore* (page 23f) suggests questions you can ask to assess the sense students are making of using the percent divisions in box plots to make comparisons.

- Investigation 4, Problem 4.1 *Summarize* (page 62b) suggests questions you can ask to help students think about the applications of what they have learned about sampling and sample size.

ACE Assignments

An ACE (Applications—Connections—Extensions) section appears at the end of each investigation. To help you assign ACE questions, a list of assignment choices is given in the margin next to the reduced student page for each problem. Each list indicates the ACE questions that students should be able to answer after they complete the problem.

Check-Up

One check-up, which may be given after Investigation 1, is provided for use as a quick quiz or warm-up activity. The check-up is designed for students to complete individually. You will find the check-up and its answer key in the Assessment Resources section.

Partner Quiz

One quiz, which may be given after Investigation 3, is provided with this unit. The quiz is designed to be completed by pairs of students with the opportunity for revision based on teacher feedback. You will find the quiz and its answer key in the Assessment Resources section. As an alternative to the quiz provided, you can construct your own quiz by combining questions from the Question Bank, this quiz, and unassigned ACE questions.

Question Bank

A Question Bank provides questions you can use for homework, reviews, or quizzes. You will find the Question Bank and its answer key in the Assessment Resources section.

Notebook/Journal

Students should have notebooks to record and organize their work. Notebooks should include student journals and sections for vocabulary, homework, quizzes, and check-ups. In their journals, students can take notes, solve investigation problems, and record their ideas about Mathematical Reflections questions. Journals should be assessed for completeness rather than correctness; they should be seen as "safe" places where students can try out their thinking. A Notebook Checklist and a Self-Assessment are provided in the Assessment Resources section. The Notebook Checklist helps students organize their notebooks. The Self-Assessment guides students as they review their notebooks to determine which ideas they have mastered and which they still need to work on.

The Unit Test

The final assessment in *Samples and Populations* is either the unit test or the unit project. The unit test focuses on creating and analyzing data representations and evaluating samples and sampling methods.

The Unit Project

The final assessment in *Samples and Populations* is either the unit test or the unit project. In the two-part unit project, students apply their understanding of samples and populations to real-world situations. In Part 1, Safe Water and Life Expectancy, students use their knowledge of statistics and data representations to analyze a set of data and determine whether there is a relationship between life expectancy and access to safe drinking water. In Part 2, Estimating Populations, they use their knowledge of random samples and data analysis to estimate populations of geese from drawings that represent fields of geese.

Introducing Your Students to Samples and Populations

The intent of this unit is to help students explore ways to compare data sets and to consider the use of sample data as a way to make estimates about a population. To introduce your students to the unit, you might begin by posing this problem:

You are asked to design a survey to get readers' reactions to the cartoon section of the local newspaper. The newspaper is considering removing some cartoons and adding others. How would you go about planning your survey?

What kinds of questions would you ask? What would your survey look like? Would you want to ask such questions as "In what age range are you?"

How would you distribute the survey? Would you publish it in the paper and ask readers to fill it out and return it? How else might you gather data? What are the advantages and disadvantages of each method?

Samples and Populations

The homecoming committee wants to estimate how many students will attend the homecoming dance, but they don't want to ask every student in the school. How could they select a sample of students to survey? How could they use the results of their survey to predict the number of students who will attend?

A cookie company claims that there are at least 1000 chips in every 1-pound bag of its chocolate chip cookies. How could you test this claim? How do you think the company guarantees this claim?

A radio talk-show host asked her listeners to call in to express their opinions about a local election. Do you think the results of this survey could be used to describe the opinions of all the show's listeners?

The U.S. census attempts to gather information from every household in the United States. Gathering, organizing, and analyzing data from such a large population is expensive and time-consuming. In most studies of large populations, data are gathered from a sample, or portion, of the population. The data from the sample are then used to make predictions or to draw conclusions about the population.

Sampling is an important tool in statistics and data analysis. Understanding how to select samples and how to use them to make predictions will help you when you consider questions like those on the opposite page.

Talk about this problem in relation to the process of statistical investigation. Newspapers often survey the cartoon preferences of their readership by publishing the survey and asking readers to respond. This discussion will raise issues of sampling and comparing data, two main themes of this unit. It will also engage students in thinking about the wording of survey questions.

Also discuss the questions on the opening page of the student edition, which are designed to get students thinking about issues related to sampling and using sampling to make predictions about populations. Invite students to share their thoughts about each situation and how to ensure that the results will be "fair"— that they will reflect what is true about the population.

Mathematical Highlights

The Mathematical Highlights page provides information for students and for parents and other family members. It gives students a preview of the activities and problems in *Samples and Populations*. As they work through the unit, students can refer back to the Mathematical Highlights page to review what they have learned and to preview what is still to come. This page also tells students' families what mathematical ideas and activities will be covered as the class works through *Samples and Populations*.

Mathematical Highlights

In *Samples and Populations*, you will explore ways of collecting and analyzing data. This unit will help you to

● Revisit and use the process of statistical investigation to explore problems;

● Compare data using measures of center (mean or median), measures of spread (range or percentiles), and data displays (tables, stem-and-leaf plots, histograms, and box-and-whisker plots);

● Distinguish between samples and populations, compare samples, and use information drawn from samples to draw conclusions about populations;

● Apply concepts from probability to explore the concept of randomness and to select random samples from populations; and

● Explore the representativeness and sample size of random and nonrandom samples to draw conclusions about the characteristics of populations.

As you work on the problems in this unit, make it a habit to ask questions about situations that involve data analysis using samples: *What is the population? What is the sample? What kinds of comparisons and relationships among the data from the sample can I explore? Can I use my results to make predictions or generalizations about the population? Is the sample representative in terms of size and the way in which the data were collected? Was there any bias in the ways the data were collected or analyzed?*

The Investigations

The teaching materials for each investigation consist of three parts: an overview, student pages with teaching outlines, and detailed notes for teaching the investigation.

The overview of each investigation includes brief descriptions of the problems, the mathematical and problem-solving goals of the investigation, and a list of necessary materials.

Essential information for teaching the investigation is provided in the margins around the student pages. The "At a Glance" overviews are brief outlines of the Launch, Explore, and Summarize phases of each problem for reference as you work with the class. To help you assign homework, a list of "Assignment Choices" is provided next to each problem. Where space permits, answers to problems, follow-ups, ACE questions, and Mathematical Reflections appear next to the appropriate student pages.

The Teaching the Investigation section follows the student pages and is the heart of the Connected Mathematics curriculum. This section describes in detail the Launch, Explore, and Summarize phases for each problem. It includes all the information needed for teaching, along with suggestions for what you might say at key points in the teaching. Use this section to prepare lessons and as a guide for teaching the investigations.

Assessment Resources

The Assessment Resources section contains blackline masters and answer keys for the check-up, the quiz, the Question Bank, and the Unit Test. Blackline masters for the Notebook Checklist and the Self-Assessment are given. These instruments support student self-evaluation, an important aspect of assessment in the Connected Mathematics curriculum. A discussion of how one teacher assessed the check-up is included, along with a suggested scoring rubric and samples of student work. The section also includes a guide to the Unit Project, with a sample scoring rubric.

Blackline Masters

The Blackline Masters section includes masters for all labsheets and transparencies. Blackline masters of grid paper, 10-section spinners, and 12-section spinners are also provided.

Additional Practice

Practice pages for each investigation offer additional problems for students who need more practice with the basic concepts developed in the investigations as well as some continual review of earlier concepts.

Descriptive Glossary

The glossary provides descriptions and examples of the key concepts in *Samples and Populations*. These descriptions are not intended to be formal definitions but are meant to give you an idea of how students might make sense of these important concepts.

Comparing Data Sets

While the central focus of this unit is samples and populations, students may not yet have encountered the strategies necessary for comparing data sets. This investigation introduces and reviews ways to compare data sets using measures of center and spread, stem-and-leaf plots (stem plots), box-and-whiskers plots (box plots), histograms, and scatter plots.

In the five problems, students analyze data from a study on the quality, sodium content, and price of a variety of peanut butters classified by four attributes: natural or regular, creamy or chunky, salted or unsalted, and name brand or store brand. In Problem 1.1, Comparing Quality Ratings, students compare the quality ratings of natural and regular brands of peanut butter. The problem offers an opportunity to review the use of tables, stem plots, and histograms as tools to represent data and the mean, median, and range as measures to describe and compare data. In Problem 1.2, Using Box-and-Whiskers Plots, students explore box plots as another tool for comparing quality ratings. In Problem 1.3, Comparing Prices, they apply their knowledge of box plots to compare the prices of regular and natural brands of peanut butter. In Problem 1.4, Making a Quality Choice, students compare the peanut butters by each of the three remaining attributes to identify which attributes may indicate higher quality. In Problem 1.5, Comparing Quality and Price, students study a scatter plot comparing quality and price and search for relationships between these two factors for regular and natural peanut butters.

Mathematical and Problem-Solving Goals

- *To engage in the process of statistical investigation*

- *To compare data using tables, stem-and-leaf plots, histograms, and box-and-whiskers plots*

- *To compare data using measures of center (mean and median) and measures of spread (range)*

- *To consider the properties of the mean and the median, particularly the influence of extreme values on each measure's calculation*

Materials

Problem	For students	For the teacher
All	Graphing calculators, computers and statistical software (optional), grid paper	Transparencies: 1.1A to 1.5 (optional); overhead graphing calculator (optional)
1.1	Labsheet 1.1 (optional; 1 per student)	Two brands of peanut butter, crackers, two knives (optional)
1.4	Blank transparencies (optional)	
ACE	Labsheet 1.ACE (optional; 1 per student)	

Comparing Data Sets

American shoppers have a greater variety of stores and products to choose from than do shoppers anywhere else in the world. With so many choices, it can be difficult to decide which product to purchase. Many people turn to information in consumer surveys and product comparisons to help them make informed decisions.

A recent consumer survey rated 37 varieties of peanut butter. Each brand was assigned a quality rating from 1 to 100 points. A panel of trained tasters made two general statements about quality:

- Peanut butters with higher quality ratings were smooth; had a sweet, nutty flavor; and were not overly dry or sticky.
- Peanut butters with lower quality ratings were not very nutty; had small chunks of peanuts; or had a burnt or slightly rancid taste.

In addition to quality ratings, the article listed the sodium content and the price per 3-tablespoon serving for each brand. Brands were classified according to three attributes: natural or regular, creamy or chunky, and salted or unsalted. The data are presented in the table on the next page. A fourth attribute, name brand or store brand, has been added to the data.

Think about this!

- Who might be interested in the results of this peanut butter study?
- What interesting questions about peanut butter can be answered with these data?
- What interesting questions about peanut butter cannot be answered with these data?

Tips for the Linguistically Diverse Classroom

Enactment The Enactment technique is described in detail in *Getting to Know Connected Mathematics*. Students act out mini-scenes using props to make information comprehensible. Example: For the information presented on this page, four or five different jars of peanut butter can be placed on a table in the front of the classroom. A student can pantomime grocery shopping down this "aisle," pondering which brand to buy. Another student can introduce a panel of "trained testers," who pantomime what they are asked to do. The general statements about quality can be made comprehensible as the testers open jars to point to specific attributes (e.g. smoothness, chunks of peanuts) and pantomime actions (e.g. frowning after pretending to sample a bad-tasting brand, feigning difficulty in opening their mouths after tasting a sticky brand).

Comparing Quality Ratings

Grouping:
pairs

Launch

- Conduct a peanut butter taste test. *(optional)*

- Talk about the questions in "Think about this!"

- Demonstrate how stem plots and histograms are related. *(optional)*

- Have pairs explore the problem and follow-up.

Explore

- Assist students with finding statistics and creating data displays.

Summarize

- Have pairs report their findings and justify their conclusions.

- Review calculating statistics and making data displays. *(optional)*

- Review the relationship of the median and the mean to the values in a data set.

Assignment Choices

ACE questions 5 and 7

Peanut Butter Comparisons

	Brand	Quality rating	Sodium per serving (mg)	Price per serving	Regular/ natural	Creamy/ chunky	Salted/ unsalted	Name brand/ store brand
1.	Smucker's Natural	71	15	27¢	natural	creamy	unsalted	name
2.	Deaf Smith Arrowhead Mills	69	0	32	natural	creamy	unsalted	name
3.	Adams 100% Natural	60	0	26	natural	creamy	unsalted	name
4.	Adams	60	168	26	natural	creamy	salted	name
5.	Laura Scudder's All Natural	57	165	26	natural	creamy	salted	name
6.	Country Pure Brand (Safeway)	52	225	21	natural	creamy	salted	store
7.	Hollywood Natural	34	15	32	natural	creamy	unsalted	name
8.	Smucker's Natural	89	15	27	natural	chunky	unsalted	name
9.	Adams 100% Natural	69	0	26	natural	chunky	unsalted	name
10.	Deaf Smith Arrowhead Mills	69	0	32	natural	chunky	unsalted	name
11.	Country Pure Brand (Safeway)	67	105	21	natural	chunky	salted	store
12.	Laura Scudder's All Natural	63	165	24	natural	chunky	salted	name
13.	Smucker's Natural	57	188	26	natural	chunky	salted	name
14.	Health Valley 100% Natural	40	3	34	natural	chunky	unsalted	name
15.	Jif	76	220	22	regular	creamy	salted	name
16.	Skippy	60	225	19	regular	creamy	salted	name
17.	Kroger	54	240	14	regular	creamy	salted	store
18.	NuMade (Safeway)	43	187	20	regular	creamy	salted	store
19.	Peter Pan	40	225	21	regular	creamy	salted	name
20.	Peter Pan	35	3	22	regular	creamy	unsalted	name
21.	A & P	34	225	12	regular	creamy	salted	store
22.	Food Club	33	225	17	regular	creamy	salted	store
23.	Pathmark	31	255	9	regular	creamy	salted	store
24.	Lady Lee (Lucky Stores)	23	225	16	regular	creamy	salted	store
25.	Albertsons	23	225	17	regular	creamy	salted	store
26.	Shur Fine (Shurfine Central)	11	225	16	regular	creamy	salted	store
27.	Jif	83	162	23	regular	chunky	salted	name
28.	Skippy	83	211	21	regular	chunky	salted	name
29.	Food Club	54	195	17	regular	chunky	salted	store
30.	Kroger	49	255	14	regular	chunky	salted	store
31.	A & P	46	225	11	regular	chunky	salted	store
32.	Peter Pan	45	180	22	regular	chunky	salted	name
33.	NuMade (Safeway)	40	208	21	regular	chunky	salted	store
34.	Lady Lee (Lucky Stores)	34	225	16	regular	chunky	salted	store
35.	Albertsons	31	225	17	regular	chunky	salted	store
36.	Pathmark	29	210	9	regular	chunky	salted	store
37.	Shur Fine (Shurfine Central)	26	195	16	regular	chunky	salted	store

Sources: "The Nuttiest Peanut Butter." *Consumer Reports* (September 1990): 588–591.
A. J. Rossman, *Workshop Statistics: Student Activity Guide.* Carlisle, Penn.: Dickinson College, 1994, pp. 5–18.

Samples and Populations

Answer to Problem 1.1

See the "Summarize" section for some ways students may have compared the data.

Natural brands of peanut butter have higher quality ratings overall than do regular brands. The mean for natural brands (61.2) is almost 20 points higher than the mean for regular brands (42.7). Similarly, the median for natural brands (61.5) is more than 20 points higher than the median for regular brands (40.0). The ranges for natural brands (34 to 89, or 55 points) and regular brands (11 to 83, or 72 points) suggest that ratings for natural brands have less spread overall than do those for regular brands, which means that natural brands are perhaps more consistently of high quality.

1.1 Comparing Quality Ratings

To help determine which peanut butter is the "best buy," you could make several comparisons. For example, you could compare the quality ratings of the regular brands with the quality ratings of the natural brands, which contain no preservatives. How would you summarize and display the data to help you decide whether natural brands or regular brands have higher quality ratings?

Problem 1.1

Apply some of the data analysis techniques you learned in earlier statistics work to compare the quality ratings for natural brands and regular brands.

In general, do natural brands or regular brands have higher quality ratings? Use the results of your analysis to justify your choice.

■ Problem 1.1 Follow-Up

1. For the quality ratings of the regular brands, the mean is greater than the median. Why do you think this is true?

2. For the quality ratings of the natural brands, the mean and the median are close in value. Why do you think this is true?

1.2 Using Box-and-Whiskers Plots

Box-and-whiskers plots, or *box plots,* are useful representations of the distribution of values in a data set. The box plot below shows the distribution of quality ratings for the natural brands of peanut butter.

Quality Ratings for Natural Brands

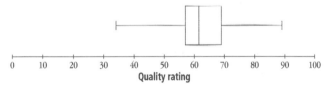

Quality rating

Using Box-and-Whiskers Plots

Grouping:
pairs

Launch

■ As a class, find the five-number summary of a data set, and make a box plot. *(optional)*

■ Have pairs explore the problem.

Explore

■ Ask questions to help students focus on the percent divisions in a box plot.

Summarize

■ Review how to make a box plot.

■ Talk about how to use the box plots to compare quality ratings.

■ Discuss how to find outliers.

■ Assign and then review the follow-up.

Answers to Problem 1.1 Follow-Up

1. The mean is greater than the median because most of the data cluster in the interval of 23 to 54 points. The median, which is centered in the entire data set, is not affected by unusually high or low values. However, the four ratings in the interval of 60 to 83 points pull the mean higher.

2. The distribution of the quality ratings of the natural brands is somewhat symmetric, with the majority of the ratings in the interval of 52 to 69 points. The few higher and lower ratings are evenly spread on either side of this interval, so the mean is not influenced by unusually high or low values.

Assignment Choices

ACE question 6 and unassigned choices from earlier problems

A box plot is constructed from the five-number summary of the data. The **five-number summary** includes the minimum value, maximum value, median, lower quartile, and upper quartile.

You know how to find the minimum value, maximum value, and median in a set of data. The **lower quartile** is the median of the data values below the median. The **upper quartile** is the median of the data values above the median. The diagram below illustrates the five-number summary for the quality ratings of the natural brands of peanut butter.

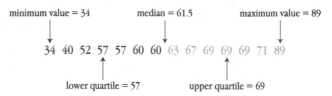

The plot below shows how the numbers in the five-number summary correspond to the features of the box plot.

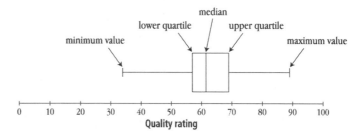

By displaying two or more box plots on the same scale, you can compare distributions. The box plots below allow you to compare the distributions of quality ratings for natural brands and regular brands.

Quality Ratings for Natural and Regular Brands

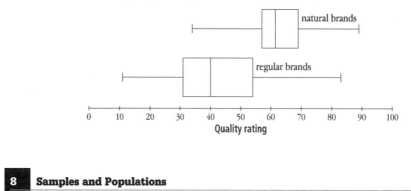

Answers to Problem 1.2

A. About 50% of the data fall below the median, and about 50% fall above the median.

B. About 25% of the data are in each quartile.

C. The box plots show that the median quality rating for natural brands is much higher than the median quality rating for regular brands. The box and the right whisker of the plot for the natural brands is higher on the scale than the upper quartile for the regular brands. This means that 75% of the natural brands have higher quality ratings than 75% of the regular brands. Based on this, natural brands have higher quality ratings overall.

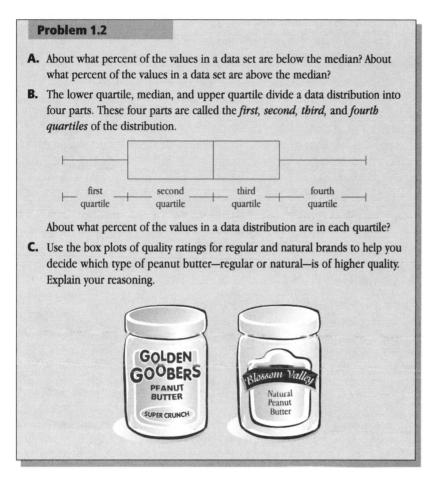

Problem 1.2

A. About what percent of the values in a data set are below the median? About what percent of the values in a data set are above the median?

B. The lower quartile, median, and upper quartile divide a data distribution into four parts. These four parts are called the *first, second, third,* and *fourth quartiles* of the distribution.

About what percent of the values in a data distribution are in each quartile?

C. Use the box plots of quality ratings for regular and natural brands to help you decide which type of peanut butter—regular or natural—is of higher quality. Explain your reasoning.

■ **Problem 1.2 Follow-Up**

Values in a data set that are much greater or much less than most of the other values are called *outliers*. To help you decide whether a value is an outlier, find the length of the box in a box plot of the data. The length of the box is the difference between the upper and lower quartiles. This length is called the *interquartile range*, abbreviated IQR. If a value is greater than 1.5 times the IQR added to the upper quartile or less than 1.5 times the IQR subtracted from the lower quartile, it is an outlier.

1. Are there outliers in the quality ratings for the natural brands? Are there outliers in the quality ratings for the regular brands?

Answers to Problem 1.2 Follow-Up

1. For the natural brands, the IQR is 69 – 57 = 12. An outlier is any value greater than (1.5 × 12) + 69 = 87 or less than 57 – (1.5 × 12) = 39. Therefore, the quality ratings of 34 and 89 are outliers. For the regular brands, the IQR is 54 – 31 = 23. An outlier is any value greater than (1.5 × 23) + 54 = 88.5 or less than 31 – (1.5 × 23) = ⁻3.5. There are no outliers in the quality ratings of the regular brands.

2. a. The whiskers are drawn to the greatest and least data values that are not outliers, which are 71 and 40.

   b. You would find the five-number summary, calculate the IQR, and determine whether any outliers exist. On the box plot, you would mark each outlier with an asterisk and then draw the box plot. The whiskers would extend to the greatest and least values in the data set that are not outliers.

Launch

- Introduce the question of whether regular or natural brands are a better buy.

- Have groups of two to four explore the problem and follow-up.

Explore

- Assist students who are confused by the box plot for the natural brands.

Summarize

- Construct the two box plots as students give the five-number summaries.

- Discuss how to choose peanut butter based on price or quality rating by looking at box plots.

2. On a box plot, outliers are sometimes indicated with asterisks (*). Both pairs of box plots below show the distribution of quality ratings for regular and natural brands of peanut butter. In the plots on the right, outliers have been indicated with asterisks.

Quality Ratings for Natural and Regular Brands

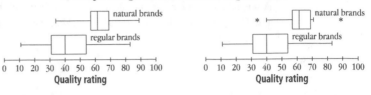

a. In the plots on the left, the whiskers extend from the box to the minimum and maximum values. What values do the whiskers in the plots on the right extend to?

b. Describe how you would construct a box plot if you wanted to show the outliers in a set of data.

1.3 Comparing Prices

Many people consider *both* quality and price when deciding which products or brands to buy. The box plots below show the distributions of per-serving prices for natural and regular brands of peanut butter.

Peanut Butter Prices

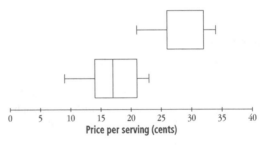

2. See page 9

Answers to Problem 1.3

A. natural brands: minimum value = 21, lower quartile = 26, median = 26, upper quartile = 32, maximum value = 34

B. regular brands: minimum value = 9, lower quartile = 14, median = 17, upper quartile = 21, maximum value = 23

C. The upper box plot shows the price distribution for the natural brands; the lower box plot shows the price distribution for the regular brands. In each plot, the left whisker extends to the minimum value, the right whisker extends to the maximum value, the left end of the box represents the lower quartile, the vertical line in the box represents the median, and the right end of box represents the upper quartile. In the upper box plot, the lower quartile and the median are both 26 and are represented by the same vertical line.

Problem 1.3

In the peanut butter data on page 6, refer to the column giving price per serving.

A. Calculate the five-number summary for the prices of the natural brands.

B. Calculate the five-number summary for the prices of the regular brands.

C. Compare the five-number summaries you found in parts A and B with the box plots shown on the previous page. Decide which plot shows the distribution of prices for the natural brands and which plot shows the distribution of prices for the regular brands. Explain how the numbers in the five-number summaries are shown by various features of the plots.

D. How do the prices of the natural brands compare with the prices of the regular brands? Explain how you can make this comparison by using the box plots.

E. If *price* were the only factor a buyer considered, would natural peanut butter or regular peanut butter be a better choice? If *quality* were the only factor a buyer considered, would natural peanut butter or regular peanut butter be a better choice? Explain your reasoning.

Problem 1.3 Follow-Up

1. About what percent of the data are in the box of a box plot? That is, what percent are between the upper and lower quartiles?

2. About what percent of the data are in the interval from the minimum value to the upper quartile?

3. About what percent of the data are in the interval from the lower quartile to the maximum value?

D. The upper box plot indicates generally higher prices per serving than the lower box plot because it is farther to the right along the price scale. In fact, most of the prices for the natural brands lie above the maximum price for the regular brands.

E. Considering only price, regular brands are a better choice because, as these box plots show, their prices are almost always lower than prices of natural brands. Considering only quality, natural brands are a better choice because, as shown in the box plots in Problem 1.2, their quality ratings are generally higher than those of regular brands.

Answers to Problem 1.3 Follow-Up

1. About 50% of the data are in the box of a box plot.

2. About 75% of the data are in the interval from the minimum value to the upper quartile.

3. About 75% of the data are in the interval from the lower quartile to the maximum value.

1.4

Making a Quality Choice

Grouping:
pairs

Launch

■ Introduce the idea of comparing quality ratings for the other three attributes.

■ Have pairs work on the problem and follow-up.

Explore

■ Have students create box plots by hand or using technology.

■ Distribute transparencies to some groups for recording box plots to share during the summary. *(optional)*

Summarize

■ Select groups to present their arguments for each attribute.

■ Discuss what their results indicate about which brands are good quality choices.

1.4 Making a Quality Choice

The 37 brands of peanut butter listed on page 6 are classified according to four attributes: natural or regular, creamy or chunky, salted or unsalted, and name brand or store brand. In Problems 1.1 and 1.2, you compared the quality ratings of regular brands with the quality ratings of natural brands. You found that natural brands are a good choice based on their quality ratings. In this problem, you will compare the quality ratings for the other three attributes.

Problem 1.4

Justify your answers to the questions below with statistics and box plots.

A. Compare the quality ratings of the creamy brands with the quality ratings of the chunky brands. Based on quality, are creamy brands or chunky brands a better choice?

B. Compare the quality ratings of the salted brands with the quality ratings of the unsalted brands. Based on quality, are salted brands or unsalted brands a better choice?

C. Compare the quality ratings of the name brands with the quality ratings of the store brands. Based on quality, are name brands or store brands a better choice?

■ Problem 1.4 Follow-Up

1. List the four attributes—natural or regular, creamy or chunky, salted or unsalted, and name brand or store brand—you would recommend to someone who wants to choose a peanut butter based on quality ratings.

2. Can you find at least one brand of peanut butter in the list that has all the attributes you recommend?

1.5 Comparing Quality and Price

In previous problems, you explored the quality and price data for natural and regular peanut butters. You may have wondered how the price of a brand of peanut butter is related to its quality. What connection would you expect between price and quality for any product?

Assignment Choices

ACE questions 1, 3, and unassigned choices from earlier problems

Answers to Problem 1.4

See page 23p.

Answers to Problem 1.4 Follow-Up

1. Based on quality ratings, peanut butters that are *natural, chunky, unsalted,* and *name brand* are good choices.

2. There are four peanut butters that meet these criteria: Smucker's Natural, Adams 100% Natural, Deaf Smith Arrowhead Mills, and Health Valley 100% Natural. (Note: It may be interesting to point out to students that the peanut butters with the indicated attributes are not necessarily those with the highest quality ratings and to ask students to hypothesize why this is so.)

To explore the relationship between two variables, you can make a coordinate graph, or **scatter plot**. The scatter plot below shows the (quality rating, price) data for all 37 brands of peanut butter.

Peanut Butter Quality and Price

Problem 1.5

For these questions, refer to the quality ratings and per-serving prices in the table of peanut butter data on page 6.

A. In the graph above, which plot symbol, • or ♦, represents data for natural peanut butter? Which represents data for regular peanut butter?

B. Is there an overall relationship between quality and price? Explain.

C. Do any (quality rating, price) data pairs appear to be unusual? Explain your reasoning.

D. In Problems 1.2 and 1.3, you used box plots to compare quality ratings and prices of natural and regular peanut butters.

  1. How can you use the scatter plot to compare the quality ratings of the natural brands with the quality ratings of the regular brands?

  2. How can you use the scatter plot to compare the prices of the natural brands with the prices of the regular brands?

Launch

■ As a class, inspect the (quality rating, price) scatter plot.

■ Have students make the scatter plot on their calculators. *(optional)*

■ Have pairs explore the problem and follow-up.

Explore

■ Ask questions to help any students who are having trouble.

Summarize

■ Ask students to share their answers and their reasoning.

Answers to Problem 1.5

A. The symbol • represents data for natural brands, and the symbol ♦ represents data for regular brands.

B. There are two clusters of data points: a group near the upper right representing high quality and high price of natural brands, and a group near the lower left representing low quality and low price of regular brands. The overall relationship in the data is "the higher the quality, the higher the price."

C. Possible answer: Two data pairs appear to be unusual, those for Hollywood Natural and Health Valley 100% Natural. Both brands have relatively low quality ratings (34 and 40, respectively) but relatively high prices (32¢ and 34¢, respectively), a combination that runs against the overall trend in the data.

D. See page 23q.

■ **Problem 1.5 Follow-Up**

Some people are concerned about the sodium content of the foods they eat. People with heart and blood-pressure problems are often put on low-sodium diets. Notice in the table on page 6 how the unsalted brands contain very little sodium compared to the salted brands. This is because table salt contains sodium.

1. Make a scatter plot of the (quality rating, sodium) data for all 37 brands of peanut butter. Use different symbols for salted brands and unsalted brands.

2. Does there appear to be an overall relationship between sodium content and quality rating? Explain.

3. Look back at the box plots you made of the quality ratings for the salted brands and of the quality ratings for the unsalted brands in part B of Problem 1.4. Is there a connection between quality rating and the salt content of peanut butter? Explain your thinking.

4. In questions 1–3, you looked for a relationship between quality rating and sodium content or added salt. Compare your conclusions about this relationship based on the scatter plot with weaknesses of each type of data display? What are the strengths and your conclusions based on the box plots.

Answers to Problem 1.5 Follow-Up

1–3. See page 23q.

4. The scatter plot and the box plots both show only a slight tendency for sodium or salt content to be related to quality. Scatter plots let you see all the data points when you compare two variables, so you can pick out individual points of interest; however, it is harder to concentrate on one variable at a time. Box plots give you a quick picture of a distribution and make it easy to pick out important values like the median and to compare distributions by percentages, but you have no idea how many data values there are or what most of the values are.

Applications • Connections • Extensions

As you work on these ACE questions, use your calculator whenever you need it.

Applications

1. Refer to the peanut butter data on page 6.

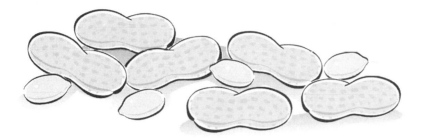

a. In Problem 1.3, you compared the prices of natural brands with the prices of regular brands. Based on price, are natural brands or regular brands a better choice?

b. Based on price, are creamy brands or chunky brands a better choice? Justify your answer with statistics and graphs.

c. Based on price, are salted brands or unsalted brands a better choice? Justify your answer with statistics and graphs.

d. Based on price, are name brands or store brands a better choice? Justify your answer with statistics and graphs.

e. List the four attributes—natural or regular, creamy or chunky, salted or unsalted, and name brand or store brand—you would recommend to someone who wants to choose a peanut butter based on price.

f. Can you find at least one brand of peanut butter that has all the attributes you recommend?

Investigation 1: Comparing Data Sets 15

Answers

Applications

1a–1c. See page 23r.

1d. See page 23s.

1e. Based on price, peanut butters that are *regular, chunky or creamy, salted,* and *store brand* are good choices.

1f. Sixteen brands of peanut butter meet these criteria.

Investigation 1 15

2a. The values on or near the horizontal axis represent brands with very low or 0 mg sodium per serving.

2b. *A* (11, 225); *B* (49, 255); *C* (76, 220); *D* (67, 105); *E* (35, 3); Each pair of coordinates tells the quality rating and sodium content of one brand of peanut butter.

3a. See box plots below right. Generally, jet planes are longer than propeller planes. From the box plots, we can see that 75% of the jet planes are longer than 100% of the propeller planes.

3b. See box plots on the following page. Generally, jet planes have greater wingspans than propeller planes. From the box plot, we can see that 75% of the jet planes have greater wingspans than 15 of the 16 propeller planes, the one outlier in the propeller planes. (Note: Students may or may not show outliers on their plots.)

4. See page 23s.

---

2. The scatter plot below shows (quality rating, sodium) data for the 37 brands of peanut butter listed on page 6.

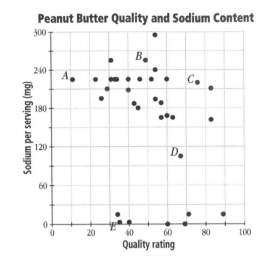

Peanut Butter Quality and Sodium Content

a. Compare the values in the table with the scatter plot. Why are some points located on or very near the horizontal axis?

b. Give the approximate coordinates of each labeled point. Explain what the coordinates tell you about the brand represented by the point.

3. The table on the next page gives the engine type, body length, and wingspan of several airplanes flown by major airlines.

a. Based on body length, how do propeller planes compare to jet planes? Justify your answers with statistics and graphs.

b. Based on wingspan, how do propeller planes compare with jet planes? Justify your answers with statistics and graphs.

4. Make a scatter plot of the (wingspan, body length) data given in the table on page 17. Describe the overall relationship between these two variables.

3a.

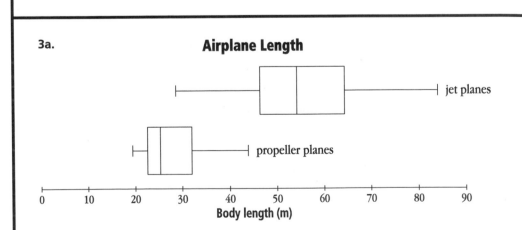

Airplane Length

Airplane Data

Plane	Engine type	Body length (m)	Wingspan (m)
Boeing 707	jet	46.6	44.4
Boeing 747	jet	70.7	59.6
Ilyushin IL-86	jet	59.5	48.1
McDonnell Douglas DC-8	jet	57.1	45.2
Antonov An-124	jet	69.1	73.3
British Aerospace 146	jet	28.6	26.3
Lockheed C-5 Galaxy	jet	75.5	67.9
Antonov An-225	jet	84.0	88.4
Airbus A300	jet	54.1	44.9
Airbus A310	jet	46.0	43.9
Airbus A320	jet	37.5	33.9
Boeing 737	jet	33.4	28.9
Boeing 757	jet	47.3	38.1
Boeing 767	jet	48.5	47.6
Lockheed Tristar L-1011	jet	54.2	47.3
McDonnell Douglas DC-10	jet	55.5	50.4
Aero/Boeing Spacelines Guppy	propeller	43.8	47.6
Douglas DC-4 C-54 Skymaster	propeller	28.6	35.8
Douglas DC-6	propeller	32.2	35.8
Lockheed L-188 Electra	propeller	31.8	30.2
Vickers Viscount	propeller	26.1	28.6
Antonov An-12	propeller	33.1	38.0
de Havilland DHC Dash-7	propeller	24.5	28.4
Lockheed C-130 Hercules/L-100	propeller	34.4	40.4
British Aerospace 748/ATP	propeller	26.0	30.6
Convair 240	propeller	24.1	32.1
Curtiss C-46 Commando	propeller	23.3	32.9
Douglas DC-3	propeller	19.7	29.0
Grumman Gulfstream I/I-C	propeller	19.4	23.9
Ilyushin IL-14	propeller	22.3	31.7
Martin 4-0-4	propeller	22.8	28.4
Saab 340	propeller	19.7	21.4

Source: William Berk and Frank Berk. *Airport Airplanes.* Plymouth, Mich.: Plymouth Press, 1993.

3b.

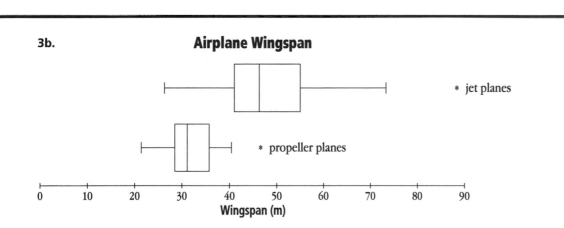

Airplane Wingspan

* jet planes

* propeller planes

Connections

5. The graphs below compare prices (in U.S. dollars) of 2-liter bottles of soft drink in cities around the world. The titles and the axis labels are missing.

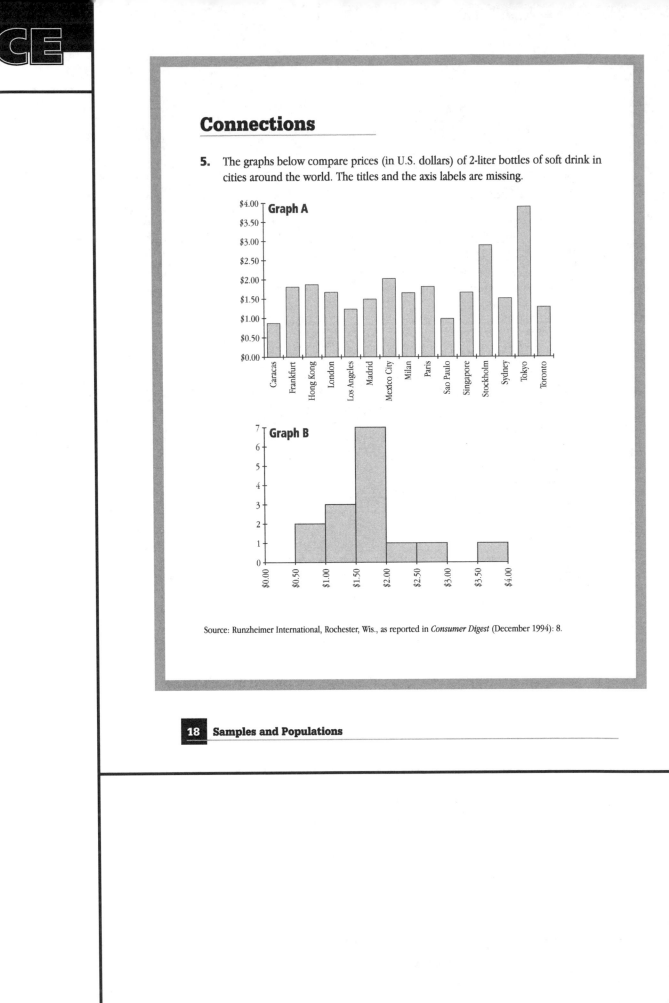

Source: Runzheimer International, Rochester, Wis., as reported in *Consumer Digest* (December 1994): 8.

a. Which graph could you use to identify the cities with the highest and lowest soft-drink prices? Give the names of these cities and the prices.

b. Which graph could you use to find the typical price of a 2-liter bottle of soft drink for all the cities? What is the typical price? Explain how you found your answer.

c. What title and axis labels would be appropriate for each graph?

d. If you were given only graph A, would you have enough information to make graph B? Explain your reasoning.

e. If you were given only graph B, would you have enough information to make graph A? Explain your reasoning.

6. Two students were comparing snack-size boxes of two brands of raisins, TastiSnak and Nature's Best. The brands sell for the same price. Tim said that TastiSnak raisins are a better deal because there are more raisins in each box. Kadisha disagreed. She said that since a box of either brand contains half an ounce, the brands give you the same amount for your money.

To test these claims, the students determined the actual number of raisins and the mass in grams for 50 boxes of each brand. The results are shown in the box plots below. Based on the mass and the number of raisins, which brand is a better deal? Explain how you used the graphs to determine your answer.

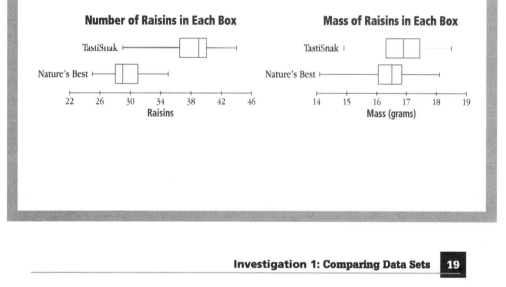

6. Possible answer: From the box plot of the number of raisins per box, it can be seen that 75% of the boxes of TastiSnak raisins contain more raisins than 100% of the boxes of Nature's Best raisins. From the box plot of the mass in grams per box, it can be seen that the brands are quite similar; the medians differ by about $\frac{1}{2}$ gram. In terms of which is a better deal, if a consumer wants more raisins, TastiSnak is the better deal. However, it may be that TastiSnak raisins are less plump than Nature's Best raisins.

7a. The number of data values in the set must be 250 ÷ 25 = 10. One possible set of values is 15, 10, 18, 7, 34, 26, 21, 19, 57, and 43.

7b. Any set of 10 values with a sum of 250 will work, so other students probably gave different data sets. (Note: This helps students understand that some problems have more than one answer and points out that the mean may be a summary value for many different sets of values.)

7c. The median and the mean don't have to be close in value. If there are some very high or very low values, the mean might be quite different from the median. In the data set in part a, the mean is 25 and the median is 20. The mean is affected by the relatively high values 43 and 57.

7. The sum of the values in a particular set of data is 250, and the mean is 25.

   a. Create a data set that fits this description.

   b. Do you think other students in your class created the same data set you did? Explain.

   c. Must the median of the data set be close in value to the mean? Explain.

Extensions

8. In many sports, the length of a game or match is determined by a time clock. In baseball, however, a game ends when nine innings have been completed and one team is ahead. If the teams are tied after nine innings, extra innings are played until one team is ahead. The graph below displays data about the duration of professional baseball games (in minutes). The title and the axis labels are missing.

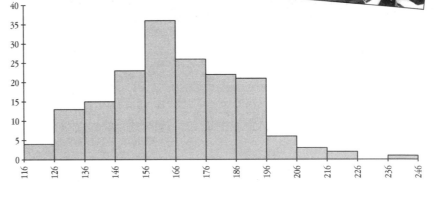

Source: *Student Poster Projects: Winners of the American Statistics Poster Competition, 1991–1992.* Palo Alto, Calif.: Dale Seymour Publications, 1994, p. 20.

a. What title and axis labels are appropriate for this graph?

b. What does the shape of the graph tell you about the length of a typical baseball game?

c. About how many games are represented in the graph?

d. Estimate the lower quartile, the median, and the upper quartile for these data. What do these numbers tell you about the length of a typical baseball game?

9. The scatter plot below shows (body length, wingspan) data for jet and propeller planes. The plot shows that, in general, greater body lengths are associated with greater wingspans. It's often useful to model such a trend with a linear graph and an equation.

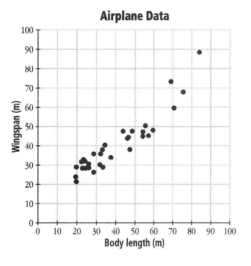

Airplane Data

8a. The graph could be titled "Length of Baseball Games," with a horizontal axis label of "Game length (minutes)" and a vertical axis label of "Number of games" or "Frequency."

8b. The distribution indicates that most games last between 136 and 196 minutes. The typical game length is about 160 minutes.

8c. About 172 games are represented.

8d. Estimates will vary. The lower quartile is approximately 150, the median is approximately 160, and the upper quartile is approximately 180. These numbers indicate that approximately 25% of games last less than 150 minutes, 25% last between 150 and 160 minutes, 25% last between 160 and 180 minutes, and 25% last more than 180 minutes.

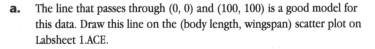

9a. See page 23t.

9b. $y = x$

9c. The slope is 1; the y-intercept is 0. The slope indicates that the wingspan will increase about 1 m for every 1-m increase in body length.

9d. Points above the line represent airplanes with wingspans that are greater than what you would expect for other planes of similar body length.

9e. Points below the line represent airplanes with wingspans that are less than what you would expect for other planes of similar body length.

9f. Points on the line represent airplanes with wingspans that are about what you would expect for other planes of similar body length.

a. The line that passes through (0, 0) and (100, 100) is a good model for this data. Draw this line on the (body length, wingspan) scatter plot on Labsheet 1.ACE.

b. Write an equation for the line.

c. What are the slope and the y-intercept of the line? What does the slope tell you about the relationship between body length and wingspan?

d. What can you conclude about the wingspan and body length of an airplane that is represented by a point *above* the line?

e. What can you conclude about the wingspan and body length of an airplane that is represented by a point *below* the line?

f. What can you conclude about the wingspan and body length of an airplane that is represented by a point *on* the line?

Mathematical Reflections

In this investigation, you reviewed your knowledge of statistics and data displays. You learned how to use the five-number summary of a data set to make a box plot. And, you used box plots to compare data distributions. These questions will help you summarize what you have learned:

1. Describe how you would construct a box plot for a set of data.

2. **a.** What is true about the values in a data set if the mean is *greater than* the median?

   b. What is true about the values in a data set if the mean is *close in value* to the median?

   c. What is true about the values in a data set if the mean is *less than* the median?

3. How can you use box plots to compare two or more data sets?

4. **a.** In what types of situations is a scatter plot useful?

   b. Describe how you would construct a scatter plot.

   Think about your answers to these questions, discuss your ideas with other students and your teacher, and then write a summary of your findings in your journal.

Tips for the Linguistically Diverse Classroom

Original Rebus The Original Rebus technique is described in detail in *Getting to Know Connected Mathematics*. Students make a copy of the text before it is discussed. During the discussion, they generate their own rebuses for words they do not understand; the words are made comprehensible through pictures, objects, or demonstrations. Example: Question 1—Key words and phrases for which students might make rebuses are *construct* (step 1, step 2, step 3), *box plot* (sketch of one), *set of data* (numbers).

Possible Answers

1. To construct a box plot, first calculate the five-number summary of the data set. Then, draw a number line with a scale that will encompass all the data values. Draw the first whisker starting at the minimum data value and extending to the first quartile, parallel to the scale. Draw a box extending from the lower quartile to the upper quartile, and indicate the median with a line perpendicular to the scale and inside the box. Draw the second whisker from the upper quartile to the maximum data value. If outliers are being considered, find the IQR to determine what points, if any, are outliers. Use asterisks to mark any outliers, and shorten the whiskers to the next value higher or lower than the outliers.

2a. If the mean is greater than the median, there are some unusually high values in the data set that are pulling the mean up.

2b. If the mean is close in value to the median, there are generally no unusually high or low values.

2c. If the mean is less than the median, there are some unusually low values in the data set that are pulling the mean down.

3, 4. See page 23t.

1.1 • Comparing Quality Ratings

In this problem, students are introduced to the data set they will be analyzing throughout Investigation 1. From a consumer-product study, the data consist of information about the quality, sodium content, and price of 37 brands of peanut butter classified by four attributes: natural or regular, creamy or chunky, salted or unsalted, and name brand or store brand. In Problem 1.1, students first review what they already know about data analysis by comparing the quality ratings for natural and regular brands of peanut butter.

Launch

One way to introduce this investigation is to engage students in a simple taste test of two varieties of peanut butter. If possible, choose brands from the table of data in the student edition, selecting one with a low quality rating (perhaps a store brand from your local supermarket) and one with a high quality rating (for example, Jif). Make sure to check whether any students have an allergy to peanuts.

One way to conduct the taste test is as follows:

■ Remove the labels from the jars.

■ Label one jar A and the other jar B.

■ Prepare, or have a student prepare, enough crackers with peanut butter A and enough crackers with peanut butter B for each student to have one cracker for each brand. (This is a good opportunity to discuss important criteria for taste tests, such as using the same type of cracker for each brand and spreading the same amount of peanut butter on each cracker.)

■ Have students take one of each cracker at the same time to do their taste tests. (Teachers have found that students need to taste the peanut butters at the same time to be able to make comparisons.)

■ Ask students to rate the taste of each product on a scale of 1 to 10, with 10 being the highest.

Students' ratings for each of the two peanut butters can be displayed on separate line plots. Once the two line plots are displayed, ask students to discuss which brand is better based on their ratings. Use this as an opportunity to help the class consider what kind of criteria might be used to determine a quality rating for a particular brand of peanut butter and to help students realize how similar their ratings may be to one another. Ratings will likely cluster in one section of each line plot. Students are not trained tasters, yet they share a sense of how good a peanut butter tastes.

Use the questions in the "Think about this!" feature preceding the table of data in the student edition to have a conversation with students about the data and about questions that the data might help to answer. In considering the questions, students will become familiar with the table of data.

Who might be interested in the results of this study?

Peanut butter is a common food in many households; these data may be of interest to anyone who eats peanut butter. With the increasing attention being paid to healthful diets, such nutritional information is important. Ask the class who might be the audience for *Consumer Reports,* the magazine in which the initial study was reported. Many people have an interest in comparative shopping; this magazine presents such data so that consumers may make more informed purchasing decisions.

What interesting questions about peanut butter can be answered with these data?

A few of the questions that can be asked about brands of peanut butter guide students' work in this investigation, but many other questions are possible. Here are a few questions that can be addressed by analyzing this set of data:

■ Is there a lot of salt in peanut butter?

■ Is there much variation in quality ratings among different kinds of peanut butter?

■ What's the best buy if I am most interested in quality?

■ What's the best buy if I am most interested in price?

■ I like Jif chunky peanut butter. How does it stack up against the other peanut butters in this study?

What interesting questions about peanut butter can't be answered with these data?

Here a few questions that might be asked but that cannot be addressed by analyzing this set of data:

■ Who eats peanut butter?

■ What preferences for peanut butter do students in our class have?

■ Does peanut butter contain a high amount of fat? Do different brands differ widely in their fat content? (Information on fat content is not shown in the table. These questions might make an interesting research topic, especially with reduced-fat peanut butters now on the market.)

■ Which brands shown in the table are sold in our local grocery stores?

■ If we conducted our own taste test, trying some of the higher-rated peanut butters and some of the lower-rated peanut butters, would our results agree with these?

Problem 1.1 is stated in a general way. It asks students to apply their knowledge of data analysis to compare quality ratings for natural brands and regular brands and to draw conclusions about which category of peanut butter has an overall higher quality rating. Make sure students understand the task.

You may want to use the problem to assess what students already know by providing very little direction as to how they should approach the question. Alternatively, you may chose to review students' earlier experiences in data analysis by specifically asking students to compute measures of center (mean and median) and spread (range) and to display the data using back-to-back stem plots and histograms.

If students have not had much experience with making histograms, you may want to work through an example to demonstrate how stem plots and histograms are related. The following example is reproduced on Transparency 1.1B.

A stem plot can be constructed from the quality ratings of the regular peanut butters, as shown on the left below. The plot can then be rotated, as shown on the right.

Quality Ratings for Regular Brands

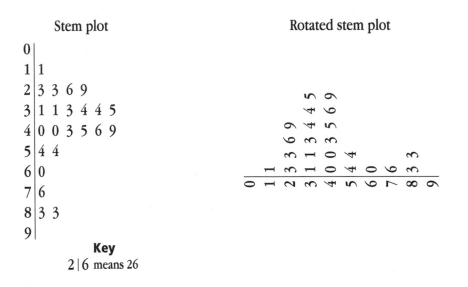

Stem plot   Rotated stem plot

```
0|
1| 1
2| 3 3 6 9
3| 1 1 3 4 4 5
4| 0 0 3 5 6 9
5| 4 4
6| 0
7| 6
8| 3 3
9|
```

Key
2 | 6 means 26

Enclosing each column of numbers in the rotated stem plot with a rectangle demonstrates the connection between a stem plot and a histogram. Note that a stem plot displays the *actual values* in a data set; a histogram shows the *distribution* of continuous data—in this case, quality rating.

Transforming a Rotated Stem Plot into a Histogram

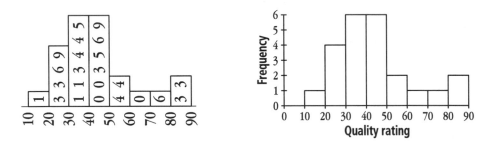

Have students work on the problem and the follow-up in pairs. The table of data is reproduced on Labsheet 1.1, which you may want to distribute.

Explore

As you circulate, you may need to review strategies for finding the median, mean, and range and for creating stem plots and histograms.

Summarize

Have pairs of students report their findings. Ask for justification of the conclusions they reach. Use the information reported to review the statistics of the mean, the median, and the range. Also review some of the ways to display data, such as histograms and stem-and-leaf plots. The examples shown below are reproduced on Transparency 1.1C, which you may want to use for reviewing important ideas with the class.

This is a back-to-back stem plot that students might construct in answering this question.

Quality Ratings for Natural and Regular Brands

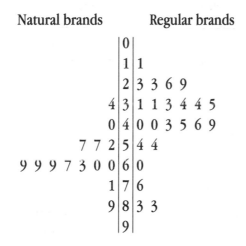

```
Natural brands            Regular brands
                       |0|
                       |1|1
                       |2|3 3 6 9
              4|3|1 1 3 4 4 5
              0|4|0 0 3 5 6 9
          7 7 2|5|4 4
    9 9 9 7 3 0 0|6|0
              1|7|6
              9|8|3 3
               |9|
```

Below are two histograms that students might make in answering this question.

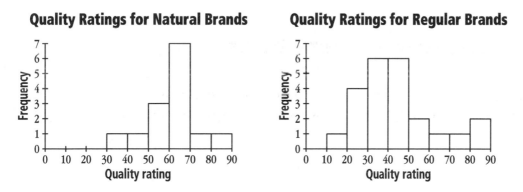

Quality Ratings for Natural Brands   **Quality Ratings for Regular Brands**

Students might compute the mean, median, and range of the data sets.

Natural brands		Regular brands
61.2	mean	42.7
61.5	median	40
34 to 89	range	11 to 83

Involve students in a discussion about what information they can "see" with each graph and in what ways each type of graph helps or hinders making comparisons. With histograms, the shape of the data may be described and compared; this includes noting the range of the data and any clusters, gaps, and peaks. A back-to-back stem plot makes the comparisons clearer because the two distributions are shown against each other, rather than next to each other as with histograms.

As is appropriate whenever students have analyzed data to answer specific questions, ask students to think about other questions or comparisons that might be interesting to investigate with a different analysis of the data.

In the discussion of the follow-up, review the fact that the median and the mean provide two ways to summarize data. The median as a value is considered to be more *stable*—unchanging with changes in data—than the mean. That is, in an ordered list of values, the values at either end may be anything; the median will not vary. For example, consider these three data sets:

			Median		
Set A:	16	34	**42**	56	62
Set B:	16	34	**42**	56	162
Set C:	16	34	**42**	56	252

While the median is 42 in each set of values, the means are 42, 62, and 80, respectively.

Review with students the idea that if the mean is greater than the median, there are some unusually high values in the data; if the mean is less than the median, there are some unusually low values in the data.

1.2 • Using Box-and-Whiskers Plots

In this problem, students are introduced to five-number summaries and box-and-whiskers plots, or box plots. They use box plots as another tool for comparing the quality ratings of regular and natural brands of peanut butter.

Launch

The discussion preceding Problem 1.2 in the student edition opens with a box plot showing the distribution of quality ratings for the natural brands of peanut butter. You may want to walk students through the creation of this graph to help them understand the information contained in a box plot. These steps are outlined on Transparency 1.2A.

First, ask students to help you list the data values in order: 34, 40, 52, 57, 57, 60, 60, 63, 67, 69, 69, 69, 71, and 89.

Next, work with students to find the five-number summary. The minimum value is 34, the maximum value is 89, and the median is 61.5 (the average of the two center values, 60 and 63). The lower quartile is the median of the data values below the median—or the median of 34, 40, 52, 57, 57, 60, and 60—which is 57. The upper quartile is the median of the data values above the median—or the median of 63, 67, 69, 69, 69, 71, and 89—which is 69.

Now, ask students to use these numbers to draw the number line and make the box plot.

Quality Ratings for Natural Brands

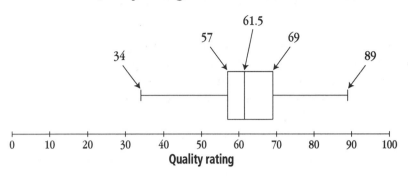

You might have students practice this skill by asking them to construct a box plot showing the distribution of quality ratings for the regular brands on the same scale as the box plot for the natural brands. They can compare their box plots to those shown in their books.

Quality Ratings for Natural and Regular Brands

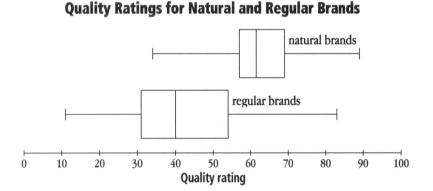

Have students work in pairs to answer the questions in the problem. Save the follow-up until after you have summarized the problem and talked about how to determine outliers.

Explore

As you circulate, ask questions to help students focus on the percent divisions of data in a box plot.

What percent of the data fall below the median? *(about 50%)* Above the median? *(about 50%)*

What percent of the data fall below the lower quartile? *(about 25%)* Above the upper quartile? *(about 25%)*

What percent of the data fall between the median and the lower quartile? *(about 25%)* Between the median and the upper quartile? *(about 25%)*

Summarize

Review with students the procedure for making a box plot for a set of data: order data from least to greatest, identify the five-number summary, and draw the box and the whiskers in relation to a number line.

Ask students to share what they learned about how the numbers that summarize the data also separate the data into standard percent groupings. Generally speaking, if the data are in an ordered list, we know that about 50% of the data fall before the median and about 50% fall after the median. The lower and upper quartiles separate the data set below or above the median in half again. This means that the actual box in a box plot accounts for about 50% of the data, and each whisker accounts for about 25% of the data. Ask questions to assess students' comprehension of these ideas.

> What percent of the data in a box plot fall above the lower quartile? *(about 75%)* Below the upper quartile? *(about 75%)*

For the Teacher: More About Box Plots

The student edition shows box plots constructed along a horizontal axis; they can also be constructed along a vertical axis. Both plots below show the distribution of quality ratings for natural brands of peanut butter.

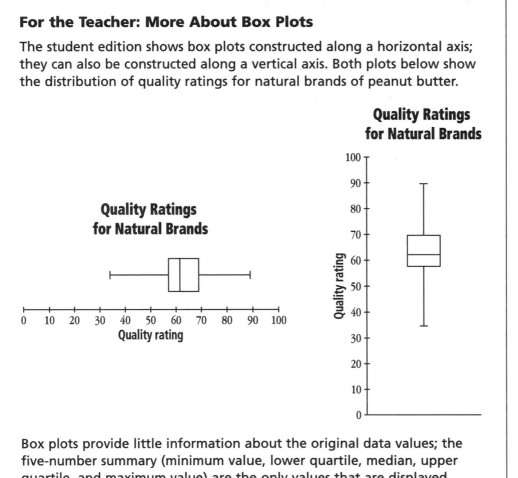

Box plots provide little information about the original data values; the five-number summary (minimum value, lower quartile, median, upper quartile, and maximum value) are the only values that are displayed. Moreover, box plots do not offer a way to do detailed analysis of a single distribution. They must be joined with such representations as histograms in order to conduct such analyses.

Ask students to explain their thoughts on how they used the box plots to decide whether regular or natural brands of peanut butter are of higher quality.

Introduce the concept of *outliers,* data value much greater or much less than most of the other values in a set. Talk about determining whether a data set contains outliers by first calculating the *interquartile range (IQR),* the difference between the upper and lower quartiles. Outliers are then defined as follows:

$$\text{values} > 1.5(\text{IQR}) + \text{upper quartile}$$
$$\text{values} < \text{lower quartile} - 1.5(\text{IQR})$$

Have pairs work on the follow-up questions. When they finish, review how to find outliers and talk about the value of showing outliers in box plots.

Outliers are generally only a few values; the actual box and whiskers show the spread of *most* of the data. Looking at this adjusted spread makes it easier to compare most of the data and to make generalizations without being distracted or misled by outliers. *Throughout the rest of this unit, encourage students to compute outliers whenever they make box plots.* Even if they make their box plots on a calculator that does not show outliers, they can easily compute the interquartile range and determine whether there are any outliers in the data sets.

For the Teacher: Benchmarks in Box Plots

Box plots may be used to comment on relative frequency by taking note of where the benchmarks of 0%, 25%, 50%, 75%, and 100% of the data fall. For example, we can say that 50% of the data represented by box plot A exceed 75% of the data represented by box plot B because the median in box plot A exceeds the upper quartile in box plot B.

box plot A

box plot B

However, it is often true that several values in a data set are equal to a quartile or the median. When this is the case, it may be, for example, that 50% of the data *items* fall between the two quartiles but that more than 50% of the data *values* occur in the same interval. In the data set 4, 5, 6, 8, 9, 11, 11, 11, 11, 15, for example, the interval from 6 to 11 includes more values than fall between the lower and upper quartiles.

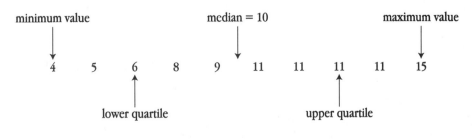

For the Teacher: Using Technology to Make Box Plots

In their work in this unit, students might make box plots using graphing calculators or computer software. However, is advisable that they make box plots by hand first, as exploring with a calculator requires some understanding of what is being displayed.

Some calculators and software programs (for example, Statistics Workshop) display outliers or offer the option to do so (for example, the TI-83 graphing calculator) while others do not display outliers (for example, the TI-80). Box plots displayed on a calculator do not show a number line marked with numbers but with tick marks, so students need a clear understanding of what is being displayed in order to identify which box plot is which. Below is a TI-80 display of the box plots of quality ratings for natural and regular brands of peanut butter.

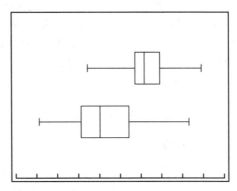

Below is a display of the same box plots made with Statistics Workshop software.

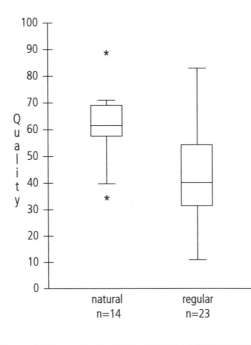

On the TI-80, using the trace function and the arrow keys will cause the cursor to move through the five summary numbers on each box plot as the values are displayed in the lower-left corner of the screen. Using this feature will help students understand how the box plots are related to the work they did by hand. For more assistance with using the graphing calculator to make box plots, see the technology section in the front of this book.

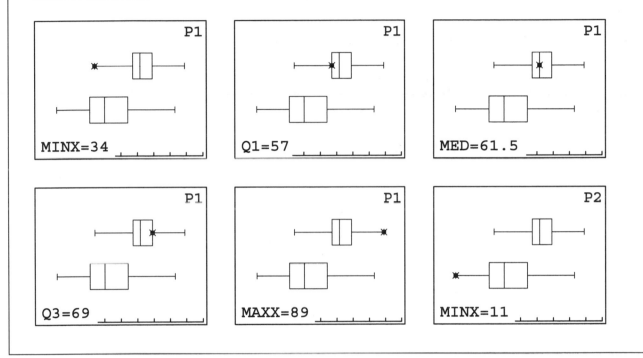

1.3 • Comparing Prices

In Problem 1.2, students investigated box plots of the quality ratings of natural and regular peanut butters. In this companion problem, they study box plots comparing prices of natural and regular peanut butters. Students apply what they have learned in working on Problem 1.2, and they encounter a situation in which the median and a quartile have the same value.

Launch

In the previous problem, students used box plots to determine that natural peanut butters are a better choice for a consumer who is primarily interested in quality rating. In essence, results of the study indicate that natural peanut butters taste better. In this problem, students investigate which type of peanut butter is a better buy for a consumer for whom price is of most importance. Introduce the problem by posing this question.

> We have found that natural brands of peanut butter are probably a better choice for a consumer who is most concerned about quality rating. Do you think they are also a better buy for a consumer who is most concerned about price?

Review the concept of a five-number summary, the five values from which a box plot is constructed. Have students work in groups of two to four on the problem and follow-up.

Explore

In their groups, students will calculate five-number summaries for the prices of natural brands and regular brands and use them to identify which box plot in the student edition represents which set of data.

Some students may be confused by the fact that in the upper box plot, which is for the natural brands of peanut butter, there is no vertical line inside the box. Because the lower quartile and the median are both 26, they are represented by the same vertical line. If students need help, ask them to indicate where the lower quartile is represented in the box plot and then where the median is represented.

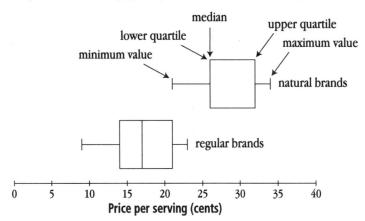

Peanut Butter Prices

Summarize

Have students share the values they found for each five-number summary as you construct the box plots at the board or the overhead. Students should have discovered that the median and the lower quartile of prices for the natural brands are the same and thus are represented by a single vertical line on the box plot.

> Is natural peanut butter or regular peanut butter a better choice if you are concerned only with price? If you are concerned only with quality?

As students found out earlier, the quality ratings for the natural brands are generally higher than those for the regular brands. The box plots of quality ratings show that more than 75% of the natural brands have greater quality ratings than do the regular brands. The reverse is true for price: when students look at the box plots, they can immediately say that regular brands cost less than natural brands.

> What do the box plots tell you about how prices for natural brands and regular brands compare?

Make sure students recognize that the plots show that the prices for 100% of the natural brands are higher than the prices for 75% of the regular brands. That is, the lowest price of the natural brands falls approximately at the upper quartile of the regular brands. The five-number summaries verify that the minimum value for the prices of the natural brands is equal to the upper quartile for the prices of the regular brands, or 21¢.

1.4 • Making a Quality Choice

Students have already looked at quality ratings for natural versus regular brands of peanut butter. Now they will compare the quality ratings for the remaining three attributes by which the brands are classified: creamy or chunky, salted or unsalted, and name brand or store brand.

Launch

Introduce the idea of comparing the quality ratings for attributes other than natural versus regular.

> In your previous work, you have discovered that natural brands have an overall higher quality rating than do regular brands.
>
> In this problem, you will look at how the quality ratings are related to the other attributes of peanut butter: creamy or chunky, salted or unsalted, and name brand or store brand. For example, how do you think the quality ratings of creamy peanut butters might compare to the quality ratings of chunky peanut butters?

Have students work in pairs to analyze the quality ratings for the three remaining attributes and to answer the follow-up questions.

Explore

Have students create their box plots by hand or using their calculators or statistics software (if it is available). You may want to distribute blank transparencies to some pairs for recording their box plots to one part of the problem for sharing during the class summary.

The five-number summaries for the quality ratings for each of the three attributes are given here and on page 23n for your information. You may need to remind students that if a median or a quartile falls between two values, those two values are averaged to determine the median or quartile.

Quality Ratings of Creamy Brands
 minimum value: 11
 lower quartile: 33
 median: 43
 upper quartile: 60
 maximum value: 76

Quality Ratings of Chunky Brands
 minimum value: 26
 lower quartile: 40
 median: 51.5
 upper quartile: 69
 maximum value: 89

For the Teacher: Creating Box Plots with Statistics Software

Shown here are box plots comparing the quality ratings for each of the four attributes by which the peanut butters are sorted. These box plots were made with Statistics Workshop software, which indicates outliers with asterisks. Some calculators and statistical software packages extend the whiskers to the minimum and maximum values; others apply the interquartile-range rule (see Problem 1.2 Follow-Up) to determine whether some of the very low or very high values are unusual and, if so, marks them as outliers. Statistics Workshop displays box plots vertically; other programs display them horizontally.

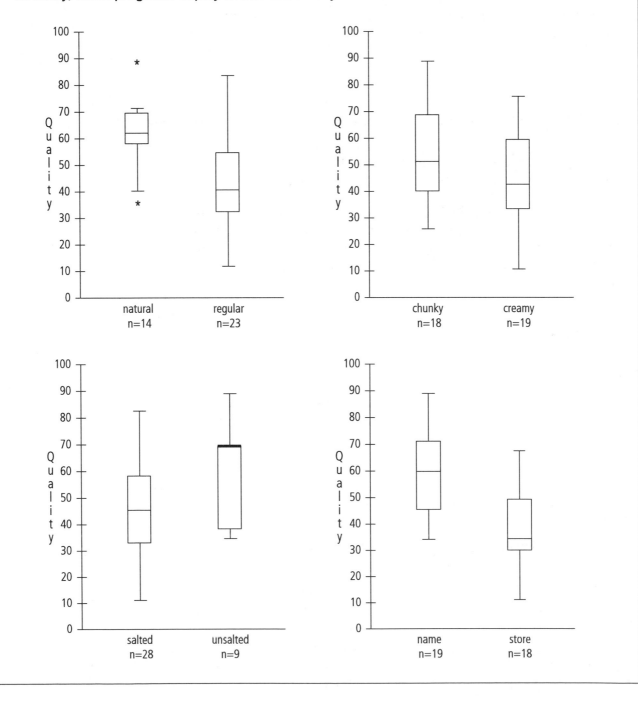

Quality Ratings of Salted Brands
> minimum value: 11
> lower quartile: 32
> median: 45.5
> upper quartile: 58.5
> maximum value: 83

Quality Ratings of Unsalted Brands
> minimum value: 34
> lower quartile: 37.5
> median: 69
> upper quartile: 70
> maximum value: 89

Quality Ratings of Name Brands
> minimum value: 34
> lower quartile: 45
> median: 60
> upper quartile: 71
> maximum value: 89

Quality Ratings of Store Brands
> minimum value: 11
> lower quartile: 29
> median: 34
> upper quartile: 49
> maximum value: 67

Summarize

Creating an argument using data is an essential component of the statistical investigation process. Each set of box plots provides an opportunity for this discussion to occur. Select one or more groups to present their arguments for each of the three attributes. If possible, display their box plots for the class to see. Then ask students which attributes and brands they would recommend to someone interested in peanut butter quality.

It may be interesting to ask students to reflect on the brands that are indicated by applying all four attributes. Health Valley 100% Natural, in particular, has a quality rating of only 40! And Jif regular chunky and Skippy regular chunky, both with a rating of 83, do not meet all four criteria. By inspecting all four sets of box plots, students can see that the variation in quality ratings between natural and regular brands and between name and store brands is more pronounced than the variation in quality ratings between creamy and chunky brands and salted and unsalted brands. Choosing a brand by applying all four criteria essentially gives the relationship between each attribute and quality equal weight and does not account for individual variation in the products.

1.5 • Comparing Quality and Price

Relationships between variables may be displayed in scatter plots. In this problem, students explore the relationship between quality and price of the regular brands versus the natural brands of peanut butter. They investigate a scatter plot of the (quality rating, price) data and then construct and interpret their own scatter plot of the (quality rating, sodium) data.

Launch

Direct the class's attention to the scatter plot displaying the (quality rating, price) data, which is reproduced on Transparency 1.5.

You may want to have students create this scatter plot on their calculators by entering the quality ratings and price-per-serving data. On the TI-80 calculator, this can be done by entering the quality ratings and price data for natural brands as pairs in two companion lists and the data for regular brands in the next two lists. Then, pairs of data for natural and regular brands would be plotted on the same graph, with different symbols chosen to show the data pairs. (If all the quality ratings are entered into one list and all the prices are entered into a second list, the data pairs will all be displayed with the same symbol, making comparisons difficult.) For more assistance using the graphing calculator to make scatter plots, see the technology section in the front of this book.

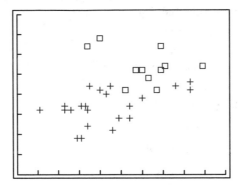

Have students work in pairs to explore the questions posed in the problem and the follow-up.

Explore

If students have trouble with part A, ask:

> Have you looked back at the original data shown? How might this help you to answer the questions here?

For part B, you might ask:

> Locate a peanut butter with a high quality rating in the original data. What is its quality rating and cost? Where is this point on the scatter plot? Now do the same for one with a low quality rating and one with a middle quality rating. How can this help you to answer the question?

For part C, you might ask:

> What does it mean when we say a (quality rating, price) data value is "unusual"? "Usual" means that the higher the quality rating, the greater (lower) the cost. So, when would a data pair be unusual?

Summarize

Talk about students' findings and their reasoning. In the follow-up, students will have found that many peanut butters have similar sodium content but different quality ratings. The same is true for unsalted peanut butters; there is no obvious relationship. The box plots show that the range of the quality ratings for the unsalted brands (34 to 71) is similar to the range of quality ratings for salted brands (11 to 83), so there are not great differences. You might point out that because salt is used as preservative, there are several natural brands in the table that do not contain added salt and thus have low sodium content.

Additional Answers

Answers to Problem 1.4

A. There is not much variation between these two distributions. Chunky brands have a slight edge over creamy: the median quality rating for chunky brands is 51.5 while the median rating for creamy brands is 43, a difference of only 8.5 points. Chunky brands seem to be a slightly better choice.

Quality of Creamy vs. Chunky Brands

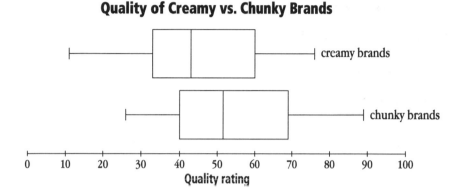

B. More than 50% of the quality ratings for unsalted brands are above the upper quartile for salted brands. And 100% of the unsalted brands have quality ratings above the lower quartile for salted brands. Thus, unsalted brands are better choice. (Note: The box plot for unsalted brands may confuse students, as the median, 69, and the upper quartile, 70, are almost identical.)

Quality of Salted vs. Unsalted Brands

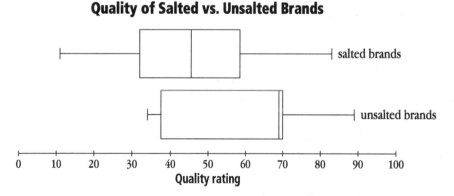

C. 100% of name brands have quality ratings that are greater than or equal to the median quality rating for store brands. Thus, name brands are a better choice.

Quality of Name vs. Store Brands

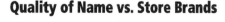

Answers to Problem 1.5

D. 1. To compare the quality ratings of the two categories, look at the relative positions of the two symbols along the horizontal axis. In general, natural peanut butters have higher quality ratings.

2. To compare the prices of the two categories, look at the relative positions of the two symbols along the vertical axis. In general, natural peanut butters have higher prices.

Answers to Problem 1.5 Follow-Up

1.

Peanut Butter Quality and Sodium Content

(scatter plot with "Sodium per serving (mg)" on the vertical axis from 0 to 275 and "Quality rating" on the horizontal axis from 0 to 100; legend: ● salted brands, ◆ unsalted brands)

2. There is no obvious relationship between quality rating and sodium content. Although the salted brands cluster between a sodium content of 105 mg to 225 mg, their quality ratings vary greatly. The same is true for unsalted peanut butters: there is no obvious relationship between the two variables.

3. The box plot shows a minor tendency for salted brands to be of lower quality, though if one chooses carefully, it is possible to get high quality in a salted peanut butter.

Quality of Salted vs. Unsalted Brands

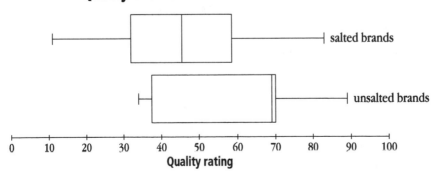

ACE Answers

Applications

1a. The lower quartile of the natural brands is greater than the maximum price of the regular brands, meaning that more than 75% of the natural brands cost more than the regular brands. Based on price, regular brands are a better choice.

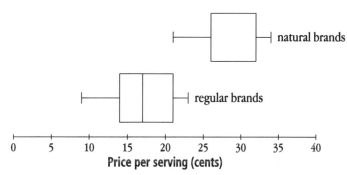

Peanut Butter Prices

1b. There is very little variation between the plots of the creamy brands and the chunky brands. This means prices are essentially the same for both, so either is a good choice.

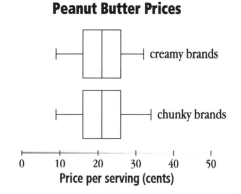

Peanut Butter Prices

1c. More than 75% of the unsalted varieties are priced higher than 100% of the salted varieties, so the salted varieties are less expensive. Note that there are 28 salted varieties and only 9 unsalted varieties.

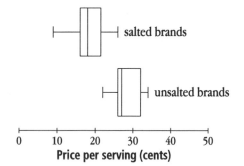

Peanut Butter Prices

1d. 100% of the name brands have prices that are greater than the median price, or 50%, of the store brands. Based on price, store brands are a better choice.

Peanut Butter Prices

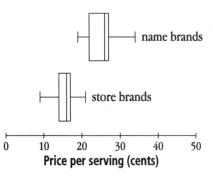

4. In general, the greater the body length, the greater the wingspan.

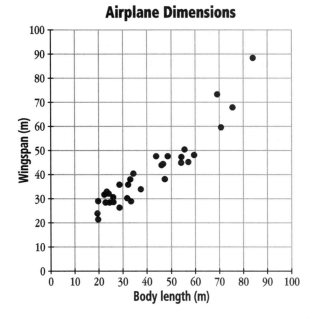

Extensions

9a.

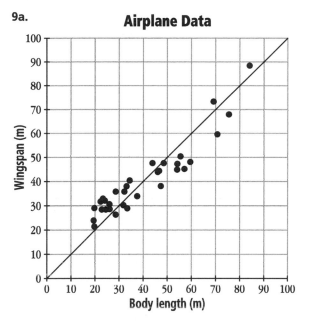

Airplane Data

Mathematical Reflections

3. The five-number summary includes the minimum value, lower quartile, median, upper quartile, and maximum value. Those five points divide the data distribution into four quartiles, which each contain about 25% of the data. We can construct box plots on the same scale and then look at whether one data set has the same, greater, or lower values than the other data set. (Note: By themselves, box plots help us see the spread in a data set, but we can't tell anything about the shape of the data.)

4a. A scatter plot is useful for displaying or looking for patterns in data sets in which each value is described by two related attributes—in other words, when the data are in ordered pairs.

4b. To make a scatter plot, set scales on the axes to include the maximum and the minimum values of each variable, and then plot the ordered pairs of the data points.

Conducting Surveys

Though we often cannot collect data from all members of a population, we usually gather data in order to describe or to better understand a population. To find a sample that accurately represents a population, we develop a sampling plan. We use results of the analysis of data from the sample to make predictions or to draw conclusions about characteristics or behaviors of the entire population. In this investigation, students consider the distinction between samples and populations and use the results of analyses of data from samples to make estimates about population characteristics and behaviors.

In Problem 2.1, Asking About Honesty, students consider the implications of making estimates about the entire U.S. population based on a telephone survey involving a few thousand people. The survey raises issues about predicting from data collected about a sample to an entire population. In Problem 2.2, Selecting a Sample, students consider a variety of sampling methods, analyzing the advantages and disadvantages of each and determining which would produce the sample most representative of the population. In Problem 2.3, Asking the Right Questions, students consider issues that are important in developing surveys. In this open-ended problem, they work with partners to design a survey to gather information about middle and high school students and their plans for the future. In the process, they practice writing both open and closed survey questions.

Mathematical and Problem-Solving Goals

- *To distinguish between a sample and a population*

- *To consider various ways of developing a sampling plan*

- *To use data from a sample to make predictions about a population*

- *To design a survey, focusing on how questions are asked*

Problem	For students	For the teacher
All	Graphing calculators, computers and statistical software (optional), grid paper	Transparencies: 2.1A to 2.3 (optional), overhead graphing calculator (optional)
2.2		Large sheets of paper (optional)
2.3	Blank transparencies or large sheets of paper (optional)	

Materials

Conducting Surveys

If you wanted to gather information about students in your class—such as their preferences for food, television programs, music, or sports—it would be fairly easy to conduct an accurate survey. But what might you do if you wanted information about all the students in your school, or all the people in your city, your state, or the entire country?

Some recent reports made these claims:

- Americans spend 44% of their food budget on meals prepared away from home.
- Of all restaurant orders, 49% are for off-premises consumption.
- More than 2 million American youths, most of them girls, participate in competitive gymnastics.
- On Tuesday, July 30, 1996, more than 45 million American households watched evening broadcasts of the Atlanta Olympic Games.

Think about this!

How could the people who reported these data know about the eating, sports, and television-viewing activities of all 260 million Americans?

Tips for the Linguistically Diverse Classroom

Rebus Scenario The Rebus Scenario technique is described in detail in *Getting to Know Connected Mathematics.* This technique involves sketching rebuses on the chalkboard that correspond to key words in the story or information that you present orally. Example: Some key words and phrases for which you may need to draw rebuses while discussing these claims: *meals prepared away from home* (McDonald's arches), *off-premises consumption* (paper bag labeled TO GO), *competitive gymnastics* (stick figure on balance beam), *watched evening broadcasts* (television set), *Olympic Games* (Olympic symbol).

You can study a large **population** by collecting data from a small part, or **sample,** of that population. You can then *make predictions* or *draw conclusions* about the entire population based on data from the sample. The challenge in such studies is to find a sample that accurately represents the population. Such a sample is called a **representative sample**.

2.1 Asking About Honesty

Newspapers, magazines, and radio and television programs conduct surveys on a variety of subjects. Such surveys often ask readers or listeners to call in to express their views. A magazine with a national circulation asked its readers to phone in their answer to five questions about honesty.

How Honest Is America?

A. If you found someone else's wallet on the street, would you
1. try to return it to the owner?
2. return it, but keep the money?
3. keep the wallet and the money?

B. If a cashier mistakenly gave you $10 extra in change, would you
1. tell the cashier about the error?
2. say nothing and keep the cash?

C. Would you cheat on an exam if you were sure you wouldn't get caught?
1. yes
2. no

D. If you found someone else's telephone calling card, would you use it?
1. yes
2. no

E. Do you feel that you are an honest person in most situations?
1. yes
2. no

 Call 1-900-555-8281, and enter your answers by pressing the appropriate number keys.

Grouping:
pairs

Launch

- Introduce Investigation 2 by discussing the situations on the opening page of the student edition.

- Talk about samples, sampling plans, and the honesty survey.

- Have groups of two to four work on the problem and follow-up.

Explore

- As you circulate, remind students to be prepared to present their answers and to describe their strategies.

Summarize

- Discuss the questions that involve percents, resolving any differences.

- Ask students to share their survey questions and their ideas on revising the sampling plan.

Assignment Choices

ACE questions 1–4 and unassigned choices from earlier problems

Launch

- Discuss the five research questions, how they might be asked, and how the research might be conducted.

- Have groups of two to four work on the problem and follow-up.

Explore

- If students have trouble identifying the sampling plans, focus them on the name of each type of sampling.

Summarize

- Ask students to share their ideas about the advantages and disadvantages of each sampling method and which gives the most representative sample.

- Talk about the follow-up.

- Review representative samples and biased samples.

Problem 2.1

A. A *sampling plan* is a strategy for choosing a sample from a population. What is the sampling plan for this survey? What are the population and the sample for this survey?

B. Suppose 5280 people answered the survey, and 4224 of them pressed 2 for question C. What percent of the callers said they would not cheat on an exam?

C. Of the 5280 callers, 1584 pressed 1 for question D. What percent of the callers said they would not use someone else's calling card?

D. The U.S. population is about 260 million. Based on the results of this survey, how many people in the United States would not cheat on an exam? How many would not use someone else's calling card?

E. List some reasons why predictions about all Americans based on this survey might be inaccurate.

▩ Problem 2.1 Follow-Up

1. The magazine conducting the survey assumes a person is honest if he or she reports honest behavior for all five questions. Suppose that, according to these criteria, 3507 people out of the 5280 who responded are honest. Based on these results, what percent of the U.S. population would you predict is honest?

2. Write two questions that could be used to gather additional information about honest behavior.

3. How could you revise the sampling plan for this survey so you would be more confident that the results would predict the percent of the U.S population that is honest?

Selecting a Sample

The results of the telephone survey in Problem 2.1 were used to make predictions about the U.S. population. Making accurate predictions about a population based on the results of a survey can be complicated, even when you are interested in a relatively small population.

ACE questions 5–11 and unassigned choices from earlier problems

Answers to Problem 2.1

A. The sampling plan is to ask people to answer the survey. The population is the population of the United States; the sample is the readers of this particular magazine who call in to answer the survey.

B. 4224 ÷ 5280 = 80%

C. 5280 – 1584 = 3696; 3696 ÷ 5280 = 70%

D. About 80% of 260 million, or 208 million people, would not cheat on an exam. About 70% of 260 million, or 182 million people, would not use someone else's calling card.

E. See page 36e.

Answers to Problem 2.1 Follow-Up

See page 36e.

Suppose you are doing a research project on the lives of students at your school and would like to answer these questions:

- How many hours of sleep do students get each night?
- How many students eat breakfast in the morning?
- How many hours of television do students watch in a week?
- How many soft drinks do students consume in a day?
- How many students wear braces on their teeth?

If your school has a large student population, it might be difficult to gather and analyze information from every student. How could you select a sample of your school population to survey?

Problem 2.2

Ms. Baker's class wants to find out how many students in their school wear braces on their teeth. The class divides into four groups. Each group devises a plan for sampling the school population.

- Each member of group 1 will survey the students who ride on his or her school bus.

- Group 2 will survey every fourth person in the cafeteria line.

- Group 3 will read a notice on the school's morning announcements asking for volunteers for their survey.

- Group 4 will randomly select 30 students for their survey from a list of three-digit student ID numbers. They will roll a 10-sided number cube three times to generate each number.

A. What are the advantages and disadvantages of each sampling plan?

B. Which plan do you think would most accurately predict the number of students in the school who wear braces? That is, which plan do you think will give the most *representative* sample? Explain your answer.

Answers to Problem 2.2

A. Possible advantages and disadvantages: *Group 1's plan* is easy to implement, but the students on a particular bus probably all live in the same neighborhood and, as a result, won't necessarily be typical of all students in the school. *Group 2's plan* seems to offer a better prospect of surveying students that represent the variety of the school, but it is possible that the students who buy cafeteria lunches aren't typical of all students; for example, it may be that students who wear braces don't buy cafeteria food as much as students who don't wear braces. *Group 3's plan* is similar to the magazine's survey about honesty, with the risk that one won't find out what shier students think. *Group 4's plan* would make each student equally likely to be chosen, but it may be more difficult to implement because each selected student would need to be tracked down.

B. Group 4's plan would probably give the most representative sample. See the explanation in part A.

▓ Problem 2.2 Follow-Up

The plans developed by the groups in Ms. Baker's class are examples of common sampling methods.

1. Group 1's plan is an example of **convenience sampling**. What do you think convenience sampling is? Describe another plan that would use convenience sampling.

2. Group 2's plan is an example of **systematic sampling**. What do you think systematic sampling is? Describe another plan that would use systematic sampling.

3. Group 3's plan is an example of **voluntary-response sampling**. What do you think voluntary-response sampling is? Describe another plan that would use voluntary-response sampling.

4. Group 4's plan is an example of **random sampling**. What do you think random sampling is? Describe another plan that would use random sampling.

5. When using sampling methods to study a large population, it is important to choose samples that are representative of the population. Samples that give misleading impressions are called **biased samples.** Which groups in Problem 2.2 are likely to get a biased sample? Explain your answers.

6. Which sampling method was used in Problem 2.1?

Answers to Problem 2.2 Follow-Up

1. Convenience sampling is choosing a sample based on the availability of respondents, people who are easy to locate and ask. Possible plans: Survey the students in a particular math class or homeroom or who belong to the same club or team.

2. Systematic sampling is choosing a sample by using a methodical technique. Possible plans: Choose every fifth name from an alphabetical list of students in each grade level, or the first person off each school bus one morning, or the student at the head of each row of seats in an auditorium assembly.

3. Voluntary-response sampling is asking people to choose to participate. Possible plan: Hand out surveys to all students, and ask them to return completed forms to a box in the school office.

You have seen that when conducting a survey, it is important to select a representative sample. You must also be careful about how you ask your questions.

When you write a survey, you need to think about whether each question should be an open question or a closed question.

An *open question* asks a person to write a response. Here are two examples of open questions:

> What is your age?
>
> After high school, what do you plan to do?

The first question has predictable responses that should be easy to organize and analyze. Although answers to the second question are less predictable, the question gives the person the freedom to answer in any way he or she chooses.

A *closed question* provides a person with a set of choices. Here, the two questions above are restated as closed questions:

What is your age?

| _____ under 12 | _____ 12 | _____ 13 | _____ 14 |
| _____ 15 | _____ 16 | _____ 17 | _____ over 17 |

After high school, which of the following do you plan to do?

_____ attend a two-year college	_____ join the service
_____ attend a four-year college	_____ get a full-time job
_____ attend a trade or vocational school	_____ other

The answers to closed questions are generally easier to organize and analyze than the answers to open questions, but closed questions limit the possible responses.

When you critique a survey you have written, you should ask yourself several things:

- Are the questions clearly stated?
- Can any of the questions be misinterpreted?
- Have I provided good, reasonable choices for the closed questions in my survey?
- What types of answers can I expect to the open questions?
- Will I be able to organize and analyze the data I collect?

At a Glance

Grouping:
pairs

Launch

- Discuss open and closed questions.

- Have students work in pairs to write questions for a survey.

- Consider having students do part of the problem as homework.

Explore

- Remind students to make their questions clear.

Summarize

- Have pairs share their questions and sampling plans.

- Develop a class survey from the students' questions. *(optional)*

---

4. Random sampling is giving every member of a population an equally likely chance of being selected. Possible plan: Choose student names or numbers by writing them all on slips of paper, mixing them in a bowl, and selecting slips of paper without looking.

5. Group 1 will get a biased sample because they are surveying only students who ride on their buses; they won't survey any students who don't take those buses. Group 2 will get a biased sample because they are surveying only students who buy lunch in the cafeteria. Group 3 will get a biased sample because they are surveying only students who are motivated enough to respond. Group 4 won't get a biased sample because they are selecting students at random.

6. The honesty survey used voluntary-response sampling.

Assignment Choices

ACE questions 12–15 and unassigned choices from earlier problems

Problem 2.3

In this problem, you will work with a partner to design a survey to gather information about middle school and high school students and their plans for the future. Your survey should include questions about characteristics of the students, such as age, gender, and favorite school subject. Your survey should also gather information about what students plan to do after graduation from high school. For example, your survey might include questions about the following topics:

- Students' plans for college or a job immediately after high school

- The types of careers students would like to pursue

- The places students would like to live

A. Work with a partner to develop a first draft of a survey. Exchange surveys with another pair of students, and critique each other's survey.

B. Prepare a final version of your survey.

C. Write a paragraph describing a sampling plan you could use to survey students in your school.

■ Problem 2.3 Follow-Up

1. At Hilltop Middle School, there are 200 sixth graders, 200 seventh graders, and 200 eighth graders. If you gave your survey to one class of 25 students in each grade, could you use the results to make predictions about all the students in the school? Explain your reasoning.

2. At Valleyview Middle School, there are 250 sixth graders, 250 seventh graders, and 250 eighth graders. About 60% of the students at each grade level are girls. How could you select a random sample of students in the school so that 60% of the students in your sample are girls and 40% are boys?

Answers to Problem 2.3

Surveys will vary. Have students share their surveys, perhaps having the class develop a single survey by choosing questions from among all those that students wrote.

Answers to Problem 2.3 Follow-Up

1. By using this convenience sample, you don't give all students an equally likely chance to be included. You would not want to use results to make predictions about all the students in the school.

2. Possible answer: List all girls by grade level and all boys by grade level. Choose the sample size to be used for each grade level (for example, 30 students). Randomly select 60% of each sample (18 students) from all the girls at that grade level and 40% of each sample (12 students) from all the boys at that grade level.

Applications • Connections • Extensions

As you work on these ACE questions, use your calculator whenever you need it.

Applications

There are 350 students in Banneker Middle School. Mr. Abosch's math class wants to find out how many hours of homework a typical student in the school did last week. Several students in the class devised plans for selecting a sample of students to survey. In 1–4, tell whether you think the plan would give a representative sample, and explain your answer.

1. Anna suggested surveying every third student on each homeroom class list.

2. Kwang-Hee suggested putting 320 white beans and 30 red beans in a bag and asking each student to draw a bean as he or she enters the auditorium for tomorrow's assembly. The 30 students who draw red beans will be surveyed.

3. Ushio suggested that each student in Mr. Abosch's class survey everyone in his or her English class.

HOMEWORK SURVEY
Please take one.

4. Kirby suggested putting surveys on a table at the entrance to the school and asking students to return completed questionnaires at the end of the day.

In 5–8, describe the population being studied and the sampling method being used.

5. A magazine for teenagers asks its readers to write in with information about how they solve personal problems.

6. To find out how much time middle school students spend on the telephone each day, members of an eighth grade class kept a record for a week of the amount of time they spent on the phone each day.

5. The population being studied is the teenagers who read the magazine. The voluntary-response sampling method is used.

6. The population being studied is middle school students. The convenience sampling method is used, as only those students in a particular class keep track of their phone time.

Answers

Applications

1. Systematic selection from class lists would probably give a representative sample, provided the lists include the names of all students in the school.

2. Selection by choosing red and white beans could produce a representative sample because every student has an equal chance of being in the sample. However, if attendance for the assembly is low, the sample may not be representative of the population.

3. Selection by surveying all members of particular classes would probably not give a representative sample because students do not have an equally likely chance of being surveyed. It may be that students in these classes are assigned more homework on average and thus spend more time doing homework.

4. This voluntary-response method would not give a representative sample because it depends on people's choosing to complete and return the surveys. Not everyone will complete a survey, and those who do may not place it in the box at the end of the day; those who complete surveys may have some special reason for responding.

7. The population being studied is middle school students. The random sampling method is used.

8. The population being studied is students who attend the particular school. The sampling method has elements of both systematic and random methods—depending on the method of choosing the student from among the A's, the B's, and so on. Even if a name is chosen at random from each letter of the alphabet, the fact that some letters are more common than others as the first letter of last names will bias the sample against certain students' chances of being selected.

9. Answers will vary. Here is one idea: *Question 8*—Survey questions could separate the three issues of drugs, alcohol, and weapons so that the results will clearly indicate which issues are deemed serious enough by students to permit the intrusion on student privacy. For example, a question might be "Do you think school authorities should be allowed to open student lockers to search for weapons?" The answers to the three questions could be analyzed separately to find the percent of students who feel each way about each issue.
(Teaching Tip: You may want students to share their questions in groups, focusing on any refinements that may be needed to make them clearer.)

7. To estimate the number of soft drinks consumed by middle school students each day, Ms. Darnell's class obtains a list of students in the school and writes each name on a card. They put the cards in a box and select the names of 40 students to survey.

8. A television news report said that 80% of adults in the United States support the right of school authorities to open student lockers to search for drugs, alcohol, and weapons. The editors of the school paper want to find out how students in their school feel about this issue. They select 26 students for their survey—one whose name begins with A, one whose name begins with B, one whose name begins with C, and so on.

9. Choose one of the issues in questions 5–8. Write a survey question you could ask about the issue, and explain how you could analyze and report the results you collect.

Connections

10. Students at Banneker Middle School were asked how much time they spent doing homework last Monday night. The results are shown in this back-to-back stem-and-leaf plot.

Minutes Spent on Monday-Night Homework

Grade 6		Grade 8
0 0 0 0 0 0	0	0
5 5 5 5 5 5	1	0 5 5
5 0 0	2	0 0 0 5 5 5
5 5 5	3	0 0 0 0 5 5 5
5 5 0	4	0 0 0 5 5 5
0 0	5	0 5
	6	0 5 5
0	7	5
5	8	0

a. Find the median homework time for each grade.

b. For each grade, describe the overall distribution of homework times. How do the homework times for sixth graders compare with the homework times for eighth graders? Explain your reasoning.

c. Could these data be used to describe what is typical of all school nights in each of the two grades? Explain your reasoning.

11. Samples of adults and eighth grade students were asked how much time they spend on the telephone each evening. The results are displayed in the box plots below.

Telephone Time

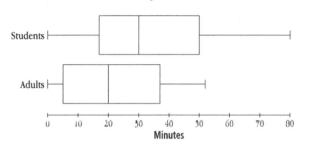

a. What are the median, lower quartile, upper quartile, and range of the telephone times for the students?

b. What are the median, lower quartile, upper quartile, and range of the telephone times for the adults?

c. Describe the similarities and differences between the distribution of telephone times for adults and the distribution of telephone times for students.

Connections

10a. median for grade 6: 20 minutes; median for grade 8: 35 minutes

10b. Time spent on homework for students in grade 6 is clustered between 0 and 20 minutes; time for students in grade 8 is clustered between 20 and 45 minutes. Students in grade 6 seem to spend less time studying on Monday nights than do students in grade 8. For both grade levels, few students spent more than 50 minutes on homework.

10c. These data may not be representative of all school nights because students may typically have more homework on some nights than on others.

11a. approximate values: median = 30, lower quartile = 17, upper quartile = 50, range = 0 to 80

11b. approximate values: median = 20, lower quartile = 5, upper quartile = 37, range = 0 to 52

11c. The students had a wider range of telephone times than did the adults. In general, the students spent more time on the telephone than did the adults.

12a. 8 ÷ 25 = 32%, and 32% × 350 = 112 students

12b. 7 ÷ 28 = 25%, and 25% × 350 ≈ 88 students

12c. Answers will vary. It is quite possible to get different results from different samples, even when using a random sample.

13a. Possible answer: People who feel strongly about the issue will be more likely to participate in the survey. The poll is surveying only those who watch this station's evening news—probably only a select part of the population in the area. It may be, for instance, that teenagers are under-represented and older adults are overrepresented in the viewer population.

13b. Possible answer: The media may conduct such polls to gain viewer participation or to help the station present stories from viewpoints consistent with those of the viewers.

---

12. There are 350 students in Banneker Middle School. Ms. Cabral's class wants to research how many students attended camp last summer. They survey two random samples of students. Here are the results:

> Sample 1: 8 of 25 attended camp
> Sample 2: 7 of 28 attended camp

a. Based on the results from sample 1, how many students in the school would you predict attended camp?

b. Based on the results from sample 2, how many students in the school would you predict attended camp?

c. Lawrence, one of Ms. Cabral's students, was confused by the results of the study. He said, "We were careful to choose our samples randomly. Why did the two samples give us different predictions?" How would you answer Lawrence's question?

13. A local television station wanted to find out how the people in the broadcast area felt about women serving in combat roles in the military. During its evening news broadcast, the station asked viewers to call in with their opinions about this question:

Should women be allowed to have combat roles in the military?

a. What possible biases could there be in the results of this opinion poll?

b. Why do you think the media conduct such polls, even though they know the results are biased?

Extensions

14. Television stations, radio stations, and newspapers often predict the winners of important elections long before the votes are counted. They make these predictions based on polls.

    a. What factors might cause a preelection poll to be inaccurate?

    b. Political parties often conduct their own preelection polls to find out what voters think about their campaign and their candidates. How might a political party bias such a poll?

    c. Find out how a local television station, radio station, or newspaper takes preelection polls. Do you think the method they use is sensible?

15. In times of war, our government has set up a selective-service, or draft, system to identify young men who will be called into military service. For reasons of fairness, the selective-service system must make every effort to be sure that everyone eligible for the draft has the same chance of being selected. What do you think would be a fair system for selecting people to be drafted?

---

15. The design of a fair draft system is a sensitive issue. Students may have some good ideas about how to do this task fairly. For example, one might assume that all birthday anniversary dates are equally likely and then devise a system for randomly ordering those dates in priority; a similar scheme was used by the U.S. government during the Vietnam War. Or, one could have a computer select names at random from a database of all eligible people.

Extensions

14a. Possible answer: Preelection polls can be inaccurate as a result of a poor sampling method. When sensitive issues are being contested in an election, polled voters may not accurately report their views, especially if those views are unpopular or are believed to be unacceptable for voicing in public. (Note: Pollsters now often ask people whether or not they are likely to actually vote. Also, it is known that polls in recent years about voting issues that involve race and gender have led to inaccuracies.)

14b. Possible answer: A political party may poll people from areas in which the majority of people are of their same party or hold views similar to those held by the candidates. They might frame questions in a way that encourages responses favorable to their candidate in an intent to create a public impression that their candidate is "on a roll" in the hopes that others will be persuaded to join that side.

14c. Answers will vary. (**Teaching Tip:** It might be interesting to invite a representative of one of the local media to visit your class to describe how they conduct polls. This would make a nice culminating activity for the unit.)

1. Collecting data from a sample rather than from an entire population simplifies the task. If the sample is chosen wisely, you can tell a lot about what is true for the population.

2. *Convenience sampling* is selecting a sample of people who are easy to reach. The easiest sample to reach, though, might not be representative of the entire population. *Systematic sampling* is a regular procedure for choosing from a population. It may be a fairer method than convenience sampling, but one must be careful that the systematic procedure does not bias selection toward or away from some sector of the population. *Voluntary-response sampling* produces data from people who choose to respond. It may be easy to implement, but the data can be misleading because you get reports from either those who are atypically responsible or those who care strongly about an issue. *Random sampling* is a system that gives every member of a population an equal chance of being selected. It can be harder to implement, but it may give the best results.

3a. See right.

3b. A sample may not be representative of a population in that it represents some opinions or values more than or less than their actual occurrence in the entire population.

Mathematical Reflections

In this investigation, you learned about several sampling techniques, and you practiced writing effective survey questions. These questions will help you summarize what you have learned:

1 Why are data often collected from a sample rather than from an entire population?

2 Describe several methods for selecting a sample from a population. Discuss the advantages and disadvantages of each method.

3 **a.** What does it mean for a sample to be *representative* of a population?

   b. In what ways might a sample *not* be representative of a population?

Think about your answers to these questions, discuss your ideas with other students and your teacher, and then write a summary of your findings in your journal.

3a. A sample is representative of a population if the distribution of responses from the sample is very similar to the distribution of responses one would expect if the population were surveyed—similar five-number summaries, stem plots, scatter plots, and so on.

Tips for the Linguistically Diverse Classroom

Diagram Code The Diagram Code technique is described in detail in *Getting to Know Connected Mathematics.* Students use a minimal number of words and drawings, diagrams, or symbols to respond to questions that require writing. Example: Question 3b—A student might respond to this question by writing this using words and pictures: *How many* (basketball going through hoop) *can an 8th grade* (stick figure) *make?* The student might draw very tall stick figures in uniforms saying *All-Stars* under the heading *Not Representative,* and stick figures of various heights in regular clothes under the heading *Representative.*

TEACHING THE INVESTIGATION

2.1 • Asking About Honesty

In this problem, students consider the implications of predicting the behavior of all Americans based on the answers of a few thousand people who responded to a magazine survey about honesty.

Launch

Introduce the topic of Investigation 2 by talking with the class about the claims mentioned on the opening page of the investigation in the student edition. For each situation, encourage students to think about the part of the population on which the report is focused by asking such questions as the following:

> What is the situation being described? Who is it about?
>
> Do you think that the entire population was surveyed?
>
> How can the report make this claim if not all the people in that population were surveyed?
>
> If we collected information about this topic from the people in our class, could we use our answers to make predictions about the entire U.S. population?

Explain that we can often study a large population by analyzing only part of the population, which is called a *sample*. We can use data about a sample to help us draw conclusions about an entire population.

Introduce the survey about honesty, which is reproduced on Transparency 2.1A. Ask students to read through the survey and to consider how it describes what honesty is. They may mention other ways to pursue the question of what constitutes honest behavior; ask that they save their ideas for the follow-up.

You may want to ask the class how they think students in their school might respond to each of the survey questions.

> If you wanted to use this survey to study the honesty of the students in our school, how would you go about collecting the data?
>
> In order to draw conclusions about the students in our school, is it necessary to ask *everyone* in the school to complete the survey?

Explain what a sampling plan is. Essentially, a *sampling plan* involves identifying the population that is to be described—in the case of the magazine's survey, the population of the United States—and identifying the sample of the population that will be involved in the survey—in this case, anyone who reads the magazine and phones in a response.

> If you wanted to gather information from a sample of students in our school, how would you decide whom to ask? In other words, what would your *sampling plan* be?

Have students work in groups of two to four on the problem and the follow-up.

Explore

Circulate as groups work. Remind students to be prepared to present their answers and to describe the strategies they used.

Summarize

Parts B, C, and D and follow-up question 1 are rather straightforward mathematically and offer a brief review of percents. However, take time to discuss students' various solution strategies. If more than one answer is presented, analyze the different interpretations to resolve any questions about working with percents.

Have students share their responses to part E, which asks why the results of this survey may not apply to all Americans. Any call-in survey runs the risk of gathering the views of an atypical collection of people—those who listen to certain kinds of radio or television shows or who read certain kinds of newspapers or magazines; those who are willing to invest money and time making a call to express their opinions; and, generally, those who feel strongly about the issue being considered. Though we might assume that the magazine has a national circulation, we don't know what type of magazine it is and so cannot identify the audience. There are other things we don't know about the characteristics of the people in the sample; students might offer some insight into the problem of drawing valid generalizations from such surveys. If so, they are identifying questions related to what makes a sample *representative* of a population, which will be considered later in this investigation.

Ask students to share the survey questions they wrote for follow-up question 2. For example, they might suggest asking people if they have ever encountered one of the situations mentioned and how they responded—hypothetical situations are always different from the real thing!

Students will have a variety of ideas about revising the sampling plan in response to follow-up question 3. Ask them to provide reasons for how they propose to revise the plan and to identify the problems they are trying to remedy by using a plan other than the one developed by the magazine. Gently challenge each suggestion by asking the following:

> Will that approach be certain to give results that represent the entire population?

2.2 • Selecting a Sample

This problem raises a number of issues about sampling and surveying. Students consider four sampling plans, analyzing the advantages and disadvantages of each and determining which method would produce the sample most representative of the population under study.

Launch

Introduce the topic by reading, or having students read, the five questions in the hypothetical research project. Ask:

> How might you word each of these as a survey question to ask students?

The questions might be phrased as follows:

- How many hours of sleep do you get each night?
- Do you eat breakfast in the morning?
- How many hours of television do you watch in a week?
- How many soft drinks do you consume in a day?
- Do you wear braces on your teeth?

> Do you think your questions are clear? What would happen if you asked students in your school each question?

If students do not see that some of the questions might be ambiguous, point out, for example, that asking how many hours of sleep a student gets each night raises issues about including weekends or how many nights' data are needed in order to determine what is "typical."

> What kind of sampling plan might you design to conduct this research?
>
> Suppose there are more students in one grade than another and you want to represent both grades. How will you address this in your sampling plan?
>
> What are some of the ways you might represent and analyze the data you collect?
>
> When you are finished with the research project, what might you be able to say about the lives of students in the school?

It is not necessary to bring closure to these questions; they simply help students think about the many issues that must be considered in such a study.

Have students work on the problem and the follow-up in groups of two to four.

Explore

If students have trouble understanding a particular sampling method, ask them to focus on the name of the strategy. Each title—*convenience sampling, systematic sampling, voluntary-response sampling,* and *random sampling*—is descriptive of the important feature of that method.

Summarize

One way to summarize the sampling methods used by the four groups of students in Problem 2.2 is to post four large sheets of paper at the front of the classroom. Divide each sheet into two halves titled "Advantages" and "Disadvantages." Add to the charts as students share their ideas about each sampling method.

After the class has reviewed the four sampling plans used by the groups, ask students to share their ideas about which plan would give the most representative sample. Make reference to the summary notes that the class has developed. Ask students to explain their ideas and to critique the ideas of the other students.

As you review the follow-up, add the name of each sampling method to the appropriate chart.

Review the ideas of representative samples and biased samples.

> When we say the results from a sample are *biased,* we mean that there may be special properties associated with the sample that are not characteristics of the population. For example, surveying only sixth graders and then making a prediction about the responses of *all* students in the sixth, seventh, and eighth grades would give a *biased* prediction. The sample of sixth grades is not *representative* of the population.

Educational research has shown that students will often evaluate a situation for bias from a "fairness" perspective. They will think about whether a particular sample would be fair—fair meaning that all members of the population have a chance to be part of the sample. If so, it makes sense to use sample data to draw conclusions about all members of the population.

2.3 • Asking the Right Questions

In this open-ended problem, students work with partners to design a survey to gather information about middle and high school students and their plans for the future. In the process, they consider issues about how to write good survey questions, both open questions and closed questions.

Launch

Discuss the difference between *open questions,* which simply ask for a response, and *closed questions,* which offer a set of choices. Ask students for examples of each type of question, and talk about the advantages and disadvantages of each. One type of closed question not described in the student edition is one that asks people to indicate how strongly they feel about something or to rate something using a given scale.

Have students work with partners to develop a set of questions for a survey. You might have students do part of this problem as homework.

Explore

Make sure students understand the three phases to this problem:

- Write and edit your questions.
- Have another group of students read your questions and offer suggestions for revision.
- Rewrite the questions based on the feedback you receive.

Encourage students to try to be as clear as possible about what kinds of answers they are anticipating for each question.

Summarize

You might ask each group to prepare a display of their proposed questions (perhaps on an overhead transparency or a large sheet of paper) and have a class discussion of the questions. Similar presentation and discussion of the sampling plans should lead to lively debate and insight into the pitfalls of careless questions and sampling strategies.

You may want to work as a class to identify a single set of questions to make up a final survey. It is not expected that the class will conduct this survey; however, it is possible for students to complete the survey with their class or with a sample of students in the school.

Additional Answers

Answers to Problem 2.1

E. Possible answer: Only people who read this magazine and have the time and interest to respond will answer this survey. This group of people might be very different from an "average" group of U.S. citizens, and some people may have answered the survey more than once.

Answers to Problem 2.1 Follow-Up

1. Since 3507 of 5280 is about 66%, we could predict that about 66% of the U.S. population is honest. (Note: You may want to emphasize the fact that many respondents could have indicated honesty in response to some, but not all five, of the questions. The overall percent is likely different from the response to only question A, to only question B, and so on.)

2. Questions will vary.

3. Answers will vary.

Random Samples

In this investigation, students consider how to choose samples randomly from a population and why random samples are often preferable. They then investigate the idea that sample size affects the accuracy of population estimates. Through sampling and calculating statistics, students learn that by taking larger samples they can often reduce the variability in sample distributions and make more accurate predictions.

In Problem 3.1, Choosing Randomly, students consider various strategies for choosing a friend to attend a concert, focusing on which sampling plan involves making a random selection. In Problem 3.2, Selecting a Random Sample, they explore variability as it relates to sample data and statistics. Using various tools—such as spinners, numbers cubes, and random-number generators on calculators—they select random samples of 25 from a database of 100, and they analyze their samples to help them draw conclusions about the population. In Problem 3.3, Choosing a Sample Size, students explore and compare predictions made from samples of size 5, 10, and 25. They make distributions of sample medians and discuss which size samples seem to have medians that are most similar to the population median.

Mathematical and Problem-Solving Goals

- **To select a random sample from a population**

- **To use sampling distributions, measures of center, and measures of spread to describe and compare samples**

- **To use data from samples to estimate a characteristic of a population**

- **To apply elementary probability work with spinners or calculators to choosing random samples of data**

Materials

Problem	For students	For the teacher
All	Graphing calculators, computers and statistical software (optional), grid paper	Transparencies: 3.1 to 3.3C (optional), overhead graphing calculator (optional)
3.2	Labsheet 3.2A (optional; 1 per group), Labsheet 3.2B and/or transparencies of Labsheet 3.2B (optional; 2 per group), 10-section spinners (provided as a blackline master), 10-sided number cubes (as many as are available), paper clips or bobby pins (for spinners)	Transparency of Labsheet 3.2B (optional)
3.3	Labsheet 3.3 (optional; 1 per student), spinners and number cubes from Problem 3.2 (optional)	Transparency of Labsheet 3.3 (optional)

INVESTIGATION 3

Random Samples

What is the best way to choose a sample from a large population? In most situations, statisticians agree that it is preferable to use a procedure that gives each member of the population the same chance of being chosen. Sampling plans with this property are called *random sampling plans*. Samples chosen with a random sampling plan are called *random samples*.

3.1 Choosing Randomly

This problem will help you think about what it means to use a random sampling plan. Keep in mind that for a sampling plan to be random, all members of the population must have an equally likely chance of being selected.

> ### Problem 3.1
>
> Imagine that you have two tickets to a sold-out rock concert, and your six best friends all want to go with you. To choose a friend to attend the concert, you want to use a strategy that gives each friend an equally likely chance of being selected. Which of the three strategies below would accomplish this? Explain your reasoning.
>
> *Strategy 1:* The first person who calls you on the phone tonight gets to go with you.
>
> *Strategy 2:* You assign each friend a different whole number from 1 to 6. Then, you roll a six-sided number cube. The number that is rolled determines who attends the concert.
>
> *Strategy 3:* You tell each friend to meet you by the rear door right after school. You toss a coin to choose between the first two friends who arrive.
>
> | Max Productions presents: |
> |---|
> | **RAWLY & THE ZOOSTERS** |
> | WORLD JAMMIN' TOUR |
> | Saturday November 23 |
> | AT THE ORANGEVILLE COLISEUM |
>
> | SECTION B |
> |---|
> | 27 AA |
> | ROW SEAT |
> | RAWLY & THE ZOOSTERS |
> | WORLD JAMMIN' TOUR |
> | 8:00pm Saturday November 23 |
> | THE ORANGEVILLE COLISEUM |

■ Problem 3.1 Follow-Up

Describe another strategy you could use that would give each of your friends an equally likely chance of being selected.

Choosing Randomly

At a Glance

Grouping: *pairs*

Launch

- Talk with students about random samples, in which each member of a population has an equal chance of being selected.

- Introduce the problem, and have pairs explore the problem and follow-up.

Explore

- Have pairs discuss the three strategies in terms of which produces a random sample and then develop a strategy of their own.

Summarize

- Talk about what it means for a sampling plan to be random.

- Ask students to share their random sampling plans.

Answers to Problem 3.1

Strategy 1 is not a random sampling plan because the friend who is most eager to speak with you gets to go. Strategy 2 is a random sampling plan because each friend has the same chance of being selected. Strategy 3 includes a tool for random selection, tossing a coin, but not all six friends have an equally likely chance to be included in the coin toss.

Answer to Problem 3.1 Follow-Up

One strategy is the "put everyone's name in a hat" procedure. Another is to number the friends from 1 to 6, generate a random number between 1 and 6 using a calculator or computer, and use this number to identify the friend who goes to the concert.

Assignment Choices

ACE questions 7, 8, and unassigned choices from earlier problems

3.2

Selecting a Random Sample

Grouping:
groups of three

Launch

- Discuss the data set of 100 students and the idea of selecting a random sample from it.

- Distribute Labsheets 3.2A and 3.2B. *(optional)*

- Have groups of three explore the problem.

Explore

- Ask groups to draw their three box plots on a single grid.

Summarize

- Have groups share their box plots.

- Discuss what conclusions can be drawn about the movie-viewing behavior of the 100 students.

- Assign and review the follow-up.

Assignment Choices

ACE question 9 and unassigned choices from earlier problems

3.2 **Selecting a Random Sample**

The table on the next page contains data for 100 eighth graders at Clinton Middle School. The data were collected on a Monday. They include the number of hours of sleep each student got the previous night and the number of movies, including television movies and videos, each student watched the previous week.

You could describe these data by calculating five-number summaries or means, and you could display the distribution of the data by making stem plots, histograms, or box plots. However, doing calculations and making graphs for the entire data set would require a lot of work.

> **Think about this!**
>
> Instead of working with the entire data set, you can select a random sample of students. You can look for patterns in the data for the sample and then use your findings to make predictions about the population.
>
> - What methods might you use to select a random sample of students?
>
> - How many students would you need in your sample in order to make accurate estimates of the typical number of hours of sleep and the typical number of movies watched for the entire population of 100 students?

One way to select a random sample of students is to use two spinners like these:

You can use the spinners to generate random pairs of digits that correspond to the two-digit student numbers. What two-digit numbers can you generate with these spinners? How can you make sure that student 100 has an equally likely chance of being included in your sample?

There are many other ways to select a random sample of students. For example, you can roll two 10-sided number cubes, or you can generate random numbers with your calculator.

Grade 8 Database

Student number	Gender	Sleep (hours)	Movies	Student number	Gender	Sleep (hours)	Movies
01	boy	11.5	14	51	boy	5.0	4
02	boy	2.0	8	52	boy	6.5	5
03	girl	7.7	3	53	girl	8.5	2
04	boy	9.3	1	54	boy	9.1	15
05	boy	7.1	16	55	girl	7.5	2
06	boy	7.5	1	56	girl	8.5	1
07	boy	8.0	4	57	girl	8.0	2
08	girl	7.8	1	58	girl	7.0	7
09	girl	8.0	13	59	girl	8.4	10
10	girl	8.0	15	60	girl	9.5	1
11	boy	9.0	1	61	girl	7.3	5
12	boy	9.2	10	62	girl	7.3	4
13	boy	8.5	5	63	boy	8.5	3
14	girl	6.0	15	64	boy	9.0	3
15	boy	6.5	10	65	boy	9.0	4
16	boy	8.3	2	66	girl	7.3	5
17	girl	7.4	2	67	girl	5.7	0
18	boy	11.2	3	68	girl	5.5	0
19	girl	7.3	1	69	boy	10.5	7
20	boy	8.0	0	70	girl	7.5	1
21	girl	7.8	1	71	boy	7.8	0
22	girl	7.8	1	72	girl	7.3	1
23	boy	9.2	2	73	boy	9.3	2
24	girl	7.5	0	74	boy	9.0	1
25	boy	8.8	1	75	boy	8.7	1
26	girl	8.5	0	76	boy	8.5	3
27	girl	9.0	0	77	girl	9.0	1
28	girl	8.5	0	78	boy	8.0	1
29	boy	8.2	2	79	boy	8.0	4
30	girl	7.8	2	80	boy	6.5	0
31	girl	8.0	2	81	boy	8.0	0
32	girl	7.3	8	82	girl	9.0	8
33	boy	6.0	5	83	girl	8.0	0
34	girl	7.5	5	84	boy	7.0	0
35	boy	6.5	5	85	boy	9.0	6
36	boy	9.3	1	86	boy	7.3	0
37	girl	8.2	3	87	girl	9.0	3
38	boy	7.3	3	88	girl	7.5	5
39	girl	7.4	6	89	boy	8.0	0
40	girl	8.5	7	90	girl	7.5	6
41	boy	5.5	17	91	boy	8.0	4
42	boy	6.5	3	92	boy	9.0	4
43	boy	7.0	5	93	boy	7.0	0
44	girl	8.5	2	94	boy	8.0	3
45	girl	9.3	4	95	boy	8.3	3
46	girl	8.0	15	96	boy	8.3	14
47	boy	8.5	10	97	girl	7.8	5
48	girl	6.2	11	98	girl	8.5	1
49	girl	11.8	10	99	girl	8.3	3
50	girl	9.0	4	100	boy	7.5	2

Problem 3.2

In this problem, each member of your group will select a random sample of students and calculate the five-number summary for the movie data. Use spinners, 10-sided number cubes, a graphing calculator, or some other method to select your sample.

A. Select a random sample of 25 students. For each student in your sample, record the number of movies watched. (Each sample should contain 25 *different* students, so if you select a student who is already in the sample, select another.)

B. Calculate the five-number summary for the movie data for your sample.

C. With your group, make box plots of the movie data for your group's samples on Labsheet 3.2.

D. What can you conclude about the movie-viewing behavior of the population of 100 students based on the patterns in the samples selected by your group? Explain how you used the data from your samples to arrive at your conclusions.

E. Compare your findings with those of other groups in your class. Describe the similarities and differences you find.

▦ Problem 3.2 Follow-Up

1. Select a random sample of 25 students, and record the number of hours of sleep for each student. Calculate the five-number summary for these sleep data, and make a box plot of the distribution. Use your findings to estimate the typical hours of sleep for the population of 100 students. Compare your box plot and estimate with those of the other members of your group, and describe the similarities and differences.

2. The data on page 39 were collected by conducting a survey. The students who wrote the survey considered two possible questions for finding the number of movies watched.

   • How many movies and videos did you watch last week?
   • How many movies did you watch at a theater, on television, or on video last week? Include all movies and videos you watched from last Monday through this Sunday.

   a. Which question do you think is better? Why?
   b. Can you write a better question? If so, write one, and explain why you think your question is better.

Answers to Problem 3.2

Answers will vary. Students might discuss the medians for samples; they will find that for most samples, the medians will be similar. They might also look at the range of data in the box, from the lower quartile to the upper quartile, and how this range compares across samples.

Answers to Problem 3.2 Follow-Up

1. Box plots will vary, but there will likely be less variability in the data than was present in the movie data. Again, students might discuss medians, the presence of outliers, and the range from the lower quartile to the upper quartile.

2. a. The second question is less ambiguous than the first and is likely to get a more thoughtful response.

   b. Answers will vary. Have students share their ideas.

3.3 Choosing a Sample Size

In Problem 3.2, you selected random samples of 25 students to estimate the sleep and movie-viewing habits of all 100 students. You might wonder whether you could make good estimates with less work by selecting smaller samples.

If you took the time to analyze the movie data for all 100 students, you would find that the median number of movies and videos watched is 3. Do you think you could make a good estimate of this figure by analyzing samples of 5 or 10 students?

Problem 3.3

In this problem, you will explore how the size of a sample affects the accuracy of statistical estimates.

A. In Problem 3.2, you calculated five-number summaries for the movie data for random samples of 25 students. Work with your class to make a line plot of the medians found by all groups. Compare these results with the median for the population of 100 students.

B. 1. Select three random samples of 5 students, and find the median movie value for each sample. Compare the medians for your samples with the population median.

 2. Compare the medians for your samples with the medians found by other members of your group. Describe the similarities or differences you find.

 3. Record the medians found by your group on the board. When all groups have recorded their medians, make a line plot of the medians.

C. 1. Select three random samples of 10 students, and find the median movie value for each sample. Compare the medians for your samples with the population median.

 2. Compare the medians for your samples with the medians found by other members of your group. Describe the similarities or differences you find.

 3. Record the medians found by your group on the board. When all groups have recorded their medians, make a line plot of the medians.

D. Compare the distribution of medians for samples of size 5, 10, and 25. Write a paragraph describing how the median estimates for samples of different sizes compare with the actual population median.

Answers to Problem 3.3

A. The medians for samples of size 25 should cluster about the population median of 3.

B. The medians for samples of size 5 should show considerable variability, perhaps with a tendency to cluster around 2, 3, and 4.

C. The medians for samples of size 10 should show less variability than the medians of samples of size 5 but more than the medians for samples of size 25.

D. Descriptions will vary. The sample median for a larger sample is more likely to be a good predictor of the population median.

Choosing a Sample Size

At a Glance

Grouping:
groups of three

Launch

- Ask what students would expect if they were to analyze smaller samples.
- Do part A as a class
- Distribute Labsheet 3.3 to each student. *(optional)*
- Have groups explore the problem.

Explore

- Have groups record their medians for sample sizes of 5 and 10 on the board.

Summarize

- Make class line plots for sample sizes of 5 and 10.
- Talk about the distributions.
- Do the follow-up as a class.

Assignment Choices

ACE questions 1–6, 10, 11, and unassigned choices from earlier problems (In 1 and 2, students add their data to class line plots.)

Assessment

It is appropriate to use the quiz after this problem.

■ **Problem 3.3 Follow-Up**

1. With your class, use the sleep data to explore the relationship between sample size and the accuracy of median estimates. The median sleep value for the population of 100 students is 8 hours.

a. In Problem 3.2 Follow-Up, you calculated the median sleep value for random samples of 25 students. Work with your class to make a line plot of the medians found by all the students in your class. Compare these results with the median for the population.

b. Select a random sample of 5 students and a random sample of 10 students. Find the median sleep value for each sample.

c. Work with your class to make a line plot of the medians for the samples of 5 students and a line plot for the samples of 10 students.

d. Compare the distribution of medians for samples of size 5, 10, and 25. How do the median estimates for samples of different sizes compare with the median for the population?

2. If each student in your class chose a sample of 50 students and found the median sleep value, what would you expect the line plot of the medians to look like? Explain your reasoning.

Answers to Problem 3.3 Follow-Up

1. Sampling of the sleep data should produce results comparable to those of the movie data. However, in this case, the sample medians are likely to be closer to the population median because the sleep data show less variability.

2. From samples of size 50, the medians on the line plot should cluster very close to the population median of 8 hours of sleep because data would have been gathered from nearly half the population.

As you work on these ACE questions, use your calculator whenever you need it.

Applications

1. a. Refer to the data on page 39. Select three random samples from the population of 100 students: one sample of 5 students, one sample of 10 students, and one sample of 25 students. Record the sleep values for the students in each sample.

   b. Calculate the mean sleep value for each sample.

   c. Your teacher will display axes for three line plots: one for means for samples of size 5, one for means for samples of size 10, and one for means for samples of size 25. Add your data to the line plots.

   d. The mean sleep value for the population is 7.96 hours. Compare this value with the estimates shown in the three line plots. Write a paragraph describing how the mean estimates for samples of different sizes compare with the mean for the population.

2. a. Refer to the data on page 39. Select three random samples from the population of 100 students: one sample of 5 students, one sample of 10 students, and one sample of 25 students. Record the movie values for the students in each sample.

   b. Calculate the mean movie value for each sample.

   c. Your teacher will display axes for three line plots: one for means for samples of size 5, one for means for samples of size 10, and one for means for samples of size 25. Add your data to the line plots.

   d. The mean movie value for the population is 4.22. Compare this value with the estimates shown in the three line plots. Write a paragraph describing how the mean estimates for samples of different sizes compare with the mean for the population.

Answers

Applications

Note: In 1 and 2, students generate and analyze data individually and then add their data to class line plots.

1. Samples of size 25 should produce estimates of the mean that are closer to the population mean of 7.96 hours than will samples of size 5 or size 10.

2. Samples of size 25 should produce estimates of the mean that are closer to the population mean of 4.22 movies than will samples of size 5 or size 10.

Note: Answers to 3–6 will vary. Students should support their ideas with sound reasoning.

3. The company could randomly select a certain number of video-game systems as they come off the production line. Or, the company could systematically select every *n*th video game as it comes off the production line. The company might increase the frequency of testing when a tested item shows flaws.

4. The company could randomly test a certain sample of compact discs for each recording artist. The number would depend on the difficulty, and thus the cost, of testing. It also depends on the number of defects found in previous samples.

5. The company may want to use a systematic sampling method or randomly select a certain percent of fireworks to test. However, since fireworks that have been tested cannot then be sold, keeping testing numbers to a minimum while still assuring safety is important.

6. See right.

Connections

7a. The mean is 23; the range is 20 to 25, or 5.

7b–7d. See right.

In 3–6, use this information: Manufacturers often conduct quality-control tests to ensure that their products perform well and are safe. Depending on the type of item and the quantity produced, a manufacturer may test every item or select samples to test. For each situation described below, imagine that you are the quality-control manager for the company. Describe the testing program that you would recommend, and justify your recommendation.

3. Happy Bug Toys produces 5000 video-game systems each day.

4. The Spartan Music company manufactures a total of about 200,000 compact discs for 100 recording artists each day.

5. Fourth of July Fireworks, Incorporated, produces rockets used in fireworks displays. In the spring and early summer, they produce more than 1500 rockets each day.

6. The Clear Spring bottling company produces 25,000 bottles of spring water each day.

Connections

7. Consider the following data set: 20, 22, 23, 23, 24, 24, 25.

   a. Find the mean and the range of the values.

   b. Add three values to the data set so that the mean of the new data set is greater than the mean of the original data set. What is the range of the new data set?

   c. Add three values to the original data set so that the mean of the new data set is less than the mean of the original data set. What is the range of the new data set?

   d. Look at the ranges for the original data set and the data sets you created in parts b and c. How do the ranges compare? Why do you think this is so?

---

6. Since tested bottles probably cannot be sold, it makes sense to use a sampling strategy that involves inspecting only a small sample of all bottles produced. A systematic sample might make sense because the machinery could be programmed to select every *n*th bottle and move it aside for testing.

7b. Answers will vary. Possible answers: Add 44, 45, and 45, which gives a new mean of 29.5 and a range of 20 to 45, or 25. Or add 0, 0, and 10,000, which gives a new mean of 1016.1 and a range of 0 to 10,000, or 10,000.

7c. Answers will vary. Possible answer: Add 5, 9, and 8, which gives a new mean of 18.3 and a range of 5 to 25. Or add 22, 22, and 22, which gives a new mean of 22.7 and a range of 20 to 25.

7d. Answers will vary. Generally speaking, students may find that the ranges change. Adding values above the mean will shift the mean higher; adding values below the mean will shift the mean lower.

8. A geyser is a spring from which columns of boiling water and steam erupt. The data displayed in the graph below were collected for the Grand Geyser in Yellowstone National Park. Each point represents the height of an eruption and the time since the previous eruption.

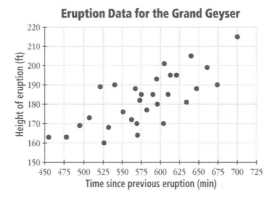

Eruption Data for the Grand Geyser

a. Describe the overall relationship between the height of an eruption and the time since the previous eruption.

b. The data above were collected for one particular geyser. What additional information would you need to decide whether the relationship you described in part a is true for most geysers?

8a. The more time has passed since the previous eruption, the greater the height of the eruption.

8b. We can't make a prediction about other geysers from just one situation. We would need data from other geysers in order to analyze whether this behavior is typical for all geysers.

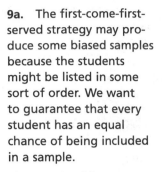

9a. The first-come-first-served strategy may produce some biased samples because the students might be listed in some sort of order. We want to guarantee that every student has an equal chance of being included in a sample.

9b. Again, this strategy does not give every student a chance of being included in the sample, and the students might be listed in some order—perhaps with odd-numbered students differing from even-numbered students in some way.

Extensions

10a. 1000 ÷ 190,000,000 ≈ 0.00053%

10b. Possible answer: The sample is probably taken from a cross section of people rather than just of people in one geographical location, occupation, political party, age group, gender, or the like.

11a. Answers will vary.

11b. The largest sample will generally produce the most accurate estimate. Red candies constitute about 23% of the distribution of colors in the table.

9. a. Suppose that instead of choosing random samples of 25 students from the population of 100 students, you selected the first 25 students for the first sample, the next 25 students for the second sample, and so on. How might this sampling procedure bias the statistical results?

b. Suppose you had chosen your samples systematically, by choosing students 1, 5, 9, 13, 17, 21, 25, . . . for the first sample; students 2, 6, 10, 14, 18, 22, 26, . . . for the second sample; students 3, 7, 11, 15, 19, 23, 27, . . . for the third sample; and so on. How might this sampling procedure bias the statistical results?

Extensions

10. Polls conducted prior to presidential elections commonly use samples of about 1000 eligible voters.

a. There are about 190 million eligible voters in the United States. What percent of eligible voters are in a sample of 1000?

b. How do you think this small sample is chosen so that the results will predict the winner with reasonable accuracy?

11. M&M's® candies are coated in six colors: green, yellow, orange, blue, brown, and red. The company produces a fixed percent of each color, but the percents are not equal. The table on the next page shows the distribution of colors in 100 bags of plain M&M's candies.

a. From the table, select random samples of 5, 15, and 25 bags, and use the samples to estimate the percent of red candies in a typical bag of M&M's.

b. Calculate the percent of red M&M's in all 100 bags. Which sample from part a produced a percent estimate closest to the overall percent? Why do you think that sample gave the closest estimate?

 Samples and Populations

Data from 100 Bags of Plain M&M's Candies

Bag	Green	Yellow	Orange	Blue	Brown	Red	Total	Bag	Green	Yellow	Orange	Blue	Brown	Red	Total
1	3	10	9	5	10	18	55	51	9	9	6	6	17	10	57
2	5	12	4	6	19	11	57	52	4	13	4	6	17	13	57
3	7	10	9	4	16	12	58	53	6	12	3	8	13	12	54
4	4	14	2	1	14	19	56	54	11	8	8	12	9	8	56
5	12	7	8	7	14	13	61	55	1	16	7	3	22	10	59
6	10	9	6	5	15	8	55	56	6	11	6	4	19	11	57
7	11	11	6	6	12	12	58	57	7	7	7	3	10	21	55
8	8	15	5	3	16	10	57	58	7	2	8	10	15	13	55
9	2	11	4	4	24	12	57	59	6	10	6	7	12	15	56
10	5	7	4	1	26	13	56	60	6	16	7	3	16	9	57
11	6	13	4	4	15	18	60	61	6	10	4	5	23	10	58
12	5	8	4	2	23	16	58	62	10	7	2	6	19	9	53
13	9	13	4	4	14	11	55	63	4	12	8	6	10	15	55
14	9	10	5	5	14	14	57	64	9	12	8	6	8	15	58
15	5	19	5	2	13	14	58	65	10	6	5	4	12	16	53
16	3	15	5	2	19	11	55	66	4	11	3	2	21	15	56
17	3	10	4	3	23	14	57	67	6	15	4	8	10	10	53
18	6	7	5	5	15	22	60	68	6	8	7	1	19	14	55
19	5	7	3	4	21	14	54	69	6	8	8	6	10	16	54
20	8	7	8	2	20	16	61	70	9	11	7	4	15	10	56
21	10	11	7	7	8	14	57	71	6	9	8	2	19	14	58
22	7	10	3	5	20	12	57	72	3	10	9	5	10	18	55
23	3	8	6	3	25	10	55	73	5	12	4	6	19	11	57
24	6	11	9	3	10	17	56	74	7	10	9	4	16	12	58
25	10	12	1	2	15	17	57	75	4	14	2	1	16	19	56
26	4	12	4	7	14	16	57	76	1	8	10	1	22	14	56
27	6	9	6	7	13	15	56	77	5	13	4	9	11	11	57
28	5	11	6	7	17	7	53	78	3	11	6	3	24	10	57
29	1	10	6	5	22	14	58	79	10	9	4	1	23	10	57
30	10	4	8	0	26	9	57	80	5	10	7	1	21	13	57
31	4	14	6	4	18	12	58	81	6	14	7	7	14	5	53
32	6	18	2	4	19	14	58	82	9	11	2	6	13	16	57
33	6	7	8	4	20	11	56	83	7	7	9	0	13	20	56
34	12	11	6	4	11	11	55	84	8	10	4	5	13	10	50
35	5	10	6	2	12	16	51	85	4	11	2	1	24	15	57
36	8	9	4	4	16	17	58	86	4	12	6	3	21	12	58
37	2	12	2	6	11	21	54	87	5	8	7	4	20	13	57
38	5	7	3	4	21	19	59	88	7	11	7	7	13	10	55
39	8	7	8	2	20	16	61	89	9	11	4	2	12	18	56
40	10	11	7	7	8	14	57	90	4	15	8	4	16	10	57
41	7	10	3	5	20	12	57	91	7	11	6	4	18	11	58
42	3	8	6	3	23	10	50	92	5	8	8	3	20	12	56
43	6	11	9	3	10	17	56	93	7	3	2	6	26	11	55
44	10	12	1	2	15	17	57	94	9	6	3	1	28	12	59
45	5	13	2	4	22	11	57	95	12	11	9	2	18	5	58
46	6	10	9	5	14	13	57	96	9	11	3	3	17	12	55
47	6	16	7	3	16	9	57	97	5	12	6	5	17	13	58
48	6	10	4	5	23	10	58	98	4	11	9	3	21	10	58
49	10	7	2	6	19	9	53	99	11	12	5	3	17	9	57
50	4	12	8	6	10	15	55	100	6	16	6	6	16	4	54

1. In a random sample, every individual in a population has the same chance of being selected. With the other three types—convenience, in which people who are present are sampled; voluntary response, in which people choose to respond; and systematic, in which some rule is used to select the sample—everyone does not have an equally likely chance to be part of the sample.

2. Random sampling is less likely to produce a biased sample—a sample that is not representative of the actual population.

3. Identify each individual with a code number, letter, or name; then select the sample by generating random numbers (using spinners, a calculator or a computer, or number cubes). Or, draw names or numbers from a bowl without looking. Using a calculator or a computer to generate random numbers is probably the most efficient method. Using spinners or number cubes will work but is more time-consuming. Drawing names from a bowl may be even more time-consuming because you must first write each value on a slip of paper.

4. See right.

5. In general, the larger the sample, the more accurate the estimates of population statistics.

Mathematical Reflections

In this investigation, you made predictions about a population by examining data for random samples. These questions will help you summarize what you have learned:

① How are random samples different from convenience, voluntary-response, and systematic samples?

② Why is random sampling preferable to convenience, voluntary-response, and systematic sampling?

③ Describe three methods for selecting a random sample from a given population. What are the advantages and disadvantages of each method?

④ If several random samples are selected from the same population, what similarities and differences would you expect to find in the medians, means, ranges, and quartiles of the samples?

⑤ How does the size of a sample affect its accuracy in estimating statistics for a large population?

Think about your answers to these questions, discuss your ideas with other students and your teacher, and then write a summary of your findings in your journal.

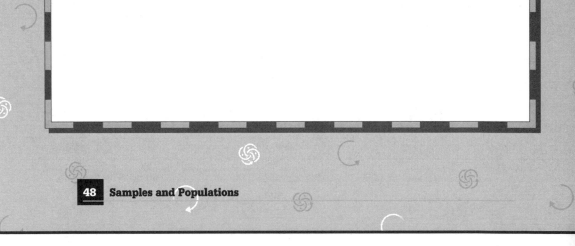

4. Several samples from the same population should have similar distributions (as shown in box plots, stem plots, and line plots) and summary statistics (median, quartiles, and mean). However, similarity among small samples will be less likely than among larger samples.

Tips for the Linguistically Diverse Classroom

Original Rebus The Original Rebus technique is described in detail in *Getting to Know Connected Mathematics*. Students make a copy of the text before it is discussed. During the discussion, they generate their own rebuses for words they do not understand; the words are made comprehensible through pictures, objects, or demonstrations. Example: Question 3—Key words and phrases for which students might make rebuses are *random sample* (spinner with equal sections), *given population* (several cars), *advantages* (thumbs up), *disadvantages* (thumbs down).

TEACHING THE INVESTIGATION

3.1 • Choosing Randomly

In this short problem, students analyze three plans for choosing a sample, keeping in mind that for a sampling plan to be random, all members of a population must have an equally likely chance of being selected. They then develop their own random sampling plans for the situation.

Launch

Talk with students about the desirability of sampling plans that produce *random samples*, samples in which each member of a population has the same chance of being selected. Introduce the problem, and have students work in pairs on the problem and the follow-up.

Explore

Have pairs of students discuss the three strategies in terms of which produces a random sample and then develop a random sampling strategy of their own.

Summarize

Have students share their responses to the problem. Then ask:

> What do you think it means to use a random sampling plan?

Ask students to share some of the other strategies they developed that would give each friend an equally likely chance of being selected. Three strategies students often propose are the following:

■ Put the six names on sheets of paper into a container and mix them. Draw one piece of paper; the name will be the friend who goes with you.

■ Assign each friend a number from 1 to 6, put these numbers on a spinner divided into six equal sections, and spin to determine who attends the concert.

■ Number the friends from 1 to 6, and use a calculator to generate a random number between 1 and 6 to select the friend.

3.2 • Selecting a Random Sample

This problem is designed to help students build an understanding of how to use randomly generated digits as a tool for identifying members of a random sample. In addition, students discover that different samples taken from the same population may produce different distributions and statistics, but that these results are generally similar to one another.

Launch

Introduce the data set of 100 students that is shown in the student edition. Talk about the idea of selecting a random sample of students to study rather than calculating statistics and making statistical representations for the entire set of data, or population.

The student edition proposes three methods for choosing a random sample from the data set: spinning two spinners, rolling two number cubes, and using a calculator to generate random numbers. Students can use these methods or invent others to choose their samples.

Have 10-sided number cubes and 10-section spinners available for students to use if they choose. (If number cubes are not available, students can choose another method.) A blackline master of 10-section spinners is provided. Students can mark the sections from 0 to 9, place the point of a pencil or a pen through the rounded end of a bobby pin or a paper clip on the center of the spinner, and flick this "pointer" to generate digits.

The student database is reproduced on Labsheet 3.2A; you may want to distribute a copy to each group. It may also be useful to provide students a template on which to draw their box plots. If the template is supplied on a transparency, the results from different groups can be super-imposed on an overhead projector. A template, similar to that shown on the opposite page, is provided on Labsheet 3.2B.

For the Teacher: Representativeness and Randomness

A central issue in sampling is the need for representative samples. Students often have intuitive notions about representativeness: they can discuss ways in which certain samples may or may not be "fair"; that is, may or may not represent selected characteristics of all the members of a population. The terms *representative* and *bias* will help students focus on whether they think data taken from a sample may be used to give a "fair" reflection of what is true about a population.

To ensure representative or fair samples, we try to choose *random* samples. The concept of randomness is not an easy one for many students to grasp. One context that will help students think about what it means to choose randomly is the draw-names-from-a-hat strategy, which gives everyone an *equally likely chance* to be included as part of a sample. The situations involving randomly choosing a sample that are encountered in this unit may all be likened to the idea of "writing each data value on an identical slip of paper, putting each piece of paper in a hat and mixing thoroughly, and then drawing out one or more slips of paper."

A number of strategies for selecting random samples are mentioned in this unit, such as spinning spinners, tossing number cubes, and generating lists of values using a calculator. These strategies rely on prior knowledge about probability that students bring with them: that there is an equally likely chance for any number to be generated by any spin, toss, or key press, and that this number may be used to select a member of a population as part of a sample—which means there is an equally likely chance for any member of a population to be included in the sample.

In addition to random sampling, students will consider other types of sampling: convenience sampling, voluntary-response sampling, and systematic sampling. It is possible to describe one or more ways in which samples selected using one of these three methods have a greater potential to be biased, or not representative, of the population from which they are drawn.

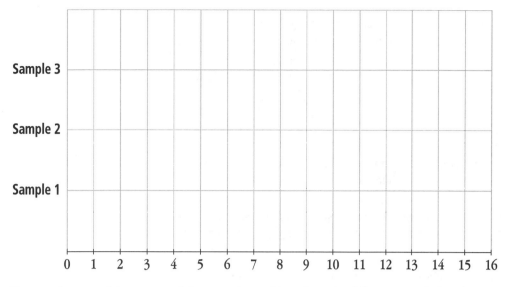

Have students work in groups of three on the problem. Save the follow-up until after the summary of the problem.

Explore

Every student in each group of three should select a random sample of 25 students from the database. The fact that each sample will probably be different allows students to explore variability as it relates to sample data and statistics.

For the Teacher: Generating Random Numbers with Calculators

In this problem, the numbers 1 to 100 must have an equally likely chance of occurring. You will need to think about how random digits are generated on the calculators students are using. Most graphing calculators and many non–graphing calculators have a function for generating decimal numbers; the number of digits in each decimal may be specified (for example, .42 is a two-digit decimal). Students can treat the decimal numbers .00 to .99 as whole numbers for selecting students from the database, with .00 representing student 100.

Some calculators have a random-integer generator, which takes an *argument;* that is, one or more numbers are entered as part of the command. The argument consists of the lower and upper bounds of the range within which you are working. For example, on the TI-80 graphing calculator, RANDINT (1, 100) designates the range of whole numbers from 1 to 100.

It is also important to check whether students' calculators generate the same ordered set of random numbers each time the calculator is turned on. If so, the calculator uses a "seed value" that causes it to begin generating random numbers in a specific way. See the technology section in the front of this book or consult the manual for each calculator to learn how to change the seed value so that each student can generate a different list of random numbers.

Have groups draw the box plots of the three distributions on the same grid, perhaps using Labsheet 3.2B. Remind students to label the axes on their box plots. Showing outliers on their plots will permit students to examine variability without their representations being distorted by outliers. Together, each group can prepare a response to part D of the problem, which they will present when they display their box plots in the class discussion.

Summarize

In Investigation 1, students were given a number of opportunities to make comparisons using box plots; some of the comparisons showed clear differences between sets of data. Other comparisons involved box plots that were quite similar; in those cases, there wasn't any essential difference between the data sets. As the class view sets of box plots generated by various groups of students in this problem, ask students to evaluate the plots from this perspective.

> Are there any apparent differences in the variability among the three samples drawn by each group of students?

If groups have made their box plots on transparencies of Labsheet 3.2B, you can superimpose the transparencies at the overhead projector. This will help the class to investigate whether there are any apparent differences in variability among the distributions of the various samples of data. Pictured below is an example of one group's box plots.

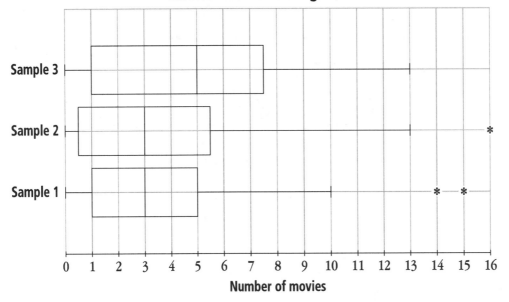

Once students have seen the box plots produced by other groups of students, ask them to again address the question asked in part D.

> What can you conclude about the movie-viewing behavior of the population of 100 students based on the patterns you have seen in the samples selected by the various groups?

Once students have considered the results from several samples, choose data from a single sample and show just the one box plot. Have students think about what they might be able to say about the population based on using the results from a *single* sample.

What if we had data from only a single sample? What can you conclude about the moving-watching behavior of the population of 100 students?

The samples were all chosen from a single population. The goal is to have students recognize that, while there may be variation among the samples, the results—the statistics and the box plots—are similar for the majority of the samples.

Students will need to save their five-number summaries and box plots for the movie data for use in Problem 3.3.

Have students gather in their groups to explore the follow-up. They will use a similar sampling process for the hours-of-sleep data as they used for the movie data. To allow the class to explore variability among samples, you may want to distribute new copies of Labsheet 3.2B for the follow-up and again have students compare the box plots they create. Shown below is an example of one group's box plots.

Hours of Sleep During One Night

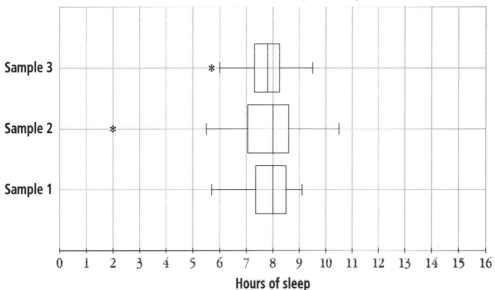

Hours of sleep

Have students share their answers to the important idea addressed in follow-up question 1.

Based on your results, what is your estimate of the typical hours of sleep for this population of students?

This question emphasizes the use of a single sample to make predictions about a population. You may want to have students describe how confident they are that they can make this prediction using just their sample data.

Allow students to share ideas for better ways to phrase the question about determining the number of movies watched, and conclude with a discussion of the difficulties that can arise in surveys.

Why might it be difficult to gather accurate data on topics like these?

Discuss the fact that acquiring accurate data about such topics as hours of sleep and number of movies watched is tricky because it can be hard for people to remember such numbers for very long. In addition, people are sometimes tempted to report numbers that are not a true measure of their behavior.

3.3 • Choosing a Sample Size

Students continue their investigation of the database of 100 grade 8 students, this time comparing the distributions of medians for various sample sizes. Students think about how well samples of various sizes estimate the actual median for the population. By collaborating as a class, students will be able to see that greater variability results from using smaller samples.

Launch

Introduce the problem, in which students will analyze the statistical estimates they make by taking smaller samples from the database of 100 grade 8 students.

> In the last problem, you analyzed samples of 25 students. Do you think you would arrive at similar estimates for the behavior of the students in this population if you were to analyze *smaller* sample sizes?

While the range of movies watched for all students in the database is 0 to 17, the actual median for any set of data will generally fall in a range of 0 to 7 movies. You may want to discuss why this would be so with your students *before* they gather any data and then revisit the idea after they have analyzed some samples.

Do part A of the problem as a class. As each group reports the medians they found for the movie data in samples of 25 students in Problem 3.2, record the medians on the board. As a class, make a line plot of the data, perhaps on a transparency of Labsheet 3.3. The scales on the labsheet are from 0 to 7 because students are unlikely to generate a median beyond this range. Ask each student to make a copy of the line plot. You may want to distribute Labsheet 3.3 to each student for making the line plots. Pictured below is an example of one such plot.

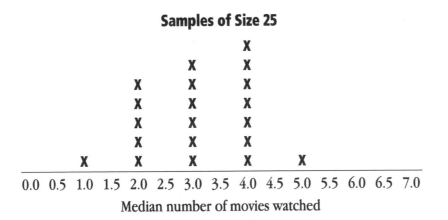

Ask the class:

> What do you observe about the overall distribution of the medians?

The *population* median for the number of movies and videos watched is 3. In the plot above, the overall distribution of medians from the samples clusters around 3 with a range of 1 to 5.

Have students work in their groups to complete the problem. Save the follow-up until after the summary of the problem.

Explore

Allow students to choose methods for generating random samples. Designate sections of the board for groups to record the medians they find for samples of 5 students (part B) and 10 students (part C). For each sample size, let the class know when all groups have recorded their results so that students can make their line plots.

Summarize

Make class line plots of the distributions of sample medians of the movie data for sample sizes of 5 and 10, perhaps adding them to the transparency of Labsheet 3.3. Here are examples of two such line plots:

Samples of Size 5

```
    X       X
    X       X       X
    X       X       X
    X       X       X       X       X       X
    X       X       X       X       X       X
_____
0.0  0.5  1.0  1.5  2.0  2.5  3.0  3.5  4.0  4.5  5.0  5.5  6.0  6.5  7.0
```
Median number of movies watched

Samples of Size 10

```
                        X   X   X
                        X   X   X
            X           X   X   X   X   X
        X   X           X   X   X   X   X               X
_____
0.0  0.5  1.0  1.5  2.0  2.5  3.0  3.5  4.0  4.5  5.0  5.5  6.0  6.5  7.0
```
Median number of movies watched

Once the class data are displayed, students can discuss their observations about the three line plots. Emphasize comparing the distributions for the different-size samples, both among the various sample sizes and to the population median.

   What do you observe about the overall distributions of the medians?

   How do the three distributions of sample medians for each sample size compare?

The medians for larger sample sizes will probably cluster more closely around the population median; for smaller sample sizes, the medians will be more spread out.

Explore the follow-up questions as a class. First, make a class line plot of the medians for the sleep data that students found in Problem 3.2 Follow-Up. Then have each student generate a sample of 5 students and a sample of 10 students and find the median hours of sleep for each sample. Construct two more line plots of these two sets of medians, and compare all three distributions. Here are examples of the line plots:

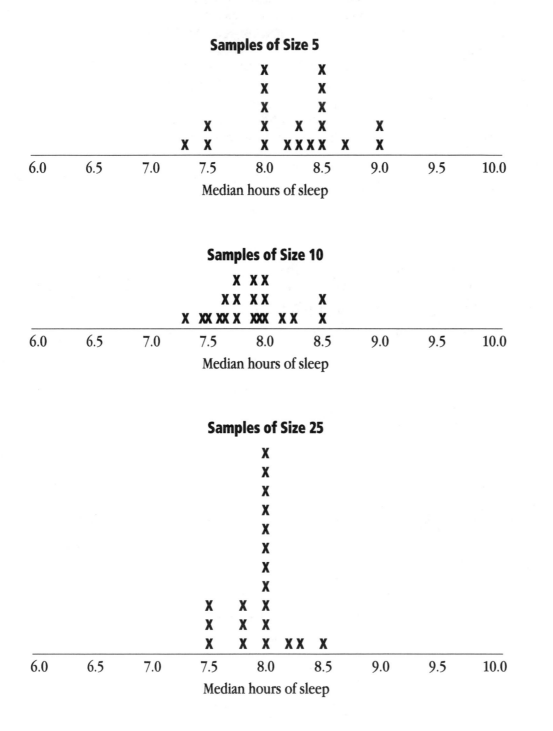

Samples of Size 5

Median hours of sleep

Samples of Size 10

Median hours of sleep

Samples of Size 25

Median hours of sleep

For the Teacher: What Is a "Good" Sample Size?

We want students to develop a sound, general sense about what makes a good sample size. In their work in this investigation, students demonstrated that samples of 25 generally had median distributions that clustered fairly closely around the actual population median. As a rule of thumb, samples sizes of 25 to 30 are appropriate for most of the settings that students at this level encounter.

Solving Real-World Problems

In this investigation, students apply what they have learned about samples to engaging real-world situations.

In Problem 4.1, Solving an Archaeological Mystery, students inspect tables of the measurements of Native American arrowheads found at six different archaeological sites. Scientists know the approximate time periods during which four of the sites were settled; the time periods for the two newly discovered sites are unknown. Students explore how data from the known sites may be used to make predictions about when each of the new sites was settled.

In Problem 4.2, Simulating Cookies, students employ a sampling procedure to investigate how many chocolate chips must be added to a batch of cookie dough to ensure that each cookie in a batch will contain at least five chips.

Mathematical and Problem-Solving Goals

- **To use data from samples to estimate a characteristic found in a population**

- **To use characteristics from a population to describe a sample**

- **To apply elementary probability in choosing random samples of data**

Materials		
Problem	**For students**	**For the teacher**
All	Graphing calculators, computers and statistical software (optional), grid paper	Transparencies: 4.1 and 4.2 (optional), overhead graphing calculator (optional)
4.2	12-section spinners (optional; provided as a blackline master), blank transparencies (optional)	

INVESTIGATION 4

Solving Real-World Problems

In this investigation, you will apply what you have learned about statistics to two real-world problems.

4.1 Solving an Archaeological Mystery

Archaeologists study past civilizations by excavating ancient settlements and examining the artifacts of the people who lived there. On digs in southeastern Montana and north-central Wyoming, archaeologists discovered the remains of two Native American settlements. They unearthed a number of arrowheads at both sites. The tables on the next page list the length, width, and neck width for each arrowhead that was found. All measurements are in millimeters.*

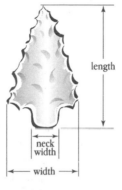

*Source: George C. Knight and James D. Keyser. "A Mathematical Technique for Dating Projectile Points Common to the Northwestern Plains." *Plains Anthropologist 28,* no. 101 (1983): 199–207.

Tips for the Linguistically Diverse Classroom

Visual Enhancement The Visual Enhancement technique is described in detail in *Getting to Know Connected Mathematics*. It involves using real objects or pictures to make information more comprehensible. Example: When discussing "Solving an Archaeological Mystery," you might display pictures of Native American settlements, various bows and arrows, and a map showing Montana and Wyoming.

At a Glance

Grouping:
small groups

Launch

■ Discuss archaeology and the arrowhead data.

■ Ask how students might compare the data from the known sites to that from the new sites.

■ Have groups of two or three explore the problem and follow-up.

Explore

■ Circulate as students create graphs, compute summary statistics, and make displays of the data.

Summarize

■ Discuss the findings and the identification of the two time periods.

■ Ask questions to help students think more deeply about what they have learned.

Assignment Choices

ACE questions 1, 4, 5, 7–11, and unassigned choices from earlier problems

Arrowheads from Two New Sites

Site I: 15 arrowheads		
Length	Width	Neck width
62	26	14
31	32	16
40	25	16
63	29	18
37	23	11
24	19	8
29	22	12
38	22	12
29	19	11
45	22	11
27	19	10
31	16	12
38	26	14
45	28	15
55	22	13

Site II: 37 arrowheads					
Length	Width	Neck width	Length	Width	Neck width
16	13	7	15	11	7
13	10	6	25	13	7
22	14	10	43	14	9
19	12	8	22	13	8
24	11	8	24	13	8
20	12	7	21	11	7
26	15	11	28	11	6
19	13	9	16	12	8
25	15	10	24	14	10
17	15	9	25	24	7
22	13	9	28	13	9
22	13	9	20	12	9
27	14	8	18	12	10
23	14	9	32	12	8
26	14	10	24	13	8
24	15	9	23	15	9
25	13	7	24	12	7
26	14	11	24	15	8
42	16	11			

The archaeologists hoped to use the arrowhead data to estimate the time period during which each site was inhabited. To help them, they used arrowhead data from four other settlement sites. The archaeologists knew that two of the sites—Laddie Creek/Dead Indian Creek and Kobold/Buffalo Creek— were settled between 4000 B.C. and A.D. 500, and that the other two sites—

Big Goose Creek and Wortham Shelter—were settled between A.D. 500 and A.D. 1600. The arrowhead data for these four sites are given on the next page.

Think about this!

How could you use these data to help you guess the settlement periods for the new sites?

Arrowheads from Four Old Sites

Big Goose Creek 52 Arrowheads				Wortham Shelter 45 Arrowheads				Laddie Creek/Dead Indian Creek: 18 Arrowheads				Kubold/Buffalo Creek 52 Arrowheads		
Length	Width	Neck width		Length	Width	Neck width		Length	Width	Neck width		Length	Width	Neck width
30	14	8		22	14	8		29	20	13		80	25	11
21	11	7		42	18	7		25	18	13		38	24	15
24	14	9		28	14	10		32	16	10		39	21	14
18	13	8		31	13	10		52	21	16		50	23	15
30	15	11		25	15	12		29	14	11		42	22	14
27	13	9		20	13	8		35	20	15		37	21	11
39	18	12		20	14	10		27	20	14		32	23	18
33	13	7		25	15	10		37	17	13		44	20	11
22	13	10		19	12	9		44	18	13		40	20	12
26	11	8		28	13	11		38	17	14		40	20	13
23	13	8		29	13	10		27	20	13		56	19	12
20	11	6		29	14	9		39	18	15		52	17	12
21	12	7		18	11	8		41	15	11		46	23	14
26	14	9		27	15	11		30	23	13		32	22	17
16	13	9		32	15	10		40	18	11		35	22	14
30	14	8		24	13	10		32	19	10		46	20	14
23	14	9		31	14	11		31	18	11		38	18	9
34	15	9		26	13	10		42	22	12		40	21	12
27	13	9		19	14	10						46	17	13
22	13	8		30	14	11						44	20	12
30	11	7		25	14	10						40	19	15
22	12	9		31	16	12						30	19	15
27	14	9		31	14	10						31	17	12
18	12	7		24	12	9						31	16	13
33	15	9		28	16	12						32	20	13
28	15	9		35	18	14						41	21	13
25	13	7		22	12	9						25	18	15
24	14	11		23	14	11						49	20	14
31	12	8		23	15	11						35	19	11
30	14	9		27	14	10						42	22	15
35	14	10		30	16	9						44	25	14
25	14	8		31	17	12						47	19	13
26	12	12		19	14	10						47	22	13
30	13	8		26	15	12						45	22	13
19	11	8		23	13	11						54	24	13
40	14	8		27	14	8						56	21	15
29	15	8		25	14	8						37	18	12
20	12	8		19	16	14						51	18	10
17	13	8		29	14	9						71	24	13
25	13	8		26	13	9						45	20	13
16	14	10		25	15	10						52	24	16
17	13	10		29	17	12						67	21	13
23	13	9		20	15	11						47	20	12
18	15	11		32	14	7						50	23	16
27	17	13		30	17	11						56	25	13
28	13	7										50	21	13
28	10	5										52	22	15
26	16	10										57	22	15
21	12	9										61	19	12
18	12	8										66	20	15
18	13	7										64	21	13
27	14	9										30	17	12

4.2

Simulating Cookies

At a Glance

Grouping:
pairs

Launch

- Discuss Jeff and Ted's business dilemma and Ted's proposal.

- Talk about the simulation students will do.

- Have pairs work on the problem and follow-up.

Explore

- Help students find ways to generate random numbers.

- Begin a stem plot for the class data.

Summarize

- Have pairs share their displays and reasoning.

- Ask questions to help students think more deeply about their work.

Assignment Choices

ACE questions 2, 3, 6, 12, 13, and unassigned choices from earlier problems

Problem 4.1

The archaeologists hypothesized that Native Americans inhabiting the same area of the country during the same time period would have fashioned similar tools.

A. Use what you know about statistics and data representations to compare the lengths of the arrowheads discovered at the new sites with the lengths of the arrowheads from the known sites. Based on your comparisons, during which time period—4000 B.C. to A.D. 500 or A.D. 500 to A.D. 1600—do you think site I was settled? During which time period do you think site II was settled? Explain how your statistics and graphs support your answers.

B. Compare the widths of the arrowheads discovered at the new sites with the widths of the arrowheads from the known sites. Do your findings support your answers from part A? Explain.

C. If the archaeologists had collected only a few arrowheads from each new site, might they have reached a different conclusion? Explain your answer.

■ Problem 4.1 Follow-Up

1. Select a random sample of 15 arrowheads from each of the six sites. For each arrowhead, find the ratio of length to width. Express each ratio as a decimal rounded to the hundredths place.

2. Compare the length-to-width ratios for the various sites. Do the ratios help you match the new sites with the sites whose settlement time is known? Explain your answer.

4.2 Simulating Cookies

Jeff and Ted operate the Custom Cookie Counter in Durham Mall. Their advertising slogan is "Five giant chips in every cookie!" One day, a customer complained that she found only three chips in her cookie. Jeff said the customer must have miscounted because he mixes 60 chips into every batch of a dozen cookies. Jeff and Ted examined a batch of cookies that were fresh from the oven. The drawing on the right shows what they found.

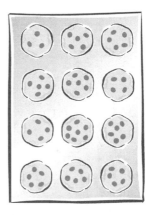

Answers to Problem 4.1

A, B. See page 62g.

C. The sample sizes for Laddie Creek and site I are somewhat small (18 and 15, respectively). However, the data from these two sites appear to reflect the trend, which indicates that it is possible to make predictions based on sample sizes that are somewhat smaller than we might like to have. (Students' work in Investigation 3 demonstrated that there was less variability in medians and means for samples of 25 than for samples of 5 or 10.) If archaeologists had collected only a few arrowheads from each new site, the data they collected might not have been representative. For example, if the shortest arrowheads from site I and the longest arrowheads from site II had been chosen, the two data sets might have been classified in the same time period. The samples from the known sites and the unknown sites are of relatively reasonable size; they can be used to predict characteristics about the populations.

Think about this!

What is wrong with Jeff's reasoning about how many chips to add to each batch of cookie dough? What advice would you give to Jeff and Ted to help them solve their quality-control problem?

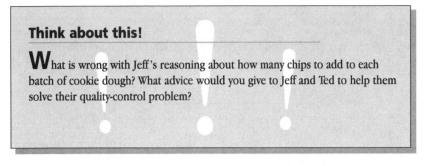

Ted had an idea about how to use random sampling to determine how many chips they should add to each batch of dough in order to be fairly confident that every cookie will contain at least five chips. He explained his idea to Jeff:

"Think about a batch of dough as 12 cookies packed in a bowl. As chips are added to the dough, each chip lands in one of the cookies. There is an equally likely chance that a chip will land in any one of the 12 cookies. We need to add chips to the dough until every cookie contains at least five chips."

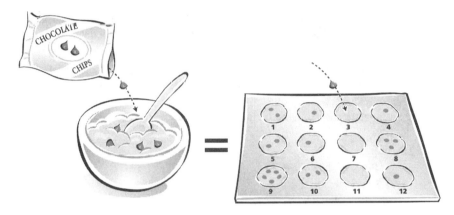

"We can simulate adding the chips by generating random integers from 1 to 12. Generating a 1 is equivalent to adding a chip to cookie 1, generating a 2 is equivalent to adding a chip to cookie 2, and so on. We can keep a tally of where the chips land and stop when each 'cookie' contains at least five 'chips.' The total number of random integers we generated will be an estimate of the number of chips we need to add to each batch to be fairly confident that each cookie will contain at least five chips."

Investigation 4: Solving Real-World Problems **53**

Answers to Problem 4.1 Follow-Up

1. Ratios will depend on the arrowheads that are sampled. For site I, there are only 15 arrowheads, so the sample consists of all the data.

2. See page 62i.

Problem 4.2

Study Ted's plan for simulating the cookie mixing until it makes sense to you.

A. Conduct the simulation Ted describes. You might use a chart like this to tally the number of chips in each cookie.

cookie 1 _____
cookie 2 _____
cookie 3 _____
cookie 4 _____
cookie 5 _____
cookie 6 _____
cookie 7 _____
cookie 8 _____
cookie 9 _____
cookie 10 _____
cookie 11 _____
cookie 12 _____

Generate random numbers until each cookie contains at least five chips. When you are finished, find the total number of chips in the entire batch.

B. Your teacher will display the stem values for a stem plot. Add your number-of-chips data to the plot.

C. Jeff and Ted want to be quite certain there will be at least five chips in each cookie, but they don't want to waste money by mixing in too many chocolate chips. Based on your class data, how many chips would you advise Jeff and Ted to use in each batch? Explain how you determined your answer.

■ Problem 4.2 Follow-Up

1. What other methods might Jeff and Ted use to be fairly confident that each cookie they sell contains at least five chips?

2. As Jeff and Ted's business becomes more successful, they decide it would be more efficient to make cookies in batches of four dozen. How many chips should they add to each batch to be confident that each cookie has at least five chips?

3. How many chips would Jeff and Ted have to put in a batch of 12 cookies to be *absolutely certain* no cookie will have fewer than five chips?

Answers to Problem 4.2

See page 62j.

Answers to Problem 4.2 Follow-Up

1. Possible answer: Perhaps a more efficient quality check would be to inspect each tray of cookies before it goes into the oven and add chips to any cookie that does not obviously contain five. Since the chips are supposedly "big," this might be an easy solution. Another option is to sell at a discount any cookie that looks like it might contain fewer than five chips.

2. Answers will vary. See the "Summarize" section for a discussion of this question.

3. Theoretically, there is no way to be absolutely certain that each cookie will contain at least five chips. However, as a practical matter, if one adds enough chips the dough will be mostly chocolate!

As you work on these ACE questions, use your calculator whenever you need it.

Applications

1. The arrowhead data on pages 50 and 51 include the neck width of each arrowhead found in the six archaeological sites.

neck width

a. Calculate five-number summaries of the neck width for each site's arrowhead data. Based on these statistics, what conclusions can you draw about the time periods in which the new sites were settled?

b. On the same scale, make box plots of the neck-width data for all the sites. Explain how the relationships among the plots illustrate your conclusions from part a.

2. Oatmeal-raisin cookies are the most popular cookie at Jeff and Ted's Custom Cookie Counter. Jeff and Ted bake these cookies in batches of four dozen. They pour a box of raisins into each batch.

a. How could you use a sample of the cookies to estimate the number of raisins in a box?

b. If there are 1000 raisins in a box, how many raisins would you expect to find in a typical cookie?

Answers

Applications

1a. See below left.

1b. See page 62k.

2a. You could randomly choose some number of cookies (say 5), find the average number of raisins per cookie, and multiply the average by 48 to estimate the number of raisins in a box.

2b. $1000 \div 48 \approx 21$ raisins

1a. The five-number summaries are shown in the table. The statistics for site I seem closest to those for Kobold/Buffalo Creek, with minimums of 8 versus 9, medians of 12 versus 13, and the same maximum of 18. The statistics for site II seem closest to those for Big Goose Creek, with minimums of 6 versus 5, medians of 8 versus 8.5, and maximums of 11 versus 13. This would indicate that site I was likely settled between 4000 B.C. and A.D. 500 and site II was likely settled between A.D. 500 and A.D. 1600.

Site	Minimum	Lower quartile	Median	Upper quartile	Maximum
Big Goose Creek	5	8	8.5	9	13
Wortham Shelter	7	9	10	11	14
Laddie Creek/Dead Indian Creek	10	11	13	14	16
Kobold/Buffalo Creek	9	12	13	15	18
Site I	8	11	12	15	18
Site II	6	7	8	9	11

3. The mean and the median for this sample are both 8, so a good estimate of the number of chips in the bag is 8 × 60 = 480 chips.

4a. The box plots below right show the age data. It looks as if the Bulls players are a bit older, on the average, than the Rockets players (with median ages of 30 and 28, respectively), although the Rockets have the oldest player (38 years) and the Bulls have the youngest (23 years). The Bulls players are closer in age to one another than are the Rockets players.

4b. The box plots below right show the height data. The Bulls players are slightly taller than the Rockets players (with median heights of 200.5 cm and 199 cm, respectively), although the difference in height seems too small to be very significant.

4c. You could estimate that the typical player on an NBA team is 29 years old and has a height of 200 cm, but this sample is fairly small and limited to only two teams and may not be very representative.

3. Keisha opened a bag containing 60 chocolate chip cookies. She selected a sample of 20 cookies and counted the chips in each cookie.

Cookie	Chips		Cookie	Chips
1	6		11	8
2	8		12	7
3	8		13	9
4	11		14	9
5	7		15	8
6	6		16	6
7	6		17	8
8	7		18	10
9	11		19	10
10	7		20	8

Use the data from Keisha's sample to estimate the number of chips in the bag. Explain your answer.

4. The tables on page 57 list age and height data for the 1995 rosters of two professional basketball teams, the Houston Rockets and the Chicago Bulls.

a. Do the players on one team seem older than the players on the other team, or are they about the same age? Use statistics and graphs to support your answer.

b. Do the players on one team seem taller than the players on the other team, or are they about the same height? Use statistics and graphs to support your answer.

c. Based on the data for these two teams, what estimates could you make for the age and height distributions of a typical NBA team? What cautions would you suggest in making generalizations from the given data?

4a.   **Age of Basketball Players**

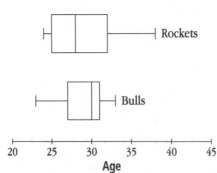

4b.   **Height of Basketball Players**

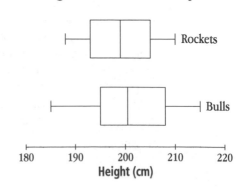

Houston Rockets		
Player	Age	Height (cm)
Breaux	25	198
Brown	27	200
Cassell	26	188
Chilcutt	27	208
Drexler	33	198
Elie	32	193
Herrera	29	203
Horry	25	205
Jones	38	203
Maxwell	30	190
Murray	24	198
Olajuwon	32	210
Smith	30	188
Tabak	25	210

Chicago Bulls		
Player	Age	Height (cm)
Armstrong	28	185
Blount	26	205
Buechler	27	195
Harper	31	195
Jordan	33	198
Kerr	30	188
Krystakowiak	31	203
Kukoc	27	208
Longley	26	215
Myers	32	195
Perdue	30	210
Pippen	30	198
Simpkins	23	205
Wennington	32	210

Connections

5. The U.S. Department of Transportation provides money to help states build new highways. However, there are strings attached. For example, if states fail to enforce the speed limits on interstate highways, they could lose their federal funding. To monitor driving speeds, states set up radar checkpoints to measure the speeds of samples of drivers.

a. Suppose you wanted to show that drivers in your state generally obey speed limits. Where and when would you set up radar checkpoints?

b. Suppose you wanted to show that drivers in your state often exceed speed limits. Where and when would you set up radar checkpoints?

Connections

5a. Possible answer: To show that drivers obey speed limits, you could set up checkpoints at heavily congested times such as during rush hours and in crowded urban areas.

5b. Possible answer: To show that drivers do not obey speed limits, you could set up checkpoints during non–rush hours and in rural areas.

6a. Graph X gives the most honest picture because it shows the full 100% scale on the vertical axis.

6b. Graphs W and Y exaggerate the growth of recycling because the vertical axes are labeled from 25%. Graph Z exaggerates the growth because the vertical axis is extended to only 60% rather than 100%. And graphs Y and Z exaggerate the growth because the *y*-axes are physically longer than those in graphs W and X.

6. Graphs are often used to support statistical arguments. However, sometimes graphs can be misleading. The graphs below all display the same data about the increase in newspaper recycling.

    a. Which graph do you think gives the most honest picture of the data pattern? Why?

    b. Why are the other graphs misleading?

Percent of Newspapers Recycled, 1980-1991

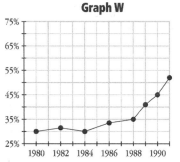

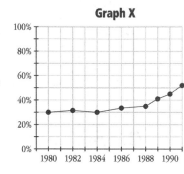

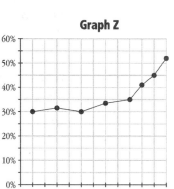

Even if you never have a job that requires you to design or analyze surveys, you will hear and read about surveys that interest you or that affect your daily life. When you are dealing with a survey, it is a good idea to ask yourself these questions:

- What was the goal of this survey?
- What was the population being studied?
- How was the sample chosen?
- How have the data been analyzed and reported?
- Do the data seem to support the conclusions?

In 7–11, use these and other relevant questions to analyze the survey.

7. In designing a television remote-control device, representatives for a manufacturer called 1000 households with television sets. They found that remote-control users sit an average of 3 meters from their television sets. Based on these findings, the manufacturer designed the remote control to work well at distances of 2.5 meters to 3.5 meters from a television set.

8. A lightbulb manufacturer wanted to know the "defect rate" for its product. One morning, the quality-control manager took 10 boxes of 50 lightbulbs from the assembly line and tried them in test sockets. All but 5 bulbs worked, so the manager concluded that production quality was acceptable.

9. A nutritionist wanted to estimate what percent of the calories in a typical U.S. teenager's diet were from fat. She asked health teachers in Dallas, Texas, to have their students keep logs of what they ate on one school day. The nutritionist analyzed the students' logs and found that the median intake was 500 fat calories per day, which is the recommended daily allowance. She concluded that calories from fat are not a problem in the diets of teenagers.

Note: In 7–11, students will have a variety of reactions to the surveys; not all are "bad" surveys or analyses. Mentioned here are some of the points for which you might look.

7. The goal of the study was to determine the distance from a television set at which a typical person might use a remote control. It appears that the population being studied was owners of television sets; the sampling procedure is unclear. The report indicates only an average viewer distance, but it seems important to consider variability as well. The remote seems to have been designed for a fairly small operational range. A box plot or stem plot of the data would help in determining the range over which the remote control should be functional. The single data piece, average distance, doesn't seem to give much confidence in the conclusion.

8. The population being studied was lightbulbs produced by a particular manufacturer. The purpose of the study was to discover the defect rate of the product. The sampling procedure is not clearly random, and testing was done on a single morning. Variability in production quality over time would not be guaranteed by this brief study. In fact, industrial production processes are generally monitored regularly. A defect rate of 1% might seem acceptable, though some companies aim for lower rates. For a product whose dependability is critical, 1% would seem a fairly high defect rate.

9. The nutritionist's study set out to find the typical number of calories derived from fat in the diet of U.S. teenagers, yet the population being studied consists solely of teenagers in Dallas. Their diets may differ significantly from those of teenagers in other parts of the country. Students in health classes might be more than typically conscious of their diets. Many students may have had the same school lunch the day of the survey, which might give results far from those that would be obtained from a random survey. Also, only the median was considered; some students may be considerably over the daily allowance.

10. The aim of the study was to test whether or not there are 1000 chips in a bag of ChipsAhoy! cookies. The company may have randomly selected the bags to be tested; however, it is not clear that the company consistently tests bags of cookies. The chips in one bag may weigh more than 1000 chocolate chips but may not actually amount to that number. It is possible that the soaking process adds weight to the remaining chips.

11. The purpose of the school cafeteria survey was to determine whether students preferred salami or bologna sandwiches. The convenience sample chosen runs the risk of not producing data that are representative of the whole school population. Therefore, the data do not strongly support the conclusion that students prefer bologna.

10. The Nabisco Company claims that there are over 1000 chocolate chips in a one-pound bag of ChipsAhoy!® cookies. A skeptical consumer asked how the company knew this was true. A spokesperson said that the company chose a sample of bags of cookies, soaked each bag in cold water to remove all the cookie dough, and weighed the chips that remained. In each case, the chips weighed more than a bag of 1000 chocolate chips.

11. In the cafeteria line, a student wrinkled his nose when he saw that salami-and-cheese subs were being served for lunch. When the cook asked what he would prefer, he replied, "I like bologna better." The cook asked the next ten students in line if they preferred bologna to salami. Seven students said yes, so she decided that in the future she would serve bologna subs instead of salami subs.

Extensions

12. Plain M&M's® candies are produced in the following percents.

Color	Percent in plain M&M's
brown	30%
yellow	20%
red	20%
orange	10%
green	10%
blue	10%

Suppose you are setting a table for a holiday party. You are placing small cups of M&M's candies at each place setting. Each cup contains 50 candies poured from a large bag of plain M&M's candies.

a. How many candies of each color would you expect to be in a typical cup?

b. How would you expect the number of candies of each color to vary across the samples?

c. You can simulate filling the cups with M&M's candies by generating random integers from 1 to 10. Which numbers would you let represent each color? How many random numbers would you need to generate to simulate filling one cup?

d. Carry out the simulation described in part c three times. Compare the distributions of colors in your simulated samples with the expected distribution from part a.

e. If you selected a random sample of 1000 candies from a large bag of plain M&M's candies, how closely would you expect the percent of each color in your sample to match the percents given in the table?

13. If you select five students at random from your class, what is the probability that at least two will have the same birth month? You can use a simulation to help you answer this question.

NOVEMBER

SUN	MON	TUE	WED	THU	FRI	SAT
					1	2
3	4	5	6	7	8	9
10	11	12	13	14	15	16
17	18	19	20	21	22	23
24	25	26	27	28	29	30

a. Design a simulation to model this situation. Tell which month each simulation outcome represents.

b. Use your birth-month simulation to produce at least 25 samples of five people. Use your results to estimate the probability that at least two people in a group of five will have the same birth month.

c. Explain how you could revise your simulation to explore this question: What are the chances that at least two students in a class of 25 have the same birthday?

Extensions

12a. brown: 15; yellow: 10; red: 10; orange: 5; green: 5; blue: 5

12b. There could be great variability in one cup because there may be an absence of some colors and an abundance of others.

12c. You could let brown be represented by 1, 2, and 3; yellow by 4 and 5; red by 6 and 7; orange by 8; green by 9; and blue by 10. Fifty random numbers would be needed to simulate filling one cup.

12d. Results will vary. (**Teaching Tip:** You might have students pool their results. The distributions for each color should cluster around the numbers given in part a. A line plot of frequencies of brown M&M's candies may have a clump around 15; a box plot for the number of brown candies may have a box from something like 12 to 18, with a median near 15.)

12e. The percent of each color should come quite close to the percents in the table because this is a relatively large sample.

13a. Generate random integers from 1 to 12, with the numbers assigned to the months January through December, using a calculator, a 12-sided number cube, or a spinner divided into 12 equal sections. Generate sets of five random numbers to simulate groups of five students; two of the five numbers matching in a set indicates two students with the same birth month.

13b. Results will vary. The theoretical probability—based on the assumption that each birth month is equally likely—that at least two individuals in a group of five will have the same birth month is about 0.6. [Note: One way to reason about this is to notice that the probability of at least two people having the same birth month is 1 minus the probability that all five people have different birth months, a calculation involving combinations and permutations. One approach is as follows: probability(no matches) = $1(\frac{11}{12})(\frac{10}{12})(\frac{9}{12})(\frac{8}{12})$. This explanation is, of course, beyond the scope of this course.]

13c. Generate random integers from 1 to 365, and inspect samples of 25 random numbers looking for samples in which at least 2 numbers match.

Possible Answers

1. If two populations have similar characteristics, samples taken from them should have comparable descriptive statistics, such as medians, means, or ranges. (Note: It is important to keep in mind that two samples will seldom be *identical* in those aspects. The question of *how much* difference is significant is the key issue in *inferential* statistics, which students will learn about in future studies. The basic idea at this point is to ask, "Is it very likely that two observed samples came from the same population, given the nature of differences in the samples?")

2. The distributions of data values for a sample should generally match the distribution in the entire population. That match will be better as sample size increases, and it depends on using an unbiased sampling procedure. It would be rare for the data values in a sample to match the distribution measures (median, mean, range, and quartiles) of the entire population exactly.

3. The larger the sample size, the closer the distribution of the sample will be to that of the population.

Mathematical Reflections

In this investigation, you applied your knowledge of statistics and data displays to two real-world problems. These questions will help you summarize what you have learned:

1 How can you use descriptive statistics such as the median, mean, range, and quartiles to compare samples and to draw conclusions about the populations from which they were selected?

2 In what ways can you expect the distribution of data values for a sample to be similar to and different from the distribution of data values for the entire population?

3 What rule of thumb can you use in thinking about the role of sample size in making accurate estimates of population properties?

Think about your answers to these questions, discuss your ideas with other students and your teacher, and then write a summary of your findings in your journal.

Tips for the Linguistically Diverse Classroom

Diagram Code The Diagram Code technique is described in detail in *Getting to Know Connected Mathematics.* Students use a minimal number of words and drawings, diagrams, or symbols to respond to questions that require writing. Example: Question 3—A student might answer this question by drawing three circles under the heading *Sample Sizes;* shading about 5% of the first circle, 15% of the second circle, and 25% of the third circle; and labeling the third circle *Most like the population.*

4.1 • Solving an Archaeological Mystery

In this problem, students inspect data consisting of the measurements of arrowheads found at six different archaeological sites and use the samples to estimate population statistics. The time periods during which four of the sites were settled are known; the time periods for the other two, newer sites are unknown. Students are asked to use statistics to compare the measurements of the arrowheads from the known sites to those of the new sites in order to estimate the time period during which each new site was settled.

Launch

You might introduce the problem by talking about archaeology and some of the methods people use to seek information about ancient civilizations.

Discuss the archaeological digs and the tables of data about the Native American arrowheads that were unearthed at each of six sites. Allow students time to familiarize themselves with the tables, which list arrowhead lengths, widths, and neck widths.

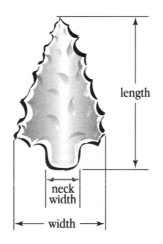

Ask students to think about how they might approach this problem.

> How could you use the data from the known sites to help you estimate the time period during which each of the two new sites was settled?

> Do you think you have enough data to make comparisons?

Have students explore the problem and the follow-up in groups of two or three. You might point out that, in real-world situations, people often work in teams to solve problems. It would be tedious for any one person to analyze these data; the task is much easier when it is shared.

Explore

The problem is stated in an open-ended way that promotes students' developing their own strategies for analysis. Students might use representations such as box plots or summary statistics such as means, medians, and ranges to make their comparisons.

Students should make summary displays of their analyses. One such display could be six parallel box plots, one for each data set. If students are using graphing calculators, it will not be possible for them to display all six box plots at one time. They may want to do their analyses with the calculator and then make a display on paper summarizing their findings. If they are using statistical software, it may be possible to display all six box plots on one scale; such a display can then be printed and analyzed.

Summarize

Ask students to discuss their findings and their conclusions and to justify their answers. An examination of the box plots students have created will yield two distinct groups of data, one with generally higher medians than the other (see the answers to Problem 4.1 for more information). These data provide a way to identify the time periods during which the new sites may have been settled.

If any students made stem plots, they will see the same patterns of spread, distribution, and clumping that emerge in the box plots.

You might ask such questions as the following to help students think about the applications of what they have learned.

> How confident are you about your predictions?
>
> We have compared different sample sizes in this problem. Why are we able to make comparisons among samples of different sizes? *(Representations such as box plots allow us to make these comparisons because they let us make a "picture" of the data and look at the shape of the data.)*
>
> Why does looking at ratios, as done in the follow-up, not reveal the same pattern of variation that we found when we analyzed separate measurements? *(Apparently the length-to-width ratio does not vary significantly from sample to sample.)*

4.2 • Simulating Cookies

In this problem, students apply what they have learned about samples and populations to address a realistic quality-control problem: How many chocolate chips must be used in a batch of a dozen cookies to ensure that each cookie contains at least five chips?

Launch

Present the problem of Jeff and Ted's cookie business: Though they advertise that there are five chocolate chips in every cookie, they received a complaint from a customer who found only three chips in her cookie. Direct students' attention to the illustration in their books of a batch of cookies.

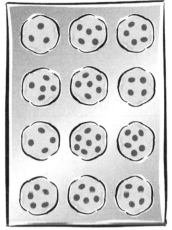

This shows how 60 chips might end up being randomly distributed among 12 cookies. Does each cookie have five chips? *(no)*

What do we want to find out? *(How many chips Jeff and Ted must add to a batch of dough to be fairly certain that every cookie will contain at least five chips.)*

Describe Ted's reasoning about the total number of chips to be added. *(Ted reasoned that if he adds 60 chips to a batch of dough, there will be an average of 5 chips per cookie: 60 ÷ 12 = 5 chips.)*

What is wrong with his reasoning? *(An average of 5 chips per cookie means that some cookies will have fewer than 5 chips and some will have more than 5 chips. Some may have exactly 5 chips, but not all will.)*

Ask students to think about ways that they might explore this problem. Discuss with them why they will be combining the results of many simulations: to obtain the results from enough samples in order to predict the typical number of chips that are needed.

It is essential that students combine their work with that of other students to get a large enough set of samples of the "total number of chips" data to make any conclusions with confidence. In Investigation 3, students generated several samples for a specific problem and then looked at the distribution of one or more sample statistics. Here, the sample statistic is the "total number of chips."

Have students work in pairs on the problem and the follow-up.

Explore

Work with students to develop ways to generate random numbers for their simulations. For example, they might generate random integers from 1 to 12 using a calculator or by spinning a 12-section spinner (provided as a blackline master).

As students conduct their simulations, display the stem values for a plot to which pairs of students will add their data. Students will use the class stem plot to answer part C. Pairs who finish their simulations early can conduct another simulation. You may want to distribute blank transparencies to some pairs for recording their displays to share in the summary.

Simulation Results

```
 0 |
 1 |
 2 |
 3 |
 4 |
 5 |
 6 |
 7 |
 8 |
 9 |
10 |
11 |
12 |
13 |
14 |
15 |
16 |
```

Shown below are the results of two actual simulations. In the first, it took 135 random numbers to achieve at least five chips per cookie (cookie 7 is the last cookie); in the second, it took 102 random numbers to achieve at least 5 chips per cookie (cookie 11 is the last cookie). Notice that there is an overall average of approximately 10 chips per cookie with the range of 5 to 15 chips in both cases. Compare this to Ted's earlier reasoning, that 60 chips is an average of 5 chips per cookie. In these two simulations, in order to guarantee 5 chips per cookie, an average of 10 chips per cookie resulted, with a range of 5 to 15 chips.

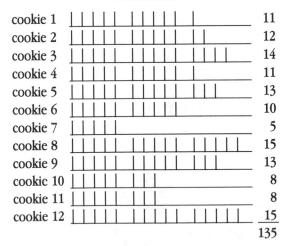

Simulation 1

cookie 1	11
cookie 2	12
cookie 3	14
cookie 4	11
cookie 5	13
cookie 6	10
cookie 7	5
cookie 8	15
cookie 9	13
cookie 10	8
cookie 11	8
cookie 12	15
	135

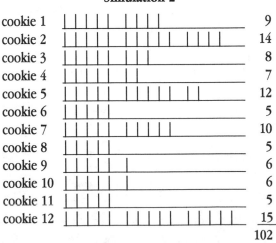

Simulation 2

cookie 1	9
cookie 2	14
cookie 3	8
cookie 4	7
cookie 5	12
cookie 6	5
cookie 7	10
cookie 8	5
cookie 9	6
cookie 10	6
cookie 11	5
cookie 12	15
	102

Summarize

Have pairs of students share their responses to part C, including their displays of the class data, and discuss their reasoning. Students should recognize that, to address this particular problem, finding the mean or the median is not sufficient; we are arguing for the least number of chips needed in order to attempt to guarantee five chips in each cookie.

There are many important ideas that might emerge in the discussion of the problem and the follow-up; for example:

What kinds of displays did the class make?

Which displays do you think are the most useful for addressing the problem?

How did you decide on the number of chips to put in a batch? Did you use the simulation that results in the greatest number of chips, or did you decide that using a number less than that would be close enough? Why?

Ask students to reflect on the meaning of their results—what they mean in terms of the actual situation. Some other questions that might be interesting to explore follow.

Were you surprised by the results of the simulations?

Is adding this many chips to a batch of a dozen cookies practical?

How do your results compare to the 60 chips that Jeff has been mixing into each batch of a dozen cookies?

What is the *average* number of chips per cookie that would result from your recommendation?

In each simulation, the cookie with the fewest chips contained 5 chips. How many chips did the cookies with the *most* chips contain? Is this many chips in a cookie realistic?

For the Teacher: Further Exploration of Follow-Up Question 2

Questions 2 asks how many chips Jeff and Ted should add to a batch of dough for *four dozen* cookies to be confident that each cookie will contain five chips. Students may reason that if it takes, on the average, some number of chips to guarantee five chips per cookie in a batch of a dozen, it will take four times that number for a batch of four dozen. You may want to suggest that students test this reasoning.

One way to test this is to conduct a number of trials for batches of various sizes: How many cookies do you need, on average, to have at least five chips per cookie in a batch of two cookies? In a batch of four cookies? In

---

a batch of eight cookies? Sixteen cookies? Or, test each batch size from two cookies on up. Students can make a coordinate graph of their (number of cookies in a batch, median number of chips) data. If the pattern is linear, the argument would make sense. If it is not, students might hypothesize other explanations.

One class found the following data. You may want to have your students explore this question, adding their data to those below.

Batch size	Trials (total number of chips)	Median
1 cookie	—	5
2 cookies	11, 12, 12, 13, 18, 18	12.5
3 cookies	17, 18, 19, 19, 25, 22	19
4 cookies	21, 24, 27, 29, 32, 34	28
5 cookies	31, 33, 34, 36, 47, 55	35
6 cookies	41, 49, 51, 55, 59, 78	53
7 cookies	46, 52, 57, 60, 68, 69	58.5
8 cookies	69, 72, 75, 82, 90, 91	78.5
9 cookies	64, 69, 70, 72, 82, 97	71
10 cookies	83, 85, 100, 103, 110, 120	101
11 cookies	76, 84, 94, 97, 111, 113	95.5
12 cookies	from Problem 4.2	107.5

The coordinate graph of these data is shown below. More data points would make the pattern in the data more evident.

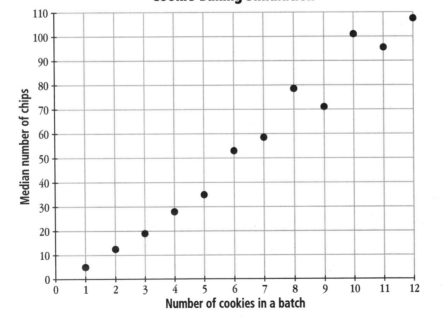

Cookie-Baking Simulation

Additional Answers

Answers to Problem 4.1

A. The box plots below display the arrowhead-length data. Lines have been drawn to highlight the relationships among the sites. (Note: Students may or may not show outliers.) Lines 1 and 2 show the similarity of site I to the Kobold/Buffalo Creek and Laddie Creek/Dead Indian Creek settlements.

Lines 2 and 3 show the similarity of site II to the Big Goose Creek and Wortham Shelter settlements, in which the data are less spread out.

Based on this, site I was likely settled between 4000 B.C. and A.D. 500, and site II was likely settled between A.D. 500 and A.D. 1600.

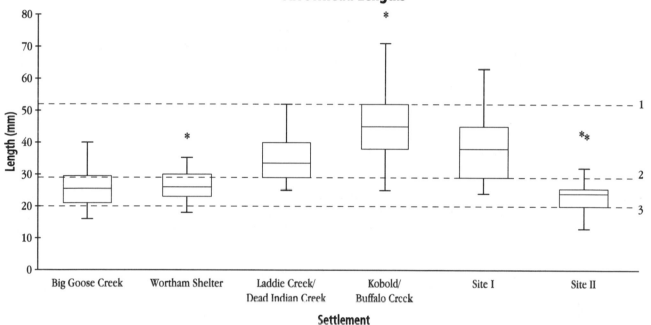

Arrowhead Lengths

B. The box plots below display the arrowhead-width data. Lines have been drawn to highlight the relationships among the sites, which support the original findings.

Lines 1 and 2 show the similarity of site I to the Kobold/Buffalo Creek and Laddie Creek/Dead Indian Creek settlements.

Lines 3 and 4 show the similarity of site II to the Big Goose Creek and Wortham Shelter settlements, in which the data are less spread out.

Again, site I was likely settled between 4000 B.C. and A.D. 500, and site II was likely settled between A.D. 500 and A.D. 1600.

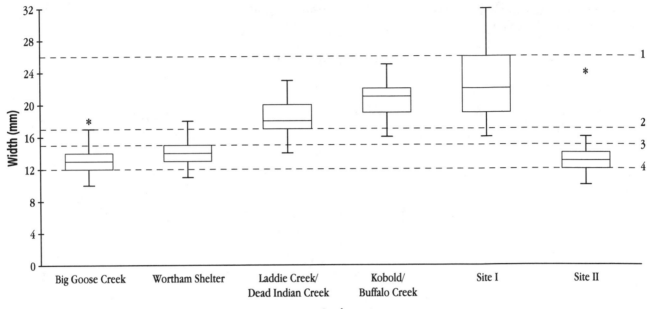

Arrowhead Widths

Answers to Problem 4.1 Follow-Up

2. The box plots below display the length-to-width ratios for all the arrowheads from each site.

   The distributions are similar in that the medians and boxes all fall within the interval of 1.5 to 2.5. While there is variation in the lengths and the widths of the arrowheads found at different sites, the small variation in the length-to-width ratios suggests that across sites, arrowheads are about twice as long as they are wide. In other words, the length-to-width ratio does not differ much from site to site, so it is not helpful for analyzing the time periods for the new sites.

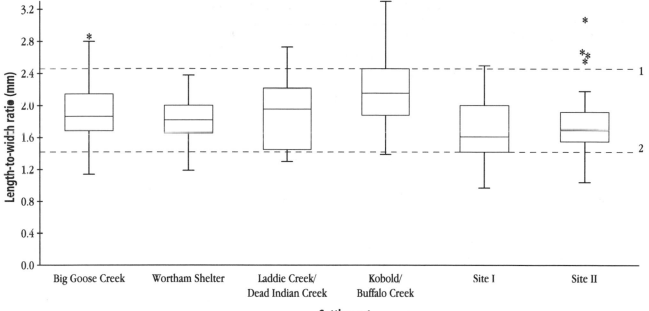

Arrowhead Length-to-Width Ratios

Answers to Problem 4.2

A, B. Simulation results will vary.

C. The distribution of chips required to meet the "at least five in each cookie" criterion can be displayed with a stem plot, a histogram, or a box plot. In their answers, students might decide to add at least as many chips as required in the worst-case batch—the greatest number of chips found in the simulation—or to settle for a number that works most of the time. Students will need to define what "most of the time" means. It could be the upper quartile; the mean, particularly if it is greater than the median; the upper limit of a particular interval on a stem plot (such as 119 in the stem plot below because the interval of 110 to 119 is the modal interval); and so on. Below are the results from a class in which 20 simulations were conducted. These results might support a variety of answers, such as 108 (the median), 117 (the upper quartile, in which 75% of the batches would consist of all cookies containing at least five chips), and 157 (the greatest number of chips required in all 20 simulations). However, since 157 turns out to be an outlier, it probably would not make sense to choose this number of chips.

Simulation Results

```
 0 |
 1 |
 2 |
 3 |
 4 |
 5 |
 6 |
 7 |
 8 | 3 5 7
 9 | 3 6 9
10 | 1 2 2 3
11 | 2 2 2 6 8 9
12 |
13 | 3 5
14 |
15 | 7
```

A box plot and a histogram of the data are shown below.

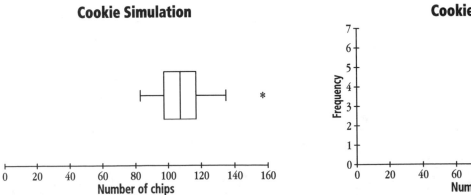

Cookie Simulation

Number of chips

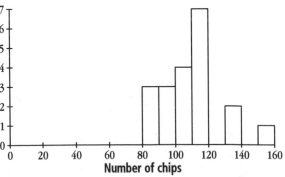

Cookie Simulation

Frequency

Number of chips

ACE Answers

Applications

1b. The box plots below show the neck-width data. Lines have been drawn to highlight the relationships among the sites. Lines 1 and 2 show the similarity of site I to the Kobold/Buffalo Creek and Laddie Creek/Dead Indian Creek settlements. Lines 2 and 3 show the similarity of site II to the Big Goose Creek and Wortham Shelter settlements. Based on this, site I was likely settled between 4000 B.C. and A.D. 500, and site II was likely settled between A.D. 500 and A.D. 1600. (Students may or may not show outliers.)

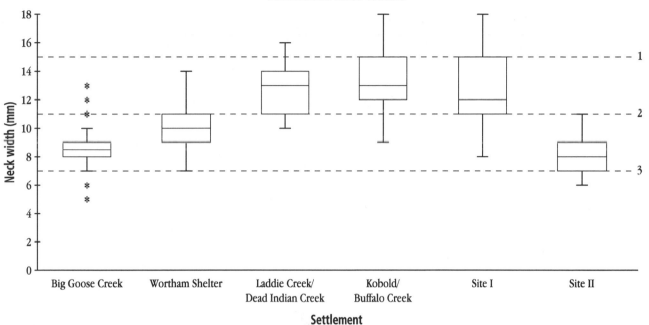

Part 1: Safe Water and Life Expectancy

In most areas in the United States, tap water is safe to drink and purified drinking water is sold in grocery stores. In many countries, however, people do not have access to safe drinking water. In this project, you will explore the relationship between life expectancy and access to safe water.

Use the data in the table below and your knowledge of statistics and data representations to prepare a report that summarizes the relationship between life expectancy and access to safe drinking water.

Country	Region	Life expectancy (years)	Percent of people with access to safe water
Oman	Near East/South Asia	49	52
Yemen, Arab Republic	Near East/South Asia	43	4
Yemen	Near East/South Asia	46	37
Afghanistan	Near East/South Asia	37	10
Bangladesh	Near East/South Asia	48	68
Kampuchea	Near East/South Asia	39	45
Laos	Far East/Pacific	43	48
Nepal	Near East/South Asia	45	11
Angola	Africa	42	17
Central African Republic	Africa	43	18
Chad	Africa	43	26
Congo	Africa	43	26
Ethiopia	Africa	46	13
Guinea	Africa	43	10
Ivory Coast	Africa	47	14
Madagascar	Africa	48	26
Malawi	Africa	44	44
Mali	Africa	45	23
Mauritania	Africa	44	17
Mozambique	Africa	49	7

Assigning the Unit Project

In this two-part unit project, which can be used as the final assessment of this unit, students apply their understanding of samples and populations to real-world situations.

In Part 1, Safe Water and Life Expectancy, students use their knowledge of statistics and data representations to analyze a set of data and determine whether there is a relationship between life expectancy and access to safe drinking water. The project can be started while Investigation 4 is in progress.

To introduce this project, you may want to display a world map so that students can locate the regions that are referenced.

Ask students to brainstorm ways that they might compare the data. The two most obvious ways are by making box plots to look at life expectancy by region and access to safe water by region, and by making a scatter plot to relate the variables of "life expectancy" and "percent of people with access to safe water."

Students are asked to prepare a report summarizing their findings. More information about the project can be found in the Assessment Resources section.

Country	Region	Life expectancy (years)	Percent of people with access to safe water
Niger	Africa	45	49
Nigeria	Africa	49	28
Rwanda	Africa	46	38
Senegal	Africa	44	35
Sierra Leone	Africa	47	9
Somalia	Africa	39	38
Sudan	Africa	47	46
Togo	Africa	48	11
Uganda	Africa	48	16
Upper Volta	Africa	44	14
Canada	Western Hemisphere	75	99
United States	Western Hemisphere	75	99
Argentina	Western Hemisphere	71	60
Costa Rica	Western Hemisphere	73	81
Cuba	Western Hemisphere	73	62
Jamaica	Western Hemisphere	71	82
Panama	Western Hemisphere	71	83
Trinidad and Tobago	Western Hemisphere	72	89
Uruguay	Western Hemisphere	71	78
Belgium	Western Europe	73	89
Denmark	Western Europe	75	99
France	Western Europe	76	97
Western Germany	Western Europe	73	99
Greece	Near East/South Asia	74	97
Italy	Western Europe	74	86
The Netherlands	Western Europe	76	97
Norway	Western Europe	76	98
Portugal	Western Europe	72	92
United Kingdom	Western Europe	74	99
Czechoslovakia	Eastern Europe	72	78
East Germany	Eastern Europe	73	82
Hungary	Eastern Europe	71	44
Poland	Eastern Europe	73	55
Austria	Eastern Europe	73	88
Finland	Western Europe	75	84
Ireland	Western Europe	73	73
Spain	Western Europe	74	78
Sweden	Western Europe	77	99
Switzerland	Western Europe	76	96
Yugoslavia	Western Europe	71	58
Israel	Near East/South Asia	73	99
Japan	Far East/Pacific	77	98
Singapore	Far East/Pacific	72	100
Australia	Far East/Pacific	74	97
New Zealand	Far East/Pacific	74	93

Source: David Nelson, Geroge Gheverghese Joseph, and Julian Williams. *Multicultural Mathematics*. New York: Oxford University Press, 1993, pp. 178 and 179.

Part 2: Estimating Populations

The three drawings below represent fields of Canadian geese. Each dot represents one goose. A 10-by-10 grid has been placed over each drawing. Use what you know about random samples and data analysis to estimate the total number of geese in each field without counting all the geese. Prepare a report describing your methods and your findings.

Field A

In Part 2, Estimating Populations, students use their knowledge of random samples and data analysis to estimate populations of geese from drawings that represent fields of geese.

Have students work in groups of two or three to make their estimates and to prepare a report summarizing their findings. You may want to distribute Labsheets U.P.A and U.P.B, on which the three fields are reproduced.

More information about the project is given in the Assessment Resources section.

Field B

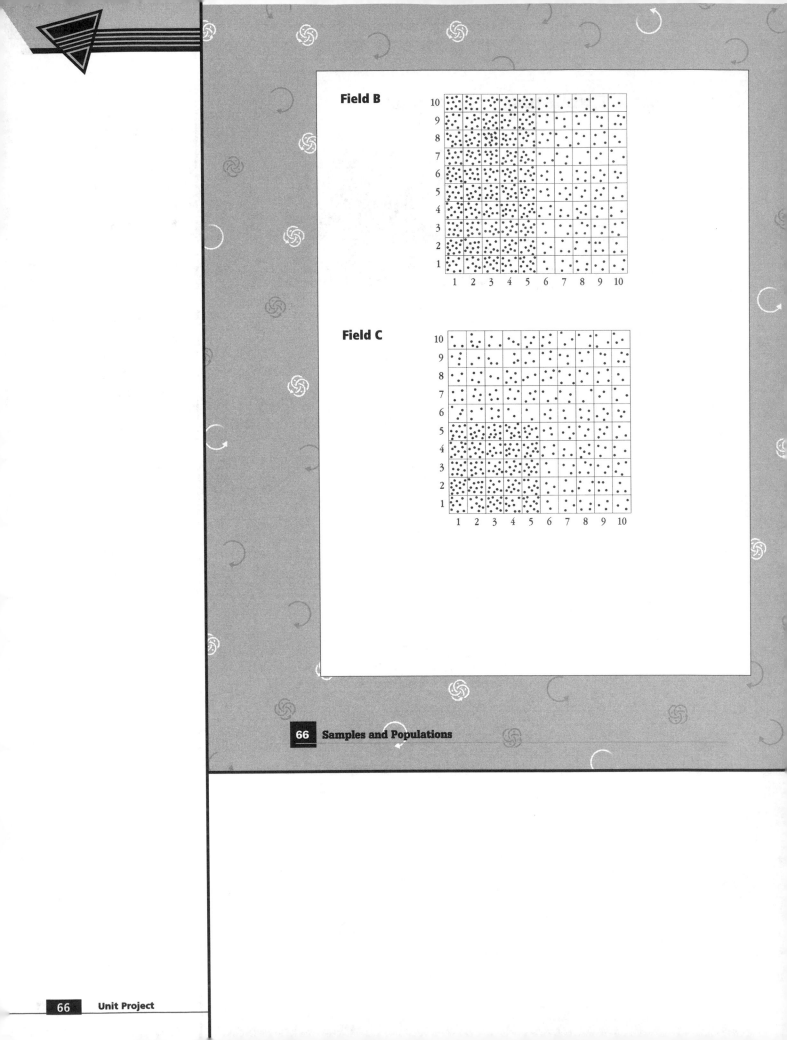

Field C

Looking Back and Looking Ahead

Unit Reflections

Working on the problems of this unit, you learned how to collect, organize, and display sample data. You learned how to *choose samples* and how to *compare samples* in order to *draw conclusions about populations* from which the samples were taken.

Using Statistical Reasoning—To test your understanding and skill in use of samples to describe populations, consider the following problems that arose when students in Elizabeth City Middle School were talking about nutrition in health class. One student objected to a cereal marketing strategy. She claimed that stores try to promote sales of cereals with high sugar content by placing them where young children will see them on the supermarket shelves.

1 *To test her claim, the class collected data on sugar content in grams per serving, calories per serving, and shelf placement—top, middle, bottom—for 77 different cereals. For example, they found Oaters on the top shelf with 110 calories and 1 gram of sugar per serving, Crunchy Critters on the middle shelf with 120 calories and 12 grams of sugar per serving, and Fancy Flakes on the bottom shelf with 140 calories and 14 grams of sugar per serving.*
The sugar content data for all 77 cereals are shown in the following calculator box plots.

Shelf Location and Sugar Content

Top shelf, $n = 20$

Middle shelf, $n = 24$

Bottom shelf, $n = 33$

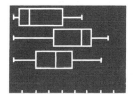

a. What is the range of sugar content in cereals on

   i. the top shelf?   **ii.** the middle shelf?   **iii.** the bottom shelf?

How to Use
Looking Back and Looking Ahead: Unit Reflections

The first part of this section includes problems that allow students to demonstrate their mathematical understandings and skills. The second part gives them an opportunity to explain their reasoning. This section can be used as a review to help students stand back and reflect on the "big" ideas and connections in the unit. This section may be assigned as homework, followed up with class discussion the next day. Focus on the *Explaining Your Reasoning* section in the discussion. Encourage the students to refer to the problems to illustrate their reasoning.

1b. **i.** 3 grams

    ii. 11 grams

    iii. 7 grams

1c. **i.** 5 or 25%

    ii. 50%

2a. Yes, the range of sugar content of the middle shelf cereals is greater than the range of sugar content of the cereals on the other two shelves. The middle-shelf cereals have a higher median for sugar content than those cereals on the other two shelves. This shelf also happens to be the closest to eye-level for children.

  b. The sample sizes for each shelf are large enough for us to be able to accurately report measures of central tendency such as the mean, median, and mode. The exact counts for each shelf do not need to be equivalent in order to make such comparisons.

  c. Answers will vary. This might be a fun follow-up activity for the class to do. We have data from only one store so it is difficult to predict using these data.

3a. Method #1

  b. Method #3

  c. Method #2

  d. Answers may vary. Method #3, however, will give results that are likely to be the most representative.

---

  b. Estimate the median grams of sugar in boxes of cereal found on the

    i. top shelf.   **ii.** middle shelf.   **iii.** bottom shelf.

  c. Use the data given for cereals found on the top and bottom shelves.

    i. How many of the 20 top-shelf cereals are in the top quartile?

    ii. What percent of the 33 bottom-shelf cereals are in the two middle quartiles?

(2) *The students wanted to look at the cereal sugar-content and shelf-placement data to test claims that cereal companies put their products where they will catch the eyes of likely customers.*

  a. Do you notice a pattern relating sugar content and shelf placement for cereals?

  b. The samples for top shelf, middle shelf, and bottom shelf have different numbers of cereals. Can you still compare the data?

  c. If you took a sample of cereals from a supermarket near you, what do you think you would find out about the sugar content in cereals on the different shelves?

(3) *Jerome decided to make a scatter plot of the cereal data to see if there is any relationship between grams of sugar and calories in the cereal. He did not want to enter the data from 77 boxes of cereal. He wanted to choose a sample of about 25 boxes of cereal. He listed three ways he might do this.*

  1. Organize the 77 cereals so they are listed in alphabetical order in one list. Choose every third cereal from this list to include in the sample.

  2. Organize the cereals on each shelf in alphabetical order and choose the first 8 cereals from each of the three lists.

  3. Number the entries in the alphabetical list of 77 cereals. Use two spinners (numbered 0 to 9) to produce two-digit numbers. Pick the first 25 cereal entries that match the numbers produced on the spinners.

  a. Which method is an example of *convenience sampling*?

  b. Which method is an example of *random sampling*?

  c. Which method is an example of a *systematic sampling*?

  d. Which method would you recommend?

④ *There are 600 students in Elizabeth City Middle School. Fifty students were selected at random to participate in a survey. They were asked the following two questions.*

1. *Using a scale of 1 to 5, how often did you eat cereal for breakfast on school days last week? (14 students responded with either a 4 or a 5.)*

2. *When you eat cereal, do you prefer unsweetened or sweetened brands? (32 students responded with a preference for sweetened cereal.)*

If all 600 students responded to both questions,

   a. How many students would you expect to answer the first question with either a 4 or a 5?

   b. How many students would you expect to answer the second question with a preference for presweetened cereal?

Explaining Your Reasoning—When you compare data sets, read graphs, choose samples, and use samples to make predictions about populations, you should be able to justify your procedures and conclusions.

1. In what types of situations are *box plots* useful tools?

2. In what types of situations are *scatter plots* useful tools?

3. When does it make sense to use data from a sample to study a population?

4. What does it mean when we say that a sample is *representative* of a population?

5. Describe three kinds of sampling methods that might *not* result in a representative sample.

6. Rules of thumb are guidelines for thinking about some topic. One rule of thumb about sampling is that it is wise to use a random sample whenever possible. What rule of thumb would you suggest about the size a sample needs to be in order to be used to make estimates about the population?

Statistical ideas and techniques for collecting and displaying data and drawing conclusions are used in nearly every branch of science, business, and government work. You'll extend and use your statistical understanding and skills in future studies, work, and reasoning about important questions faced by all people.

4a. $\frac{14}{50}$ = 28%, so find 28% of 600.

0.28 × 600 = 168 students

b. $\frac{32}{50}$ = 64%, so find 64% of 600.

0.64 × 600 = 384 students

Explaining Your Reasoning
See page 66d.

Looking Back and Looking Ahead

Possible Answers

Explaining Your Reasoning

1. Box plots are useful for comparing several data sets involving the same variable. They are especially helpful when the sets of data contain many values. Also, even if two or more sets of data have unequal numbers of values, comparisons with box plots can be made.

2. Scatter plots are useful for learning about relationships between two variables.

3. Samples are useful when the population is too large to be able to study all of its members easily.

4. When the members of a sample accurately reflect the characteristics of the population, we say the sample is representative of the population. This means that the measures of central tendency of the sample can be used to make reasonable estimates about the larger population.

5. convenience sampling, volunteer sampling, systematic sampling

6. A sample size of 30 is a good size to use.

Assessment Resources

For the quiz, students will need materials for generating random numbers, similar to what they used in Investigations 2 and 3, such as 10-sided number cubes, 10-section spinners, and graphing calculators. Students should not be directed to use a particular tool, but the equipment should be available in the room for them to self-select. In addition, they will need access to the table of data on page 47 of their books. You may want to make copies of this page rather than have them use their books during the quiz.

Check-Up

1. Which box plot below—A, B, or C—matches the stem
   plot shown at the right? Explain what you looked for
   to make the match.

```
0 | 2 3 3
1 | 4 5 6 7 7 9 9 9
2 | 2 2 3 5 5 5 8 8 9
3 | 2 4 4 5 6 6 6
4 | 0 0 1 2 6 7
5 | 1 2 3 3 4
6 | 0 5
7 | 1
8 | 4
```

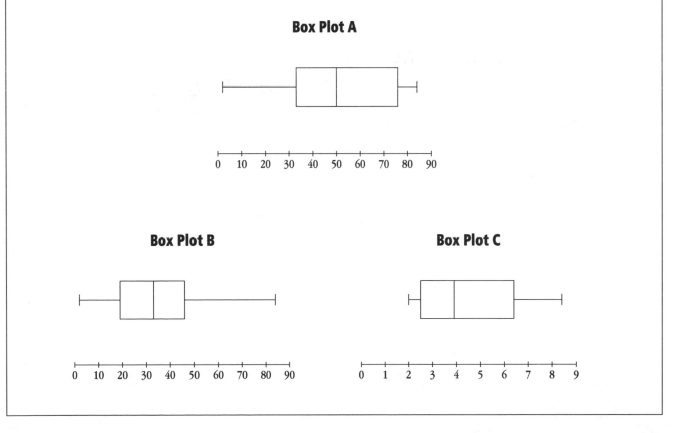

Box Plot A

Box Plot B   **Box Plot C**

Check-Up

2. **a.** This box plot shows the heights in inches of girls on a freshman basketball team. What would you say is a typical height of a team member? Give evidence to support your answer.

Heights of Basketball Players

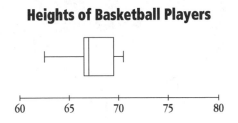

```
60      65      70      75      80
```

b. Listed below are the heights in inches of boys on a freshman basketball team. Make a box plot of these data using the same scale as used in part a.

60   60   66   66   66   67   68   69   69   69   69   70   70   71   71   71

c. Which statement do you agree with? Use the box plots to help you decide.

Statement 1: The players on the boys' team are taller than those on the girls' team.

Statement 2: The players on the girls' team are taller than those on the boys' team.

Quiz

1. a. The principal has been asked to send ten students to attend a state conference on education. She makes an announcement about the conference and selects the first ten students who contact her after the announcement. Which sampling method did she use? Explain your answer.

    i.   convenience sample

    ii. voluntary-response sample

    iii. systematic sample

    iv. random sample

    b. The principal wants to send a representative group of students to attend the conference. Do you think her method of selecting students is a good method? If yes, explain why. If no, explain how you think the principal should select students to attend the conference.

2. a. Select a random sample from the table of data about M&M's candies on page 47 in your book. For each sample, record the bag number, the number of blue candies, and the total number of M&M's in the bag. Select as many samples as you think are needed to give a reasonable sample size.

    b. Explain how you made sure that your samples were chosen randomly.

    c. Explain how you decided on the size of your sample and why it is reasonable.

    d. Use your sample to estimate the percent of blue M&M's in a typical bag of plain M&M's candies. Explain how you found your answer.

Assign these questions as additional homework, or use them as review, quiz, or test questions.

1. These box plots represent the distribution of the ratings given to four movies by 20 newspapers and magazines. Compare the box plots. Which movie do you believe is the most highly recommended? Explain your reasoning.

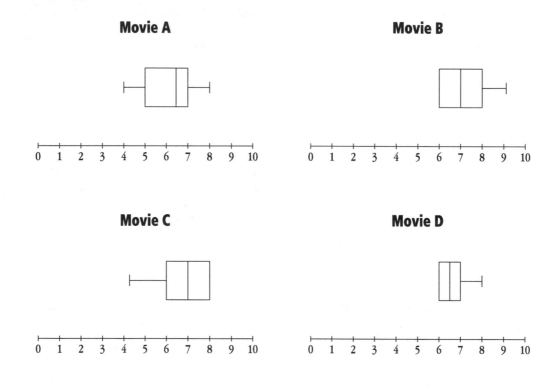

2. **a.** A class of tenth grade students counted the change in coins that they had in their pockets, backpacks, or purses. Below are their results. Make a box plot of these data.

   $1.35 $0.42 $0.85 $0.35 $0.75 $0.90 $1.02 $3.64 $0.20 $0.35 $0.45

   $0.75 $0.12 $0.10 $0.80 $1.75 $1.12 $0.41 $0.28 $0.25 $0.25 $0.40

   b. Describe what your box plot tells you about the typical amount of change carried by a student in this class.

3. A group of students wondered how many raisins were in a bowl of a particular breakfast cereal. They filled 20 identical bowls with cereal and counted the raisins in each bowl. Their results are shown below.

Bowl	Number of raisins
1	14
3	21
5	22
7	19
9	19
11	21
13	19
15	14
17	10
19	25

Bowl	Number of raisins
2	18
4	13
6	20
8	24
10	22
12	12
14	17
16	11
18	23
20	12

a. Make a box plot or a histogram showing the number of raisins in each bowl.

b. Suppose the cereal boxes are filled from a large container that holds 400 bowl-size servings. Use your sampling distribution to estimate how many raisins are in one of these large containers.

c. Are you confident about your prediction? Explain why or why not.

4. At the spring parade, the local dentists' organization was tossing packets of sugarless gum balls to all the children. Sook Leng, who was watching the parade, wondered how the gum balls had been put into the packets. A dentist told her that each packet contained 8 gum balls, which came in green, red, and yellow. A total of 40,000 gum balls had been mixed thoroughly and put into the packets. However, the dentist did not know the mix of colors in the batch of 40,000.

Sook Leng asked the children near her to tell her the number of each color of gum ball in their packets. When she went home, she made three line plots from the data she had collected from 30 packets. The line plots are shown below.

Colors of Gum Balls

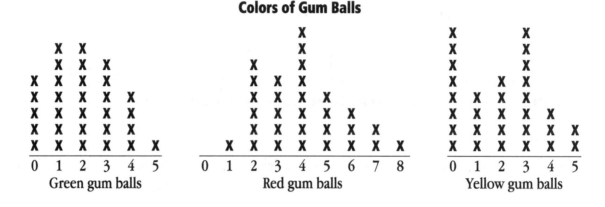

a. Make a box plot of the distribution of the number of gum balls of each color. Draw your three box plots on the same scale.

b. Using your box plots, estimate how many—or about what percent—of the 40,000 gum balls were green, how many were red, and how many were yellow. Explain your reasoning.

Several brands of raisins are packaged in half-ounce boxes. The box plots below show the distribution of the numbers of raisins found in the boxes opened for each brand.

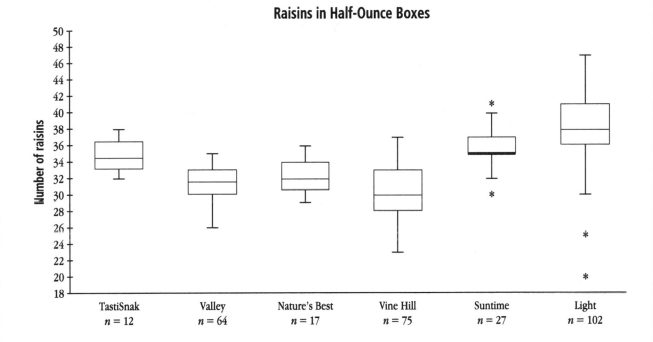

Raisins in Half-Ounce Boxes

5. Name each brand of raisins, and tell how many boxes were counted in that sample.

6. Look at the box plot for the Suntime brand of raisins. The median and the lower quartile are identical. What must be true about the data for this to be so?

7. Which brands of raisins appear to have similar numbers of raisins in their half-ounce boxes? Explain your reasoning.

8. Compare Light brand raisins with Valley brand raisins. Which brand generally has more raisins in a half-ounce box? Explain your reasoning.

Unit Test

1. Ms. Choy wants to analyze the achievement of her eighth grade classes on a quiz. These box plots represent the quiz scores of Ms. Choy's first-period, second-period, and third-period classes.

Quiz Scores

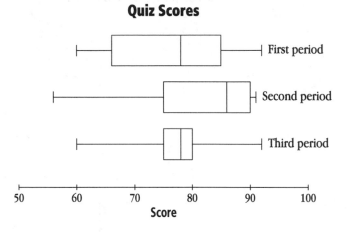

a. Describe how the box plots compare.

b. If you were Ms. Choy, which of your classes would you think was most successful on the quiz? Explain.

2. A biologist is studying a system of rivers and lakes. He takes samples by netting a quantity of fish at different places and studying the fish caught. Some of the fish are diseased because of water pollution. The biologist looks at the distribution across all the samples before drawing any conclusions. If he suspects that the percentage of diseased fish in the whole system is above 15%, he will recommend intervention.

a. The results of the biologist's samples are shown on the next page. Complete the table.

Name _____ Date _____

Unit Test

Fish-Sampling Data

Sample	Diseased fish in sample	Total number of fish caught	Percentage of diseased fish in total
1	5	15	33.3
2	8	25	32.0
3	2	12	16.7
4	3	28	10.7
5	2	40	5.0
6	2	22	
7	5	33	
8	3	27	
9	4	29	
10	4	31	
11	3	35	
12	5	40	
13	4	22	
14	1	11	
15	2	21	

b. Should the biologist call for intervention immediately after he sees the results from the first and second samples? Explain your answer.

c. Make a box plot or a histogram showing the percent of diseased fish in these samples.

Unit Test

d. Is sample 1 typical of all the samples? Explain your answer.

e. From the evidence of these samples, how should the biologist describe the general condition of the water system and what, if any, action should he propose?

f. Suppose the biologist takes a new sample and it contains 2 diseased fish out of 2. Would this change your description of the situation? Explain.

g. Based on the samples in the table, what percent of fish in this entire system do you think are diseased?

Notebook Checklist

Journal Organization

_____ Problems and Mathematical Reflections are labeled and dated.

_____ Work is neat and is easy to find and follow.

Vocabulary

_____ All words are listed.   _____ All words are defined or described.

Check-Up and Quiz

_____ Check-Up

_____ Quiz

Homework Assignments

___ _____

___ _____

___ _____

___ _____

___ _____

___ _____

___ _____

___ _____

___ _____

___ _____

___ _____

___ _____

___ _____

___ _____

___ _____

Self-Assessment

Vocabulary

Of the vocabulary words I defined or described in my journal, the word _____ best demonstrates my ability to give a clear definition or description.

Of the vocabulary words I defined or described in my journal, the word _____ best demonstrates my ability to use an example to help explain or describe an idea.

Mathematical Ideas

1. a. By studying the mathematics in *Samples and Populations*, I have learned the following . . .

    . . . about ways to choose a sample:

    . . . about problems in sample choice that might create biased conclusions:

    . . . about how to use samples to make predictions about a population:

    b. Here are page numbers of journal entries that give evidence of what I have learned, along with descriptions of what each entry shows:

2. a. These are the mathematical ideas I am still struggling with:

    b. This is why I think these ideas are difficult for me:

    c. Here are page numbers of journal entries that give evidence of what I am struggling with, along with descriptions of what each entry shows:

Class Participation

I contributed to the class discussion and understanding of *Samples and Populations* when I . . . (Give examples.)

Answers to the Check-Up

1. Box plot B matches the stem plot; explanations will vary. The range of 2 to 84 in box plots A and B fits the data in the stem plot; the range in box plot C does not. This restricts the choice to the first two plots. Half of the data in box plot A are above 50, but there are only 9 pieces of data above 50 in the stem plot, so it can't be plot A. That leaves box plot B.

2. a. Answers will vary. Based on the median, a height of about 67 inches is typical. Based on the 50% of the data in the middle of the distribution, a height of about 66.5 to 69.5 inches is typical.

   b. **Heights of Basketball Players**

   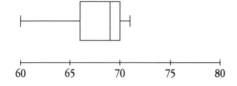

   c. Answers will vary. The middle 50% of the boys have heights ranging from 66 to 70 inches, so it would be sensible to say that a typical height is between 66 and 70 inches. However, 25% of these heights are clustered in the 69-to-70-inch range, so the most likely height appears to be from 69 to 70 inches; some students may say, that based on the median, a typical height for the boys is 69 inches. The typical girl's height is about 66.5 to 69.5 inches, so it makes sense to say that the players on the boys' team are slightly taller. (Note: Comparing only the maximum heights, which are the same, gives too much weight to a single value.)

Answers to the Quiz

1. a. This is a voluntary-response sample because the students choose to contact the principal. (Note: Students might also say this is a convenience sample. These ten students might all be in the only class whose teacher allowed them out of class to see the principal. Or they might all be in the classroom that is closest to the principal's office.)

   b. This sample would not likely be representative. Students will have various ideas about how the principal might select a representative group of students.

2. a. Samples will vary. See part d for the samples selected by one student using a calculator's random-number generator.

   b. Answers will vary. Students might roll a 10-sided die or spin a 10-section spinner once for the first digit 0–9 and once for the second digit (counting a roll of 00 as 100). They could also use the random-number generator on their calculators to choose integers from 1 to 100. Students need to account for eliminating repeats if they decide to have a sample size greater than 1.

   c. Sample sizes should be small enough to be less cumbersome than working with all 100 values, yet large enough not to be influenced by data that are not representative of the population. Typical sizes might be between 15 and 20.

d. The actual distribution of blue candies in the table is approximately 7.5%. One student's data are shown below. This student calculated the percent of blue candies in each bag. This student reported that in his sample he had a total of 44 blue candies out of a total of 566 candies, which is 7.8%. He found that the mean of the ten percents in his table is also about 7.8%. This will not always be true because the bags do not hold the same number of candies.

Bag Number	Number of blue M&M's	Total number in bag	Percent of blue candies
86	3	58	5.2%
100	6	54	11.1%
13	4	55	7.3%
26	7	57	12.3%
72	5	55	9.1%
48	5	58	8.6%
38	4	59	6.8%
59	7	56	12.5%
10	1	56	1.8%
15	2	58	3.4%

Answers to the Question Bank

1. Comparing the middle 50% of the values (from the lower quartile to the upper quartile), movies B and C have equal ratings, but comparing the maximum values of movies B and C, movie B has higher ratings.

2. **a.** Students may or may not show the outlier.

Pocket Change

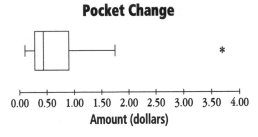

b. Answers will vary. By looking at the 50% of the data represented by the box, students could say that the typical amount of money carried is between $0.28 and $0.90. Or, by looking at the median, students could say that about $0.44 is typical.

3. a.

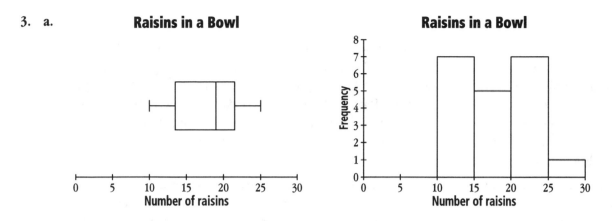

Raisins in a Bowl

Number of raisins

Raisins in a Bowl

Frequency

Number of raisins

b. Answers will vary. Using the median, a typical number of raisins is about 19, so 400 bowls would contain about 400 × 19 = 7600 raisins. Using the middle 50% of the data, a typical number is between 13.5 and 21.5, so 400 bowls would contain between 5400 and 8600 raisins.

c. The samples are fairly consistent and there are 20 samples, so these estimates should be reliable.

4. a.

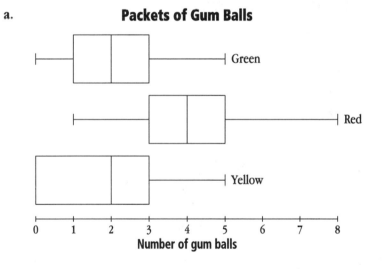

Packets of Gum Balls

Green

Red

Yellow

Number of gum balls

b. Possible answer: Using the median values (2 green, 4 red, and 2 yellow out of 8 gum balls) is one way to predict the proportion of each color in the 40,000 gum balls. This gives about 10,000 green, 20,000 red, and 10,000 yellow, or 25% green, 50% red, and 25% yellow.

5. TastiSnak: 12 boxes; Valley: 64 boxes; Nature's Best: 17 boxes; Vine Hill: 75 boxes; Suntime: 27 boxes; Light: 102 boxes

6. About 25% of the boxes of Suntime raisins had that number of raisins (35).

7. Answers will vary, but it could be argued that Valley, Nature's Best, and perhaps even Vine Hill boxes have similar numbers of raisins. Likewise, students could argue that TastiSnak and Suntime boxes have similar numbers of raisins.

8. The Light brand raisin boxes generally have more raisins. The median is noticeably greater, and about 75% of the boxes of Light raisins have more raisins than about 75% of the boxes of Valley raisins.

Answers to the Unit Test

1. **a.** Answers will vary. The range and median for the first- and third-period classes are the same, but the middle 50% of the data is much more spread out in the first period. The third-period class has a concentration of grades in the 75 to 80 range and it shows the least variability. We can say that fewer students did poorly in the third-period class, but we also have to say that fewer students in this period did really well. The second-period class has the students with the lowest grades of all three classes and does not have anyone who scored as highly as the top students in the other two classes. On the other hand, the middle 50% did better in the second-period class than in either of the other two classes.

   b. Overall, the second-period class had more successful students on the quiz than did the other two classes. About 75% of that class scored better than a 75 (as did the students in the third-period class), the median of the second-period class is higher than in the other two classes, and the middle 50% is more successful than in the other two. The middle 50% can be thought of as the typical students.

2. **a.**

Fish-Sampling Data

Sample	Diseased fish in sample	Total number of fish caught	Percentage of diseased fish in total
1	5	15	33.3
2	8	25	32.0
3	2	12	16.7
4	3	28	10.7
5	2	40	5.0
6	2	22	9.1
7	5	33	15.2
8	3	27	11.1
9	4	29	13.8
10	4	31	12.9
11	3	35	8.6
12	5	40	12.5
13	4	22	18.2
14	1	11	9.1
15	2	21	9.5

   b. No. Two samples are not enough to diagnose a whole population. The first results are alarming, but they show a higher percent of diseased fish than any of the other samples.

c.

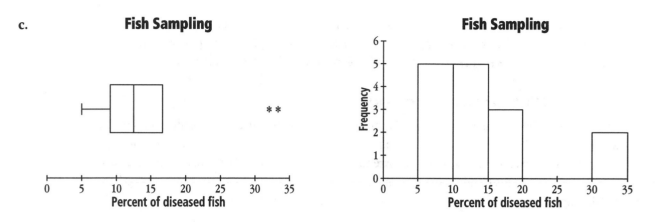

Fish Sampling

Fish Sampling

d. No. Sample 1 is one of two samples that are quite different from the others. The median of the samples is 12.5%; 33.3% is the maximum value and far from the median.

e. Answers will vary. Using the histogram, most of the samples lie in the 5% to 15% range, and using the box plot, most lie in the 9.1% to 16.7% range, so the underlying population (the fish in the whole system) is probably in this range. Some students may also calculate the mean (14.5%) or the median (12.5%) and point out that while neither of these is at the official "action" level, these percents are approaching that level, so some action may be warranted—perhaps sampling more often or putting a readiness plan into place.

f. This sample size is so small that it is probably of no use in making predictions.

g. According to the histogram, most of the samples lie in the 5% to 15% range; using the box plot, the 9.1% to 16.7% range. Using the mean or the median, students may decide that the level is actually on the upper end of this range.

The two-part unit project can be used as the final assessment in *Samples and Populations*. To complete the project, students apply their understanding of samples and populations to real-world situations. A suggested scoring rubric follows the project descriptions.

Part 1: Safe Water and Life Expectancy

In part 1, students use their knowledge of statistics and data representations to analyze a set of data and determine whether there is a relationship between life expectancy and access to safe drinking water. The two most obvious ways to compare these data are by making box plots of life expectancy by region and of access to safe water by region, and by making a scatter plot to relate the variables of "life expectancy" and "percent of people with access to safe water."

The box plots of life expectancy reveal that Eastern Europe, Western Europe, and the Western Hemisphere have the highest life expectancies and that Africa has the lowest. There is greater variation in life expectancy in the Far East/Pacific and Near East/South Asia regions than in the other regions.

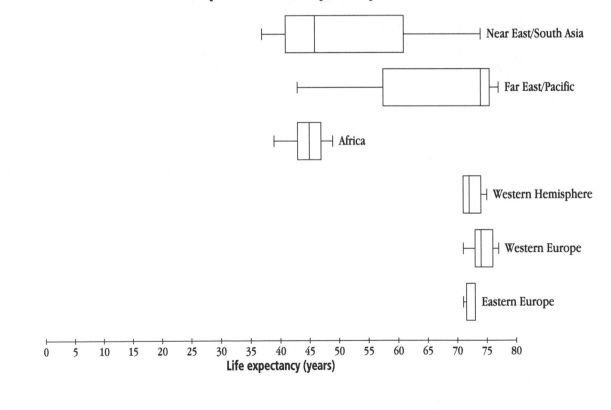

Comparison of Life Expectancy

The box plots of percent access to safe water present a picture that is less clear. For Africa, less than 50% of people have access to safe water and, as seen in the first box plot, Africans have a life expectancy of 50 years or less. Using 50 years as a benchmark, we can see that, generally, life expectancies for Eastern Europe, the Far East/Pacific, Western Europe, and the Western Hemisphere are longer than 50 years. In the Near East/South Asia region, there is tremendous variation in access to safe water.

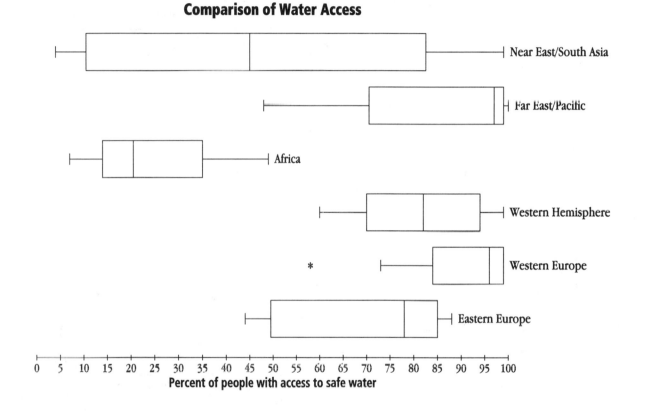

Comparison of Water Access

For all but Africa and Western Europe, the data sets are small and not necessarily well-suited to box plot displays. The scatter plot below, in which each country is represented by a data point, is more revealing of a relationship between life expectancy and access to safe water. From the graph, we can estimate that if 50% or less of a population has access to safe water, life expectancy will be less than 50 years. Similarly, if more than 50% of a population has access to safe water, life expectancy increases dramatically, to around 70 years.

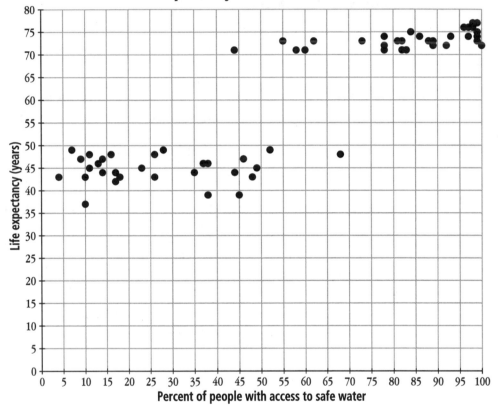

Students may want to explore other factors that might contribute to the dramatic differences in the life expectancies of people living in various countries.

Part 2: Estimating Populations

In part 2, students use their knowledge of random samples and data analysis to estimate populations of geese from drawings representing fields of geese. Using the illustrations in their books or Labsheets UP.A and UP.B, students estimate the number of geese in each of three fields.

The geese in field A are relatively evenly distributed. Students should randomly identify a reasonable number of cells and count the geese in those cells. Once a reasonable number of cells has been sampled (say, around 25), students should use the data to estimate the number of geese in the field.

In fields B and C, the geese are not evenly distributed throughout the field, but they are evenly distributed in portions of the field. In field B, the geese are distributed in two halves. Students should randomly identify a number of cells in each half of the field and count the geese in those cells. Roughly half of the sample should come from each half of the field. If students were to randomly select data from the entire field, they would run the risk of oversampling one half and undersampling the other half. In a sense, students are being introduced to a form of *stratified* sampling. This type of sampling, while random, takes into account specific characteristics of a population.

In field C, the geese are more heavily distributed in one fourth of the field than in the other three fourths of the field. Students will need to adjust their random sampling procedures to reflect this arrangement.

To randomly select cells within each grid, students will need to find a method of randomly selecting two coordinates—one to represent the horizontal grid labels, one to represent the vertical grid labels. For field A, this involves randomly generating pairs of integers, each integer being from 1 to 10. For field B, random integers must be generated in two sets: the first involving the integers $1 \leq x \leq 5$ and $1 \leq y \leq 10$, the second involving the integers $6 \leq x \leq 10$ and $1 \leq y \leq 10$. For field C, the first set involves the integers $1 \leq x \leq 5$ and $1 \leq y \leq 5$; the second involves the remaining grid. One way to identify these points is to generate random integer pairs from $1 \leq x \leq 10$ and $1 \leq y \leq 10$ and eliminate any in which $x \leq 5$ and $y \leq 5$.

Students should estimate approximately 930 geese in field A, 630 geese in field B, and 480 geese in field C.

Suggested Scoring Rubric

This rubric for scoring each part of the project employs a point scale from 0 to 4, with 4+ for work that goes beyond what has been asked for in some unique way. Use the rubric as presented here, or modify it to fit your needs and your district's requirements for evaluating and reporting students' work and understanding.

4+ Exemplary Response
- Complete, with clear, coherent work and explanations
- Shows understanding of the mathematical concepts and procedures
- Satisfies all essential conditions of the project and goes beyond what is asked for in some unique way

4 Complete Response
- Complete, with clear, coherent work and explanations
- Shows understanding of the mathematical concepts and procedures
- Satisfies all essential conditions of the project

3 Reasonably Complete Response
- Reasonably complete; may lack detail or clarity in work or explanations
- Shows understanding of most of the mathematical concepts and procedures
- Satisfies most of the essential conditions of the project

2 Partial Response
- Incomplete; work or explanations are unclear or lacks detail
- Shows some understanding of the mathematical concepts and procedures
- Satisfies some of the essential conditions of the project

1 Inadequate Response
- Incomplete; work or written explanations are insufficient or not understandable
- Shows little understanding of the mathematical concepts and procedures
- Fails to address the essential conditions of the project

0 No Attempt
- Irrelevant response
- Does not address the conditions of the project

The assessment for *Samples and Populations* includes a check-up. Below is a suggested scoring rubric and a grading scale for the check-up. Samples of two students' work and a teacher's comments about how the work was assessed follow. Note that both students chose to write their answers on separate sheets of paper.

Suggested Scoring Rubric

This rubric employs a scale with a total of 14 possible points. You may use the rubric as presented here or modify it to fit your district's requirements for evaluating and reporting students' work and understanding.

Question 1: 3 points

- 1 point for choosing the correct box plot
- 2 points for a reasonable explanation that supports the choice (If students give more information than is needed to verify the match, or if they give only one measure but it is a critical indicator that verifies the correct match, they receive full credit. This question asks students to explain what *they* looked for to match the box plot to the stem plot. It does not ask them to explain all they know about box plots, nor is it testing whether students can determine the critical piece of evidence that matches the data sets using the fewest number of measures. Students' explanation should give them the evidence they need to support their choice.)

Question 2a: 3 points

- 1 point for identifying a reasonable typical height
- 2 points for a reasonable explanation that supports the answer

Question 2b: 5 points

- 1 point for each correct summary value: minimum, lower quartile, median, upper quartile, and maximum

Question 2c: 3 points

- 1 point for selecting the boys as taller than the girls
- 2 points for using some or all of the summary numbers to support the answer

Grading Scale

Points	Grade
13 to 14	A
11 to 12	B
9 to 10	C
7 to 8	D

Sample 1

Kellie

1. I think the box plot B fits the stem and leaf plot the best. To start I looked at the minimum number. It was 2. Both box plots A & B start at about 2, but C starts at zero. Also when I saw that, I noticed the range for C went from 0–10, not 0–100 so I knew that C didn't fit the data in the stem and leaf plot. Next I looked at the maximum. Both A & B looked alright on that. Then I figured out the median. It is 33. In box plot A, it says the median is at 52 or 53, so I knew that graph A didn't fit the stem and leaf plot data. That only left B, but just to be sure I checked the 5 numbers (min. Q1, med. Q3 and max). They seemed to match up well so I know that Box plot B best fits the data in the stem plot.

2a) I think the typical height for a girl on the freshman basketball team is about 67 inches because it is the median. I think the median is typical because it is the middle number, there are the same number shorter than that there are taller. Sence I do not know what the mode is, I can't do any more to figure out what the typical height is, so I will continue to believe it is 67 inches until I know more information.

b)

c) I don't agree with either statement. I think the two teams are just about equal in height. The boys team just has two people that bring down the minimum. If you took those two peices of data you could say the boys team was taller because it would have a higher min, Q1 median and Q3 than the girls team. But sence the two low peices of data are on, the girls team has a higher min. and equal Q1 and max and the boys team has a higher median and a higher Q2 so they both equal out so I think they are equal.

Teacher's Comments on Kellie's Check-Up

Kellie earned all 14 points. She gives a reasonable, complete, and easy-to-follow explanation for each question requiring an explanation. Her box plot for question 2b is correct.

Kellie's explanation for question 2c is interesting in that she does not support either given statement. When I read her first sentence, I thought she was avoiding the issue. But after reading her entire explanation, I felt that she made a good case using all five summary numbers to support why neither statement is reasonable. She received full credit for her answer.

The work Kellie has done on the check-up indicates to me that she has made sense of the ideas presented so far in the unit.

Sample 2

José

1. B is the Box plot that goes with the stem and leaf plot. The way I determined this is first I found the high which happened to be 84 and looked for an end or wisker That was in about the middle 80's. Since all of the wiskers on each plot ended about there I decided it wouldn't help me. So after that I decided To find the low which happened to be 2. Now at this point I realized that it couldn't be plot C because according To the graph (plot) the low was at least 0. So I ruled out C and new it had to be between A or B. Then I started trying to just visually To find the median and I decided that it was either between high 20's to low 30's, or even maybe in the 40's. Now I was thinking iT was B. So I now took the paper and turned it sideways and kind of saw how the stem and leaf plot should look. I added all my evidence together and determined that it was plot B.

2a) I think the average height of a basketball player on the freshman girls team would be about 67-68 inches. I determined this by looking at where the median the plot was. Now this average height may just pertain to this basketball team but I think you could generalize the answer and say the average height of a freshman girl basketball player should be 65-70 inches.

b)

60   65   70   75   80

c) I think the boys team is taller than the girls team. Because the average height is high. There may be a few shorter ones but the median is higher. And "vise-versa" there maybe a few tall girls but the median is lower than the boys.

Teacher's Comments on José's Check-Up

José earned 11 of the 14 points. For question 1, José received full credit. For question 2a, he received 1 point for identifying a reasonable typical height but only $\frac{1}{2}$ point for his explanation. He begins by explaining that 67–68 is the median as shown in the box plot but goes on to state that the average height of a freshman girl player "should be 65–70." I am not sure what he means by "average height," and these numbers are not supported by the five summary numbers in the given box plot. His response interests me because it is as though he knows that the median is an average, but he disregards it and the other summary numbers and gives a range of 65–70. He doesn't demonstrate that he is making sense of the summary values.

José's box plot for question 2b is correct. For question 2c, he received 1 point for identifying the boys as taller but only $\frac{1}{2}$ point for his explanation. He refers only to the median in his argument for the boys being taller, and he shows no evidence of what this number tells him. He makes no reference to half the boys being as tall as or taller than the median; nor to the upper quartile measure and that the boys are taller by this measure than are the girls.

It is not clear to me how José is reasoning about the median and other measures. His work leaves me with more questions than answers. I need to have more conversations in my class about summary measures, what they do and do not reveal about data, and what is meant by the term "typical."

Blackline Masters

Peanut Butter Comparisons

	Brand	Quality rating	Sodium per serving (mg)	Price per serving	Regular/ natural	Creamy/ chunky	Salted/ unsalted	Name brand/ store brand
1.	Smucker's Natural	71	15	27¢	natural	creamy	unsalted	name
2.	Deaf Smith Arrowhead Mills	69	0	32	natural	creamy	unsalted	name
3.	Adams 100% Natural	60	0	26	natural	creamy	unsalted	name
4.	Adams	60	168	26	natural	creamy	salted	name
5.	Laura Scudder's All Natural	57	165	26	natural	creamy	salted	name
6.	Country Pure Brand (Safeway)	52	225	21	natural	creamy	salted	store
7.	Hollywood Natural	34	15	32	natural	creamy	unsalted	name
8.	Smucker's Natural	89	15	27	natural	chunky	unsalted	name
9.	Adams 100% Natural	69	0	26	natural	chunky	unsalted	name
10.	Deaf Smith Arrowhead Mills	69	0	32	natural	chunky	unsalted	name
11.	Country Pure Brand (Safeway)	67	105	21	natural	chunky	salted	store
12.	Laura Scudder's All Natural	63	165	24	natural	chunky	salted	name
13.	Smucker's Natural	57	188	26	natural	chunky	salted	name
14.	Health Valley 100% Natural	40	3	34	natural	chunky	unsalted	name
15.	Jif	76	220	22	regular	creamy	salted	name
16.	Skippy	60	225	19	regular	creamy	salted	name
17.	Kroger	54	240	14	regular	creamy	salted	store
18.	NuMade (Safeway)	43	187	20	regular	creamy	salted	store
19.	Peter Pan	40	225	21	regular	creamy	salted	name
20.	Peter Pan	35	3	22	regular	creamy	unsalted	name
21.	A & P	34	225	12	regular	creamy	salted	store
22.	Food Club	33	225	17	regular	creamy	salted	store
23.	Pathmark	31	255	9	regular	creamy	salted	store
24.	Lady Lee (Lucky Stores)	23	225	16	regular	creamy	salted	store
25.	Albertsons	23	225	17	regular	creamy	salted	store
26.	Shur Fine (Shurfine Central)	11	225	16	regular	creamy	salted	store
27.	Jif	83	162	23	regular	chunky	salted	name
28.	Skippy	83	211	21	regular	chunky	salted	name
29.	Food Club	54	195	17	regular	chunky	salted	store
30.	Kroger	49	255	14	regular	chunky	salted	store
31.	A & P	46	225	11	regular	chunky	salted	store
32.	Peter Pan	45	180	22	regular	chunky	salted	name
33.	NuMade (Safeway)	40	208	21	regular	chunky	salted	store
34.	Lady Lee (Lucky Stores)	34	225	16	regular	chunky	salted	store
35.	Albertsons	31	225	17	regular	chunky	salted	store
36.	Pathmark	29	210	9	regular	chunky	salted	store
37.	Shur Fine (Shurfine Central)	26	195	16	regular	chunky	salted	store

Sources: "The Nuttiest Peanut Butter." *Consumer Reports* (September 1990): pp. 588–591.
A. J. Rossman, *Workshop Statistics: Student Activity Guide.* Carlisle, Penn.: Dickinson College, 1994, pp. 5–18.

ACE Question 9

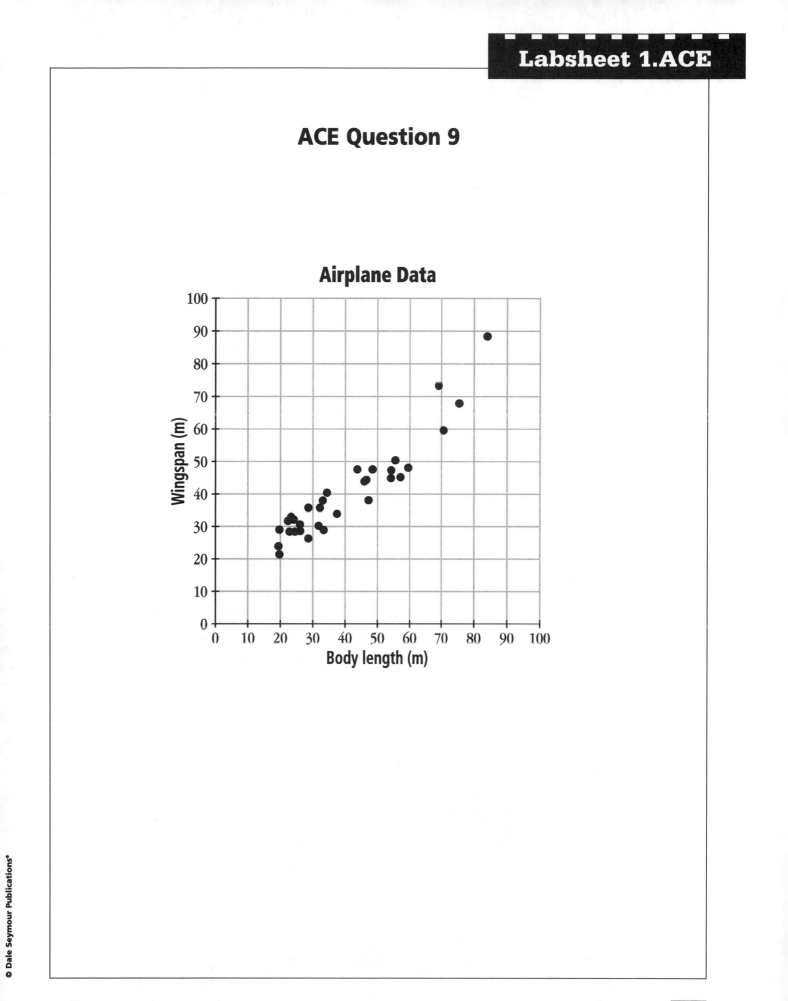

Airplane Data

Grade 8 Database

Student number	Gender	Sleep (hours)	Movies
01	boy	11.5	14
02	boy	2.0	8
03	girl	7.7	3
04	boy	9.3	1
05	boy	7.1	16
06	boy	7.5	1
07	boy	8.0	4
08	girl	7.8	1
09	girl	8.0	13
10	girl	8.0	15
11	boy	9.0	1
12	boy	9.2	10
13	boy	8.5	5
14	girl	6.0	15
15	boy	6.5	10
16	boy	8.3	2
17	girl	7.4	2
18	boy	11.2	3
19	girl	7.3	1
20	boy	8.0	0
21	girl	7.8	1
22	girl	7.8	1
23	boy	9.2	2
24	girl	7.5	0
25	boy	8.8	1
26	girl	8.5	0
27	girl	9.0	0
28	girl	8.5	0
29	boy	8.2	2
30	girl	7.8	2
31	girl	8.0	2
32	girl	7.3	8
33	boy	6.0	5
34	girl	7.5	5
35	boy	6.5	5
36	boy	9.3	1
37	girl	8.2	3
38	boy	7.3	3
39	girl	7.4	6
40	girl	8.5	7
41	boy	5.5	17
42	boy	6.5	3
43	boy	7.0	5
44	girl	8.5	2
45	girl	9.3	4
46	girl	8.0	15
47	boy	8.5	10
48	girl	6.2	11
49	girl	11.8	10
50	girl	9.0	4

Student number	Gender	Sleep (hours)	Movies
51	boy	5.0	4
52	boy	6.5	5
53	girl	8.5	2
54	boy	9.1	15
55	girl	7.5	2
56	girl	8.5	1
57	girl	8.0	2
58	girl	7.0	7
59	girl	8.4	10
60	girl	9.5	1
61	girl	7.3	5
62	girl	7.3	4
63	boy	8.5	3
64	boy	9.0	3
65	boy	9.0	4
66	girl	7.3	5
67	girl	5.7	0
68	girl	5.5	0
69	boy	10.5	7
70	girl	7.5	1
71	boy	7.8	0
72	girl	7.3	1
73	boy	9.3	2
74	boy	9.0	1
75	boy	8.7	1
76	boy	8.5	3
77	girl	9.0	1
78	boy	8.0	1
79	boy	8.0	4
80	boy	6.5	0
81	boy	8.0	0
82	girl	9.0	8
83	girl	8.0	0
84	boy	7.0	0
85	boy	9.0	6
86	boy	7.3	0
87	girl	9.0	3
88	girl	7.5	5
89	boy	8.0	0
90	girl	7.5	6
91	boy	8.0	4
92	boy	9.0	4
93	boy	7.0	0
94	boy	8.0	3
95	boy	8.3	3
96	boy	8.3	14
97	girl	7.8	5
98	girl	8.5	1
99	girl	8.3	3
100	boy	7.5	2

Box-Plot Template for Grade 8 Database

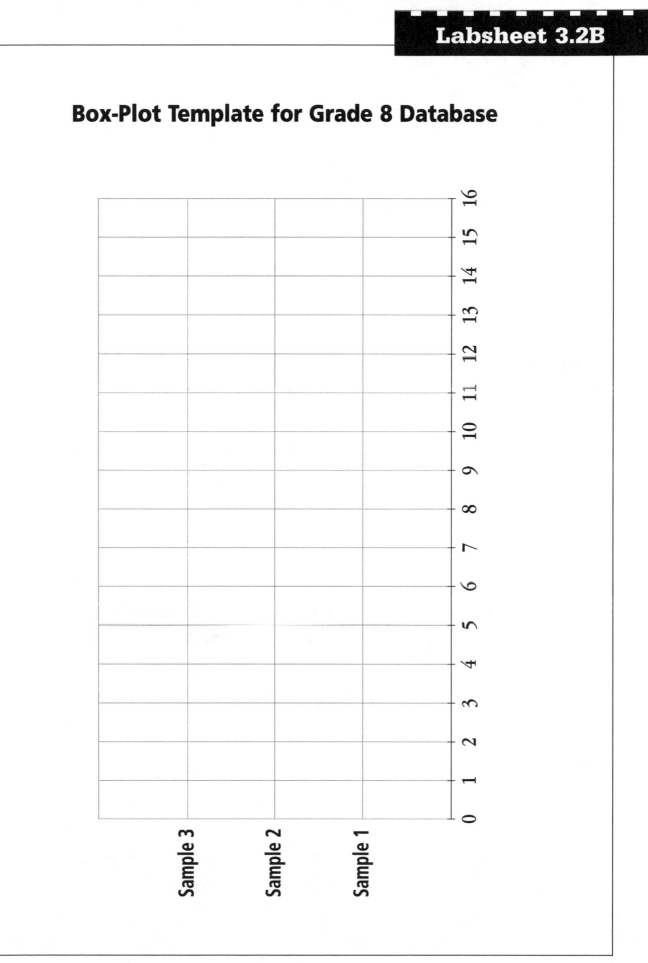

Line-Plot Template for Movie Values

Samples of Size 5

0.0   0.5   1.0   1.5   2.0   2.5   3.0   3.5   4.0   4.5   5.0   5.5   6.0   6.5   7.0
Median number of movies watched

Samples of Size 10

0.0   0.5   1.0   1.5   2.0   2.5   3.0   3.5   4.0   4.5   5.0   5.5   6.0   6.5   7.0
Median number of movies watched

Samples of Size 25

0.0   0.5   1.0   1.5   2.0   2.5   3.0   3.5   4.0   4.5   5.0   5.5   6.0   6.5   7.0
Median number of movies watched

Field A

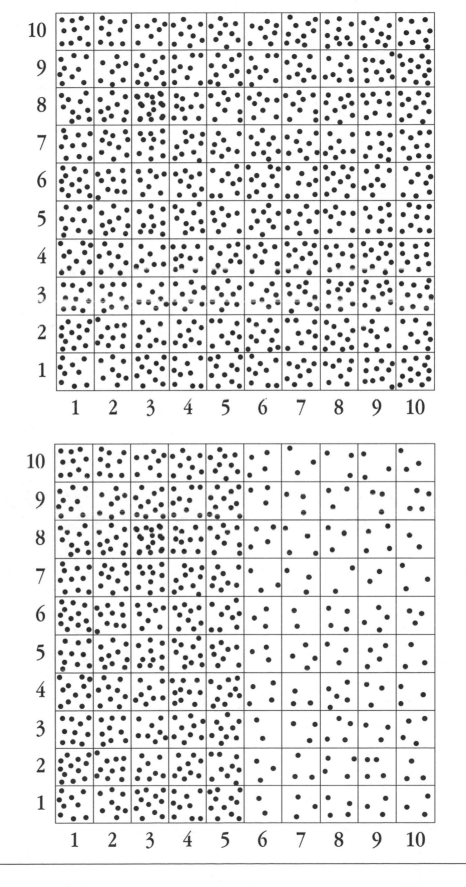

Field B

Field C

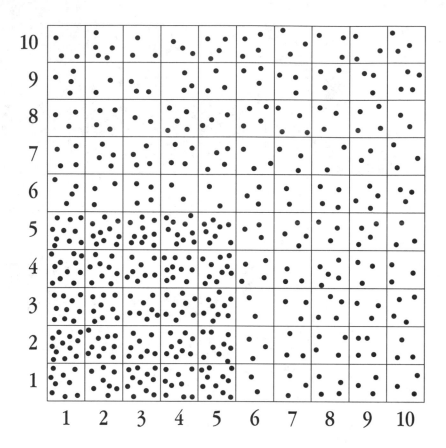

Apply some of the data analysis techniques you learned in earlier statistics work to compare the quality ratings for natural brands and regular brands.

In general, do natural brands or regular brands have higher quality ratings? Use the results of your analysis to justify your choice.

Quality Ratings for Regular Brands

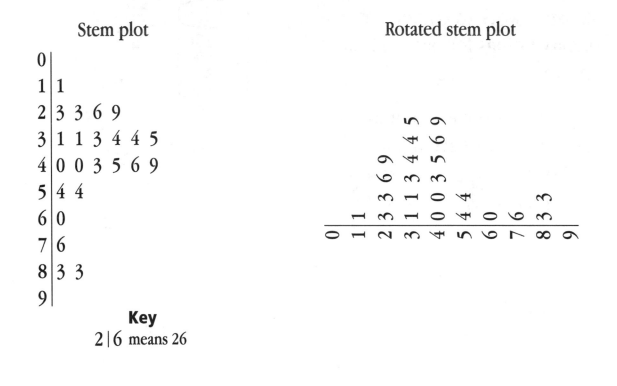

Stem plot   Rotated stem plot

```
0|
1|1
2|3 3 6 9
3|1 1 3 4 4 5
4|0 0 3 5 6 9
5|4 4
6|0
7|6
8|3 3
9|
```

Key
2 | 6 means 26

Transforming a Rotated Stem Plot into a Histogram

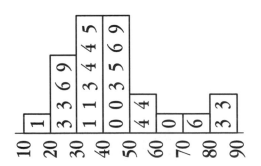

Quality Ratings for Natural and Regular Brands

Natural brands   Regular brands

```
          | 0 |
          | 1 | 1
          | 2 | 3 3 6 9
        4 | 3 | 1 1 3 4 4 5
        0 | 4 | 0 0 3 5 6 9
      7 7 | 2 | 5 | 4 4        (no, see below)
```

```
              | 0 |
              | 1 | 1
              | 2 | 3 3 6 9
            4 | 3 | 1 1 3 4 4 5
            0 | 4 | 0 0 3 5 6 9
          7 7 2| 5 | 4 4
9 9 9 7 3 0 0 | 6 | 0
            1 | 7 | 6
            9 | 8 | 3 3
              | 9 |
```

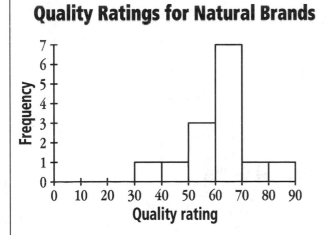

Quality Ratings for Natural Brands

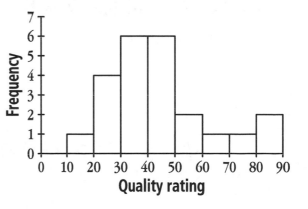

Quality Ratings for Regular Brands

To construct a box plot showing the distribution of quality ratings for the natural brands of peanut butter, first order the data and find the five-number summary. Then, draw the number line and make the box plot.

Natural brand	Quality rating	Five-number summary
Hollywood Natural	34	← minimum = 34
Health Valley 100% Natural	40	
Country Pure Brand (Safeway)	52	
Laura Scudder's All Natural	57	← lower quartile = 57
Smucker's Natural	57	
Adams 100% Natural	60	
Adams	60	← median = 61.5
Laura Scudder's All Natural	63	
Country Pure Brand (Safeway)	67	
Deaf Smith Arrowhead Mills	69	
Adams 100% Natural	69	← upper quartile = 69
Deaf Smith Arrowhead Mills	69	
Smucker's Natural	71	
Smucker's Natural	89	← maximum = 89

Quality Ratings for Natural Brands

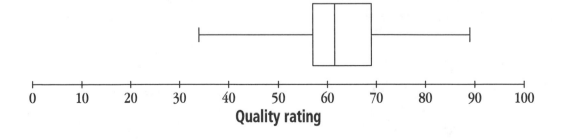

Quality rating

A. About what percent of the values in a data set are below the median? About what percent of the values in a data set are above the median?

B. The lower quartile, median, and upper quartile divide a data distribution into four parts. These four parts are called the *first, second, third,* and *fourth quartiles* of the distribution.

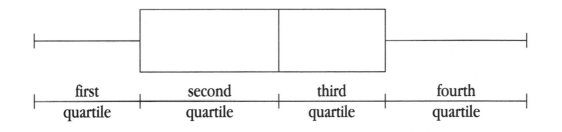

About what percent of the values in a data distribution are in each quartile?

C. Use the box plots of quality ratings for regular and natural brands to help you decide which type of peanut butter—regular or natural—is of higher quality. Explain your reasoning.

A. Calculate the five-number summary for the prices of the natural brands.

B. Calculate the five-number summary for the prices of the regular brands.

C. Compare the five-number summaries you found in parts A and B with the box plots. Decide which plot shows the distribution of prices for the natural brands and which plot shows the distribution of prices for the regular brands. Explain how the numbers in the five-number summaries are shown by various features of the plots.

Peanut Butter Prices

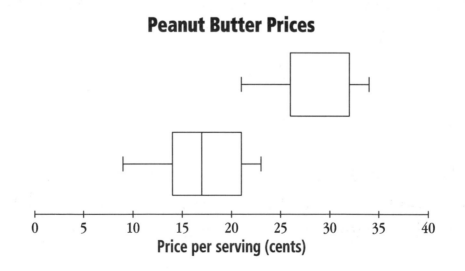

Price per serving (cents)

D. How do the prices of the natural brands compare with the prices of the regular brands? Explain how you can make this comparison by using the box plots.

E. If *price* were the only factor a buyer considered, would natural peanut butter or regular peanut butter be a better choice?

If *quality* were the only factor a buyer considered, would natural peanut butter or regular peanut butter be a better choice? Explain your reasoning.

Justify your answers to the questions below with statistics and box plots.

A. Compare the quality ratings of the creamy brands with the quality ratings of the chunky brands. Based on quality, are creamy brands or chunky brands a better choice?

B. Compare the quality ratings of the salted brands with the quality ratings of the unsalted brands. Based on quality, are salted brands or unsalted brands a better choice?

C. Compare the quality ratings of the name brands with the quality ratings of the store brands. Based on quality, are name brands or store brands a better choice?

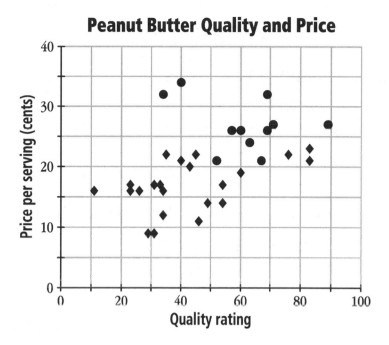

Peanut Butter Quality and Price

A. Which plot symbol, ● or ◆, represents data for natural peanut butter? Which represents data for regular peanut butter?

B. Is there an overall relationship between quality and price? Explain.

C. Do any (quality rating, price) data pairs appear to be unusual? Explain your reasoning.

D. 1. How can you use the scatter plot to compare the quality ratings of the natural brands with the quality ratings of the regular brands?

2. How can you use the scatter plot to compare the prices of the natural brands with the prices of the regular brands?

How Honest Is America?

A. If you found someone else's wallet on the street, would you
   1. try to return it to the owner?
   2. return it, but keep the money?
   3. keep the wallet and the money?

B. If a cashier mistakenly gave you $10 extra in change, would you
   1. tell the cashier about the error?
   2. say nothing and keep the cash?

C. Would you cheat on an exam if you were sure you wouldn't get caught?
   1. yes
   2. no

D. If you found someone else's telephone calling card, would you use it?
   1. yes
   2. no

E. Do you feel that you are an honest person in most situations?
   1. yes
   2. no

 Call 1-900-555-8281, and enter your answers by pressing the appropriate number keys.

A. A *sampling plan* is a strategy for choosing a sample from a population. What is the sampling plan for this survey? What are the population and the sample for this survey?

B. Suppose 5280 people answered the survey, and 4224 of them pressed 2 for question C. What percent of the callers said they would not cheat on an exam?

C. Of the 5280 callers, 1584 pressed 1 for question D. What percent of the callers said they would not use someone else's calling card?

D. The U.S. population is about 260 million. Based on the results of this survey, how many people in the United States would not cheat on an exam? How many would not use someone else's calling card?

E. List some reasons why predictions about all Americans based on this survey might be inaccurate.

Ms. Baker's class wants to find out how many students in their school wear braces on their teeth. The class divides into four groups. Each group devises a plan for sampling the school population.

- Each member of group 1 will survey the students who ride on his or her school bus.

- Group 2 will survey every fourth person in the cafeteria line.

- Group 3 will read a notice on the school's morning announcements asking for volunteers for their survey.

- Group 4 will randomly select 30 students for their survey from a list of three-digit student ID numbers. They will roll a 10-sided number cube three times to generate each number.

A. What are the advantages and disadvantages of each sampling plan?

B. Which plan do you think would most accurately predict the number of students in the school who wear braces? That is, which plan do you think will give the most *representative* sample? Explain your answer.

In this problem, you will work with a partner to design a survey to gather information about middle school and high school students and their plans for the future. Your survey should include questions about characteristics of the students, such as age, gender, and favorite school subject. Your survey should also gather information about what students plan to do after graduation from high school.

For example, your survey might include questions about the following topics:

- Students' plans for college or a job immediately after high school
- The types of careers students would like to pursue
- The places students would like to live

A. Work with a partner to develop a first draft of a survey. Exchange surveys with another pair of students, and critique each other's surveys.

B. Prepare a final version of your survey.

C. Write a paragraph describing a sampling plan you could use to survey students in your school.

Imagine that you have two tickets to a sold-out rock concert, and your six best friends all want to go with you. To choose a friend to attend the concert, you want to use a strategy that gives each friend an equally likely chance of being selected. Which of the strategies below would accomplish this? Explain your reasoning.

Strategy 1: The first person who calls you on the phone tonight gets to go with you.

Strategy 2: You assign each friend a different whole number from 1 to 6. Then, you roll a six-sided number cube. The number that is rolled determines who attends the concert.

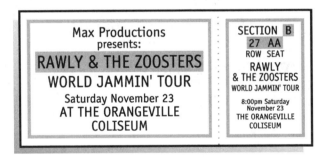

Strategy 3: You tell each friend to meet you by the rear door right after school. You toss a coin to choose between the first two friends who arrive.

In this problem, each member of your group will select a random sample of students and calculate the five-number summary for the movie data. Use spinners, 10-sided number cubes, a graphing calculator, or some other method to select your sample.

A. Select a random sample of 25 students. For each student in your sample, record the number of movies watched. (Each sample should contain 25 *different* students, so if you select a student who is already in the sample, select another.)

B. Calculate the five-number summary for the movie data for your sample.

C. With your group, make box plots of the movie data for your group's samples on Labsheet 3.2.

D. What can you conclude about the movie-viewing behavior of the population of 100 students based on the patterns in the samples selected by your group? Explain how you used the data from your samples to arrive at your conclusions.

E. Compare your findings with those of other groups in your class. Describe the similarities and differences you find.

A. In Problem 3.2, you calculated five-number summaries for the movie data for random samples of 25 students. Work with your class to make a line plot of the medians found by all groups. Compare these results with the median for the population of 100 students.

B. 1. Select three random samples of 5 students, and find the median movie value for each sample. Compare the medians for your samples with the population median.

    2. Compare the medians for your samples with the medians found by other members of your group. Describe the similarities or differences you find.

    3. Record the medians found by your group on the board. When all groups have recorded their medians, make a line plot of the medians.

C. 1. Select three random samples of 10 students, and find the median movie value for each sample. Compare the medians for your samples with the population median.

2. Compare the medians for your samples with the medians found by other members of your group. Describe the similarities or differences you find.

3. Record the medians found by your group on the board. When all groups have recorded their medians, make a line plot of the medians.

D. Compare the distribution of medians for samples of size 5, 10, and 25. Write a paragraph describing how the median estimates for samples of different sizes compare with the actual population median.

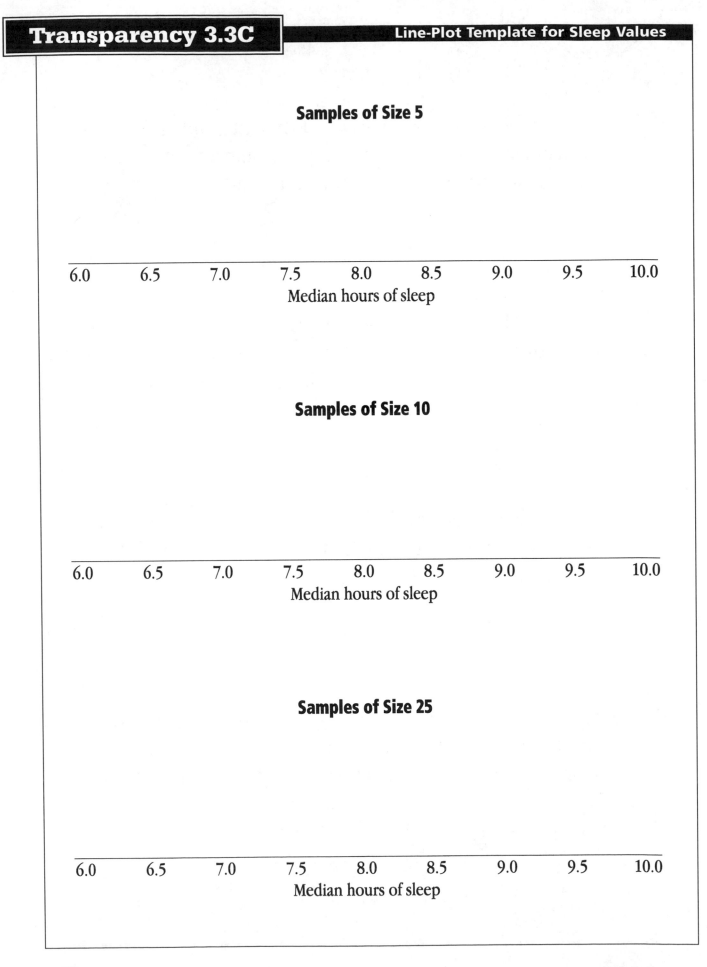

Samples of Size 5

6.0	6.5	7.0	7.5	8.0	8.5	9.0	9.5	10.0

Median hours of sleep

Samples of Size 10

6.0	6.5	7.0	7.5	8.0	8.5	9.0	9.5	10.0

Median hours of sleep

Samples of Size 25

6.0	6.5	7.0	7.5	8.0	8.5	9.0	9.5	10.0

Median hours of sleep

The archaeologists hypothesized that Native Americans inhabiting the same area of the country during the same time period would have fashioned similar tools.

A. Use what you know about statistics and data representations to compare the lengths of the arrowheads discovered at the new sites with the lengths of the arrowheads from the known sites. Based on your comparisons, during which time period— 4000 B.C. to A.D. 500 or A.D. 500 to A.D. 1600—do you think site I was settled? During which time period do you think site II was settled? Explain how your statistics and graphs support your answers.

B. Compare the widths of the arrowheads discovered at the new sites with the widths of the arrowheads from the known sites. Do your findings support your answers from part A? Explain.

C. If the archaeologists had collected only a few arrowheads from each new site, might they have reached a different conclusion? Explain your answer.

A. Conduct the simulation Ted describes. You might use a chart like this to tally the number of chips in each cookie.

cookie 1 _____

cookie 2 _____

cookie 3 _____

cookie 4 _____

cookie 5 _____

cookie 6 _____

cookie 7 _____

cookie 8 _____

cookie 9 _____

cookie 10 _____

cookie 11 _____

cookie 12 _____

Generate random numbers until each cookie contains at least five chips. When you are finished, find the total number of chips in the entire batch.

B. Your teacher will display the stem values for a stem plot. Add your number-of-chips data to the plot.

C. Jeff and Ted want to be quite certain there will be at least five chips in each cookie, but they don't want to waste money by mixing in too many chocolate chips. Based on your class data, how many chips would you advise Jeff and Ted to use in each batch? Explain your answer.

Dear Family,

The next unit in your child's mathematics class this year is *Samples and Populations.* The unit will involve your child in the process of statistical investigation. As part of this process, we will pay special attention to the ways that data are collected.

The U.S. census attempts to gather information from every household in the United States. However, in most studies of large populations, data are gathered from a *sample,* or portion, of the population. The data from the sample are then used to make predictions or draw conclusions about the population. This technique is often used, for example, by pollsters during elections.

In this unit, students will explore ways to compare sets of data by examining a national magazine's study about the quality of many brands of peanut butter. Don't be surprised if your child comes home with some recommendations for new kinds of peanut butter to try!

Students will then explore what it means to look at only a sample of a population and will think about how to design and distribute surveys. They will also explore sample size and the ways in which samples can be selected.

Here are some strategies for helping your child during this unit:

- Talk with your child about the situations presented in the unit.

- Using newspapers, magazines, television, or radio, help your child identify situations in which statistics are being used, paying particular attention to who or what was sampled.

- Talk about whether data from a particular study can be used to make accurate predictions about a larger population.

- Review your child's notebook and ask for explanations of the work.

- Encourage your child's efforts in completing homework assignments.

If you have any questions or suggestions about your child's mathematics program, please feel free to call.

Sincerely,

Estimada familia,

La próxima unidad del programa de matemáticas de su hijo o hija para este curso se llama *Samples and Populations* (Muestras y poblaciones). A través de ella su hijo o hija participará en el proceso de las investigaciones estadísticas. Y como parte de dicho proceso, prestaremos una especial atención a las diferentes maneras de recoger datos.

El censo de los Estados Unidos intenta reunir datos sobre todas y cada una de las familias que viven en este país. Sin embargo, en la mayoría de los estudios realizados sobre grandes poblaciones, los datos se recogen de una *muestra,* es decir, de una parte de los habitantes. Una vez recogidos, esos datos se utilizan para hacer predicciones o para sacar conclusiones sobre la población. Así, por ejemplo, esta técnica se emplea frecuentemente en las encuestas electorales.

En esta unidad los alumnos explorarán diversas maneras de comparar conjuntos de datos; al respecto, examinarán un estudio realizado por una revista estadounidense que trata sobre la calidad de numerosas marcas de mantequilla de maní. ¡No les extrañe que su hijo o hija les recomiende que prueben algún nuevo tipo de mantequilla de maní!

Más adelante, los alumnos explorarán lo que supone examinar sólo una muestra de la población y pensarán sobre el diseño y la distribución de las encuestas. Además, investigarán el tamaño de las muestras y las formas en que éstas pueden ser seleccionadas.

Aparecen a continuación algunas estrategias que ustedes pueden emplear para ayudar a su hijo o hija durante el estudio de esta unidad:

- Hablen con él o ella sobre las situaciones presentadas en la unidad.

- Empleen los periódicos, las revistas, la televisión o la radio para ayudarle a identificar situaciones en las que se utilicen las estadísticas; para ello, presten una especial atención tanto a las personas como a los objetos que constituyen las muestras.

- Decidan juntos si los datos de un estudio determinado pueden usarse para hacer predicciones precisas sobre una población mayor.

- Repasen su cuaderno y pídanle que les explique su trabajo.

- Anímenle a esforzarse para que complete la tarea.

Si tienen alguna pregunta o recomendación relacionada con el programa de matemáticas de su hijo o hija, no duden en llamarnos.

Atentamente,

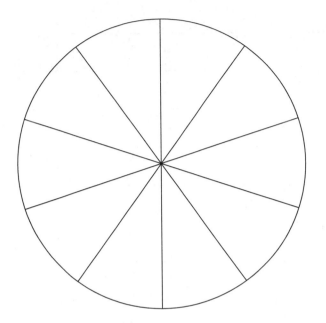

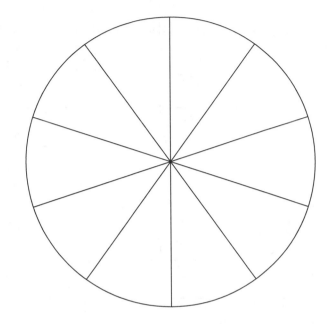

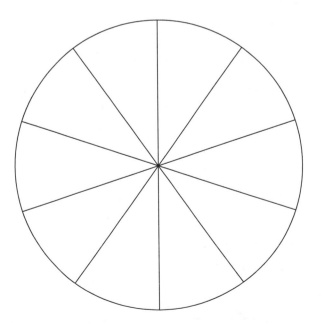

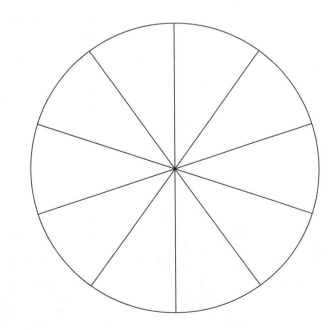

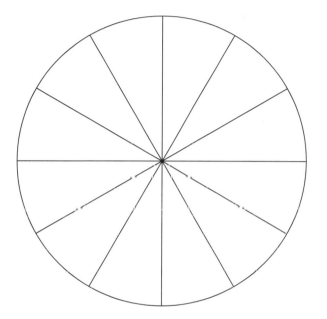
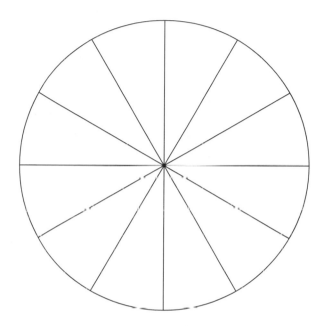
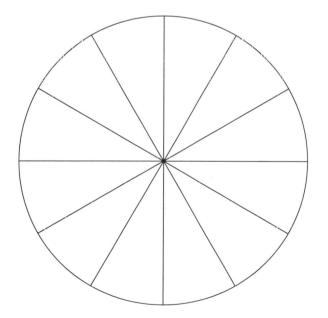
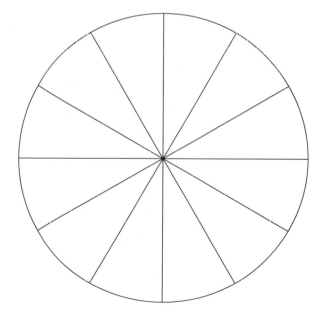

Additional Practice

Investigation 1

Use these problems for additional practice after Investigation 1.

Another peanut butter survey was conducted more recently than the survey you studied in Investigation 1. The data for natural and regular brands are presented in the table.

Peanut Butter Comparisons

Brand	Quality rating	Sodium per serving (mg)	Price per serving	Regular/ natural	Creamy/ chunky	Name brand/ store brand
Arrowhead Mills	85	0	36	natural	creamy	name
Laura Scudder's (Southeast)	79	165	25	natural	creamy	name
Adams (West)	73	173	23	natural	creamy	name
Smucker's	73	180	26	natural	creamy	name
Nature's Cupboard (Safeway)	68	240	26	natural	creamy	store
Laura Scudder's Nutty (Southeast)	84	165	26	natural	chunky	name
Arrowhead Mills	83	0	37	natural	chunky	name
Smucker's	79	180	26	natural	chunky	name
Adams (West)	75	135	23	natural	chunky	name
Nature's Cupboard (Safeway)	72	195	26	natural	chunky	store
Jif	85	225	19¢	regular	creamy	name
Simply Jif	85	98	19	regular	creamy	name
Peter Pan	82	225	17	regular	creamy	name
Skippy	82	225	18	regular	creamy	name
Kroger	79	195	15	regular	creamy	store
Skippy Roasted Honey Nut	79	180	19	regular	creamy	name
America's Choice	77	225	17	regular	creamy	store
Reese's	68	173	19	regular	creamy	name
Townhouse (Safeway)	68	240	18	regular	creamy	store
Peter Pan Very Low Sodium	57	15	18	regular	creamy	name
Peter Pan Whipped	49	173	17	regular	creamy	name
Jif Extra Crunchy	88	195	19	regular	chunky	name
Skippy Super Chunk	87	210	19	regular	chunky	name
Peter Pan Extra Crunchy	86	180	17	regular	chunky	name
Reese's	86	120	19	regular	chunky	name
Skippy Roasted Honey Nut	86	180	19	regular	chunky	name
Kroger	84	195	15	regular	chunky	store
Simply Jif Extra Crunchy	83	75	19	regular	chunky	name
America's Choice Krunchy	80	188	17	regular	chunky	store
Townhouse (Safeway)	72	195	18	regular	chunky	store

Source: "Peanut Butter: It's Not Just for Kids Anymore." *Consumer Reports* (September 1995): pp. 576–579.

1. The box plots below show the quality ratings of natural versus regular brands, creamy versus chunky brands, and name brands versus store brands. Based on these box plots, what characteristics would you look for if you wanted to choose a peanut butter based on quality rating? Explain your reasoning using the information shown in the box plots.

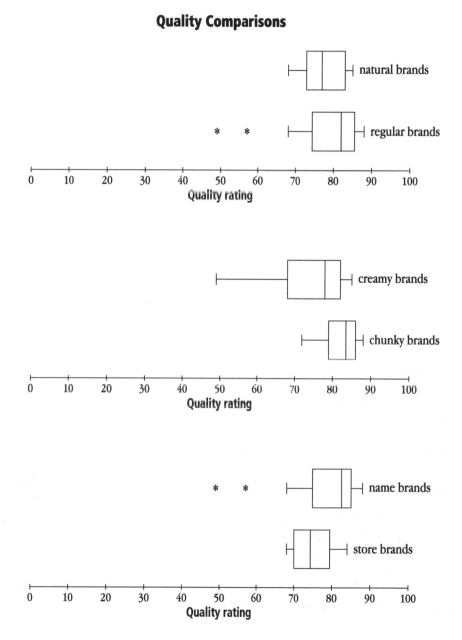

Quality Comparisons

2. Make box plots to compare the peanut butters based on price. Mark any outliers with an asterisk (*). Which characteristic(s) help identify low-price peanut butters? Explain your reasoning.

Use this information in 3–8: Ms. Humphrey asked each of the 21 students in her mathematics class to choose a number between 1 and 50. Ms. Humphrey recorded the data and made this box plot:

Ms. Humphrey's Class Data

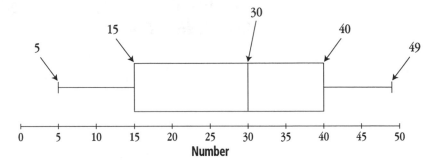

3. What is the median number that was chosen?

4. What percentage of students in Ms. Humphrey's class chose numbers above 15? Explain your reasoning.

5. About how many students chose numbers between 30 and 40? Explain your reasoning.

6. What were the least and the greatest numbers chosen?

7. Is it possible to determine from the box plot whether one of the students chose the number 27? Explain your reasoning.

8. Is it possible to determine from the box plot whether one of the students chose the number 4? Explain your reasoning.

In 9–12, refer to the table on the next page, which lists the engine type, body length, and wingspan of several airplanes flown by major airlines. The fifth column shows the ratio of wingspan to body length.

9. Finish computing the values for the fifth column.

10. What does it mean when the ratio of wingspan to body length is 1? Greater than 1? Less than 1?

11. Compute the five-number summary for jet planes and the five-number summary for propeller planes of the ratio of wingspan to body length. Explain what the medians tell you about the relationship between wingspan and body length for jet planes and for propeller planes.

12. Make box plots from your five-number summaries. Explain what your plots reveal about how jet planes and propeller planes compare based on ratio of wingspan to body length.

Airplane Data

Plane	Engine type	Body length (m)	Wingspan (m)	Wingspan-to-length ratio
Boeing 707	jet	46.6	44.4	0.953
Boeing 747	jet	70.7	59.6	0.843
Ilyushin IL-86	jet	59.5	48.1	
McDonnell Douglas DC-8	jet	57.1	45.2	
Antonov An-124	jet	69.1	73.3	
British Aerospace 146	jet	28.6	26.3	
Lockheed C-5 Galaxy	jet	75.5	67.9	
Antonov An-225	jet	84.0	88.4	
Airbus A300	jet	54.1	44.9	
Airbus A310	jet	46.0	43.9	
Airbus A320	jet	37.5	33.9	
Boeing 737	jet	33.4	28.9	
Boeing 757	jet	47.3	38.1	
Boeing 767	jet	48.5	47.6	
Lockheed Tristar L-1011	jet	54.2	47.3	
McDonnell Douglas DC-10	jet	55.5	50.4	
Aero/Boeing Spacelines Guppy	propeller	43.8	47.6	
Douglas DC-4 C-54 Skymaster	propeller	28.6	35.8	
Douglas DC-6	propeller	32.2	35.8	
Lockheed L-188 Electra	propeller	31.8	30.2	
Vickers Viscount	propeller	26.1	28.6	
Antonov An-12	propeller	33.1	38.0	
de Havilland DHC Dash-7	propeller	24.5	28.4	
Lockheed C-130 Hercules/L-100	propeller	34.4	40.4	
British Aerospace 748/ATP	propeller	26.0	30.6	
Convair 240	propeller	24.1	32.1	
Curtiss C-46 Commando	propeller	23.3	32.9	
Douglas DC-3	propeller	19.7	29.0	
Grumman Gulfstream I/I-C	propeller	19.4	23.9	
Ilyushin IL-14	propeller	22.3	31.7	
Martin 4-0-4	propeller	22.8	28.4	
Saab 340	propeller	19.7	21.4	

Source: William Berk and Frank Berk. *Airport Airplanes.* Plymouth, Mich.: Plymouth Press, 1993.

In 13–15, use the tables below, which display the results of a study of 47 half-ounce boxes of two brands of raisins. The table on the left shows the number of raisins and the mass in grams for boxes of Vine Hill raisins. The table on the right shows the results for Suntime raisins.

Vine Hill Raisins

Number in box	Mass (grams)	Number in box	Mass (grams)
29	14.78	38	16.3
35	16.59	38	16.85
35	16.01	38	17.33
35	16.55	38	17.57
36	16.99	40	16.2
38	16.34	40	16.78
38	16.3	40	17.35
39	17.83	41	17.43
39	16.66	41	16.64
39	18.36	41	16.62
39	16.93	31	14.7
40	16.25	34	16.04
40	17.92	35	16.81
40	17.12	36	16.86
40	17.37	36	16.75
42	16.95	36	17.18
42	17.45	36	15.77
44	18.48	36	16.28
35	15.64	37	16.25
36	16.88	37	17.42
36	16.36	37	16.25
36	16.3	37	15.63
37	17.25	37	17.74
37	15.61		

Suntime Raisins

Number in box	Mass (grams)	Number in box	Mass (grams)
25	14.15	31	16.13
26	16.74	31	16.6
27	15.42	32	16.6
27	16.74	33	16.55
27	15.98	33	17.11
28	17.43	34	16.88
28	16.44	34	18.1
28	16.55	35	17.63
28	15.55	35	17.32
28	15.33	26	15.34
29	16.75	28	14.11
29	16.19	29	16.94
29	16.36	29	15.16
29	17.1	29	15.75
29	16.58	29	15.65
30	16.36	30	16.5
30	16.29	31	15.83
31	15.9	31	17.17
29	16.18	32	16.6
29	15.91	32	16.59
30	16.66	32	16.38
31	15.73	33	17.11
31	16.38	34	17.24
31	16.92		

13. The two scatter plots on the next page show the data from the tables. Which scatter plot shows the data for Suntime raisins? Which shows the data for Vine Hill raisins? Explain your reasoning.

14. Is this statement true or false: "Vine Hill raisins typically have more raisins in a box than do Suntime raisins." Explain your reasoning using the two graphs.

15. Is there a relationship between the number of raisins in a box and the mass in grams? Explain your reasoning.

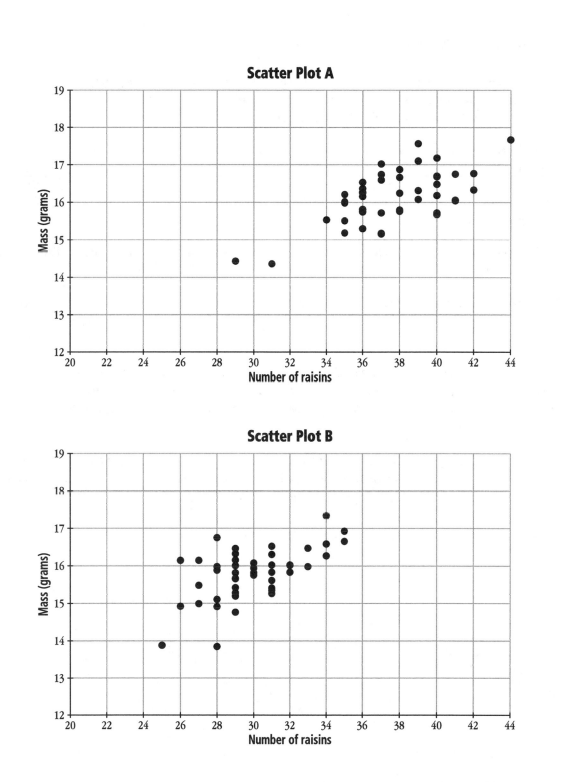

Scatter Plot A

Mass (grams) vs Number of raisins

Scatter Plot B

Mass (grams) vs Number of raisins

Investigation 2

Use these problems for additional practice after Investigation 2.

Aaron was interested in learning about how much time students at his school spend playing sports each week. To find out more about this, he asked all the boys on the basketball team and all the girls on the volleyball team to estimate how many hours per week they spent playing sports.

1. Is Aaron's sample a voluntary-response sample, a systematic sample, or a convenience sample? Explain your reasoning.

2. Suppose Aaron asked all the students in his mathematics class to estimate how many hours per week they spend playing sports.

    a. Would this be a voluntary-response sample, a systematic sample, or a convenience sample? Explain your reasoning.

    b. Would you expect the median number of hours spent playing sports for students in Aaron's mathematics class to be higher or lower than his sample from the basketball and volleyball teams? Explain your reasoning.

3. There are 1232 students enrolled at Aaron's school. The principal's office has an alphabetical list of all the students' names. Suppose Aaron asked every 20th student on the list to estimate the number of hours he or she spends playing sports each week. Would this be a voluntary-response sample, a systematic sample, or a convenience sample? Explain.

4. Aaron placed an ad in the school newspaper with a form for students to complete and return. The form asked how much time the student spent playing sports each week. Aaron received 53 responses. Is this a voluntary-response sample, a systematic sample, or a convenience sample? Explain.

Investigation 3

Use these problems for additional practice after Investigation 3.

In 1–4, use this information: In a survey of the cafeteria food at Metropolis Middle School, 50 students were asked to rate how well they liked the lunches on a scale of 1 to 10, with 1 being the lowest rating and 10 being the highest rating. The box plot below was made from the collected data.

Cafeteria Food Survey

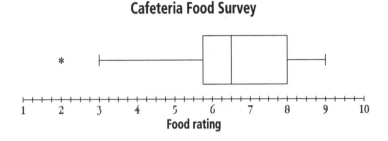

Food rating

1. What is the range of students' ratings in the sample?

2. What percent of the students in the sample rated the cafeteria food between 5.75 and 9?

3. Based on the sample data, how many of the 1000 students at Metropolis do you estimate would rate the cafeteria food 6 or higher? Explain your reasoning.

4. A rating of 8 to 10 indicates "highly satisfied" on the rating scale.

   a. What percent of students in the sample are "highly satisfied" with the cafeteria food?

   b. Estimate how many students at Metropolis Middle School would give the cafeteria food a "highly satisfied" rating.

In 5–7, use this information: Marci works on the yearbook staff at Metropolis Middle School. Of the 92 businesses in the downtown area, 41 purchased advertising space in the yearbook last year.

5. Suppose Marci wants to investigate why businesses did not advertise in the yearbook last year. Describe a sampling strategy she could use to call 10 businesses.

6. Suppose Marci wants to investigate how satisfied advertisers are with yearbook ads. Describe a sampling strategy she could use to call 10 businesses.

7. Suppose Marci wants to investigate how likely a typical downtown business is to advertise in the upcoming yearbook. Describe a sampling strategy she could use to call 10 businesses.

8. Mr. Darrow and the 29 students in his afternoon mathematics class each generated 10 random numbers between 1 and 100. Here are one student's results:

$$83 \quad 8 \quad 40 \quad 79 \quad 77 \quad 62 \quad 92 \quad 29 \quad 67 \quad 11$$

   a. Compute the five-number summary of this student's numbers and make a box plot.

   b. Select nine more samples, each containing 10 numbers between 1 and 100, using your calculator or another strategy for choosing numbers randomly. On the same scale you used in part a, make box plots for each sample.

   c. Using your box plots, about what percent of the numbers generated would you expect to fall between 29 and 79? Explain your reasoning.

9. The principal of a nearby school, Megalopolis Middle School, decided to conduct a survey of the 1107 enrolled students. She asked three teachers how many students they thought should be surveyed. One teacher said to survey 200 girls and 100 boys, the second said to randomly select and survey 50 students, and the third said to survey the first 100 students to enter the building one morning next week.

   a. Explain which of the three samples will produce data that may best represent all the students at Megalopolis.

   b. Explain why you feel that the other two samples would not be as representative of all the students as the one you chose in part a.

Investigation 4

Use these problems for additional practice after Investigation 4.

1. A group of students surveyed several pizza shops in two parts of the United States. They asked about prices and sizes of small, medium, and large cheese pizzas, and they made box plots from the data they collected.

    a. These box plots show the prices for each size pizza, including outliers. Which size appears to be the least expensive? Explain your reasoning.

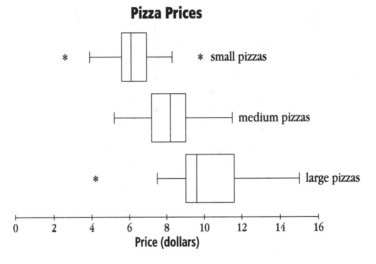

Pizza Prices

    b. One of the small pizzas had a diameter of 8 inches and a price of $3.87. Its price per square inch is $0.077. How was this calculated?

    c. These box plots show the price per square inch of pizza for each size. Which size appears to be the best buy? Explain your reasoning.

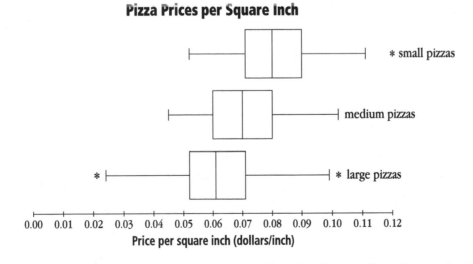

Pizza Prices per Square Inch

    d. Consider your responses to parts a and c. Which set of box plots better reflects the actual price of a pizza? Explain your reasoning.

2. Suppose Jeff and Ted decide to change their advertising slogan to "Seven giant chips in every cookie!" They mix 70 chips into a batch of dough and make 10 cookies from the dough. When they remove the cookies from the oven and inspect them, they count the number of chips in each cookie. Their results are shown below. Notice that only 5 of the 10 cookies contained 7 chips or more.

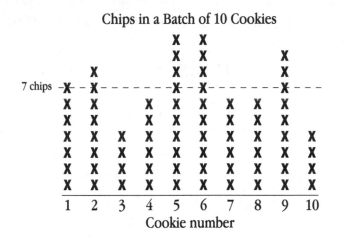

Chips in a Batch of 10 Cookies

a. Conduct a simulation to determine the number of chips needed to be added to a batch of 10 cookies until each cookie has at least 7 chips. Carry out the simulation five times so that you have five data values for the number of chips needed.

b. What is the minimum number of chips Jeff and Ted should use to be confident that each cookie will have at least 7 chips? Support your answer with statistics and graphs.

© Dale Seymour Publications®

Investigation 1

1. *Natural vs. regular:* The quality ratings for natural and regular brands are similar in terms of spread and distribution; the median for regular brands is greater than the median for natural brands, so regular brands have a slight edge. *Creamy vs. chunky:* The quality ratings for chunky brands are a bit higher than those for creamy brands; 75% of the ratings for chunky brands are greater than 50% of the ratings for creamy brands. There is less spread in the data for chunky brands. *Name brand vs. store brand:* The quality ratings for name brands are a bit higher than those for store brands; 75% of the ratings for name brands are greater than 50% of the ratings for store brands. *Conclusion:* Overall, there is less distinction among categories in this survey than in the earlier survey; however, one could say that regular, chunky, and name brand are the characteristics to look for.

2. *Natural vs. regular:* The prices for natural brands are clearly higher than those for regular brands. The box plots for these two data sets are interesting. For natural brands, a small data set, the median, upper quartile, *and* maximum value (not counting outliers) are all 26¢. For regular brands, the upper quartile and the maximum value are both 19¢. The plots suggest that there is not a great deal of variability in the price for either category. *Creamy vs. chunky:* The prices for these show little difference. *Name brand vs. store brand:* Over 75% of the name brands are more expensive than 50% of the store brands. *Conclusion:* Again, there are fewer distinctions among categories of peanut butter in this report than in the earlier report; however, one could say that natural, name-brand peanut butters are generally more expensive than regular, store-brand peanut butters.

Price Comparisons

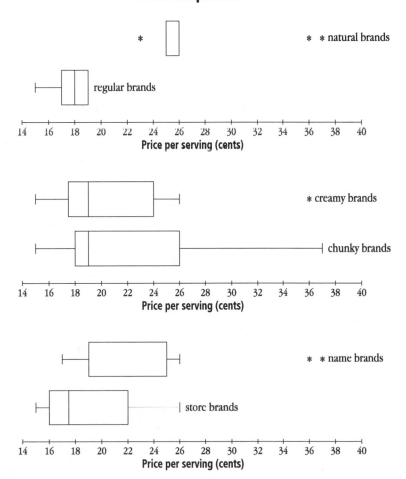

3. median = 30

4. 75%; Three quartiles fall above 15.

5. about 5 students; 25% of the data fall in this interval, and $21 \times 25\% \approx 5$.

6. 5, 49

7. It is not possible to determine whether a student chose 27. A box plot reveals no information about what values are actually represented in a quartile.

8. The minimum value is 5, so we know that no one chose 4.

9.

Plane	Engine type	Body length (m)	Wingspan (m)	Wingspan-to-length ratio
Boeing 707	jet	46.6	44.4	0.953
Boeing 747	jet	70.7	59.6	0.843
Ilyushin IL-86	jet	59.5	48.1	0.808
McDonnell Douglas DC-8	jet	57.1	45.2	0.792
Antonov An-124	jet	69.1	73.3	1.061
British Aerospace 146	jet	28.6	26.3	0.920
Lockheed C-5 Galaxy	jet	75.5	67.9	0.899
Antonov An-225	jet	84.0	88.4	1.052
Airbus A300	jet	54.1	44.9	0.830
Airbus A310	jet	46.0	43.9	0.954
Airbus A320	jet	37.5	33.9	0.904
Boeing 737	jet	33.4	28.9	0.865
Boeing 757	jet	47.3	38.1	0.805
Boeing 767	jet	48.5	47.6	0.981
Lockheed Tristar L-1011	jet	54.2	47.3	0.873
McDonnell Douglas DC-10	jet	55.5	50.4	0.908
Aero/Boeing Spacelines Guppy	propeller	43.8	47.6	1.087
Douglas DC-4 C-54 Skymaster	propeller	28.6	35.8	1.252
Douglas DC-6	propeller	32.2	35.8	1.112
Lockheed L-188 Electra	propeller	31.8	30.2	0.950
Vickers Viscount	propeller	26.1	28.6	1.096
Antonov An-12	propeller	33.1	38.0	1.148
de Havilland DHC Dash-7	propeller	24.5	28.4	1.159
Lockheed C-130 Hercules/L-100	propeller	34.4	40.4	1.174
British Aerospace 748/ATP	propeller	26.0	30.6	1.177
Convair 240	propeller	24.1	32.1	1.332
Curtiss C-46 Commando	propeller	23.3	32.9	1.412
Douglas DC-3	propeller	19.7	29.0	1.472
Grumman Gulfstream I/I-C	propeller	19.4	23.9	1.232
Ilyushin IL-14	propeller	22.3	31.7	1.422
Martin 4-0-4	propeller	22.8	28.4	1.246
Saab 340	propeller	19.7	21.4	1.086

10. If the ratio is 1, wingspan and body length are equal; if the ratio is greater than 1, wingspan is longer than body length; if the ratio is less than 1, wingspan is shorter than body length.

11. The median for jet planes is 0.902, which means that the body lengths of at least half the jet planes are slightly longer than the wingspans. The median for propeller planes is 1.176, which means that the wingspans of at least half the propeller planes are slightly longer than the body lengths.

	Jet planes	Propeller planes
Minimum	0.792	0.950
Lower quartile	0.837	1.104
Median	0.902	1.176
Upper quartile	0.954	1.292
Maximum	1.061	1.472

12. For propeller planes, the wingspan-to-body-length ratio is generally greater than 1, meaning that wingspan is generally greater than body length. The opposite is true for jet planes; the ratio is generally less than 1, meaning that wingspan is generally less than body length.

Wingspan-to-Body-Length Ratio

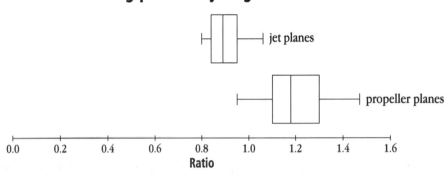

13. Scatter plot A shows the data for Vine Hill raisins; scatter plot B shows the data for Suntime raisins. The number of raisins in a box of Suntime does not exceed 35.

14. This statement is true. In the graphs, the data points for Vine Hill cluster in the interval of 34 to 42 while the data points for Suntime cluster in the interval of 28 to 31.

15. In general, the greater the number of raisins in a box, the greater the number of grams.

Investigation 2

1. This is a convenience sample because Aaron surveyed students who are on two particular sports teams.

2. a. This would be a convenience sample; Aaron's mathematics class is easy for him to survey.

   b. The median number of hours would likely be lower in the mathematics class sample because these students don't necessarily play sports at all.

3. This would be a systematic sample because a rule is being used to choose students.

4. This is a voluntary-response sample because students chose to respond.

Answer Keys

Investigation 3

1. 2 to 9

2. about 75%

3. approximately 50% of the student body, or 500 students, because the median of the sample is 6.5

4. **a.** about 25%   **b.** approximately 25% of the student body, or 250 students

5. Marci could randomly sample 10 business of the 51 who did *not* advertise last year.

6. Marci could randomly sample 10 businesses of the 41 who *did* advertise last year.

7. Marci could randomly sample 10 businesses of the total 92.

8. **a.**

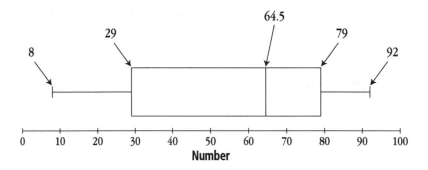

Numbers Generated by One Student

b. Answers will vary; student should show ten box plots of the samples of chosen numbers.

c. Answers will vary. Students should inspect whether most of the boxes on their plots fall in or near the interval of 29 to 79.

9. **a.** The random sample of 50 probably has the best chance of representing all students, though it is a smaller sample than the other two.

   b. Surveying 200 girls and 100 boys may produce a biased sample, depending upon the ratio of boys to girls in the school, and particularly if the survey is on a topic that might generate substantially different responses from boys than from girls. Surveying the first 100 students who enter the building may produce a biased sample, particularly if there is some reason these students are arriving early, such as attending a special meeting before school begins.

Investigation 4

1. **a.** Small pizzas are the least expensive. The median of the small pizzas is the lowest, and at least 75% of the prices are less than 75% of the prices for medium and large pizzas.

   b. The area of this pizza is $\pi r^2 = \pi (4^2) \approx 50.27$ in^2, so the price per square inch is $3.87 \div 50.27 \approx 0.077$ dollars/square inch.

   c. Large pizzas appear to be the best buy. The median for the large pizzas is the lowest, and 50% of the prices for the large pizzas are near or below 75% or more of the prices for the medium and small pizzas.

   d. The second set of box plots is a better reflector of actual price because the size of the pizza—and thus what the customer actually gets for his money—is reflected in the data.

2. a. Below are results from two simulations. In the first, it took 121 random numbers to achieve at least 7 chips per cookie (cookie 8 is the last cookie); in the second, it took 120 random numbers to achieve at least 7 chips per cookie (cookie 10 is the last cookie). Notice that there is a mean of approximately 12 chips per cookie with a range of 7 to 16 chips in both cases.

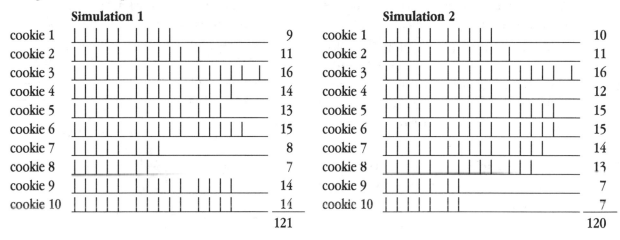

The stem plot below shows the results of five simulations. (Note: You may want to make a class stem plot of all students' data, perhaps including the five values shown here.)

Simulation Results

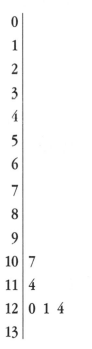

```
 0 |
 1 |
 2 |
 3 |
 4 |
 5 |
 6 |
 7 |
 8 |
 9 |
10 | 7
11 | 4
12 | 0 1 4
13 |
```

b. Answers will vary. Students might decide to add at least as many chips as required in the worst-case batch—the highest number of chips found in the simulation—or to settle for a number that works most of the time (with students defining what "most of the time" means).

Descriptive Glossary

biased sample A sample that does not accurately represent the population. Biased samples can give misleading results. If you wanted to predict how many students in your school recycle their soda cans, surveying only the ecology club would give you a biased sample.

box-and-whiskers plot (or box plot) A display that shows the distribution of values in a data set. A box plot is constructed from the five-number summary of the data. The box plot at the bottom of the page shows the distribution of quality ratings for natural brands of peanut butter.

convenience sample A sample that is selected because it is easy. If you survey everyone on your soccer team who attends tonight's practice, you are surveying a convenience sample.

distribution The arrangement of values in a data set.

five-number summary The minimum value, lower quartile, median, upper quartile, and maximum value for a data set. These five values give a summary of the shape of a distribution. The five-number summary for the quality ratings for regular brands of peanut butter, as seen in the box plot below, is as follows:

minimum value = 11
lower quartile = 31
median = 40
upper quartile = 54
maximum value = 83

histogram A display that shows the distribution of continuous data. The range of data values, divided into intervals, is displayed on the horizontal axis. The height of the bar over each interval indicates the number of data values in that interval. The histogram below shows quality ratings for regular brands of peanut butter. The height of the bar over the interval from 20 to 30 is 4. This indicates that four brands of peanut butter have quality ratings between 20 and 30.

Quality of Regular Brands

population The entire collection of people or objects under study.

**Box-and-Whiskers Plot
with Five-Number Summary**

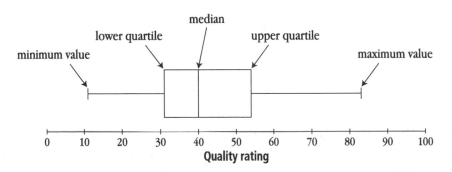

random sample A sample chosen in a way that gives every member of a population an equally likely chance of being selected.

representative sample A sample that accurately represents a population.

sample A group of people or objects selected from a population. You can study a large population by collecting data from a sample. You can make predictions or draw conclusions about the entire population based on data from the sample.

scatter plot A graph used to explore the relationship between two variables. The graph below is a scatter plot of (length, wingspan) data for several airplanes. Each point represents the length and wingspan for one airplane.

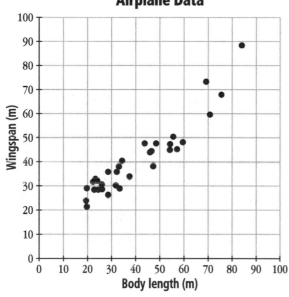

Airplane Data

stem-and-leaf plot (or stem plot) A display that shows the distribution of values in a data set. Unlike a box plot or a histogram, a stem plot allows you to see the individual values in the data set. The stem plot below shows the distribution of quality ratings for regular brands of peanut butter. In this plot, the stems are a vertical list of the tens digits of the ratings. Attached to each stem are the corresponding leaves, in this case the ones digits. The leaves 3, 3, 6, and 9 next to the stem 2 indicate that the data set includes the values 23, 23, 26, and 29.

Quality Ratings of Regular Brands

```
0 |
1 | 1
2 | 3 3 6 9
3 | 1 1 3 4 4 5
4 | 0 0 3 5 6 9
5 | 4 4
6 | 0
7 | 6
8 | 3 3
9 |
```

Key
2 | 6 means 26.

systematic sample A sample selected in a methodical way. If you survey every tenth person on an alphabetical list of names, you are surveying a systematic sample.

voluntary-response sample A sample that selects itself. If you put an ad in the school paper asking for volunteers to take a survey, the students who respond will be a voluntary-response sample.

distribución La disposición de valores en un conjunto de datos.

gráfica de dispersión Una gráfica usada para explorar la relación entre dos variables. La siguiente es una gráfica de dispersión de datos (longitud, envergadura) para varios aviones. Cada punto representa la longitud y la envergadura de un avión.

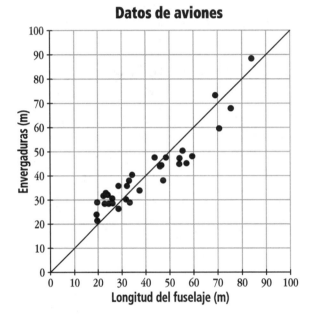

Datos de aviones

histograma Una representación que muestra la distribución de datos continuos. La gama de valores de los datos, dividida en intervalos, se representa en el eje horizontal. La altura de la barra sobre cada intervalo indica el número de valores de datos de ese intervalo. El siguiente histograma representa la calificación por calidad de las marcas de mantequilla de maní común. La altura de la barra sobre el intervalo de 20 a 30 es 4. Esto indica que hay 4 marcas de mantequilla de maní que tienen una calificación entre 20 y 30.

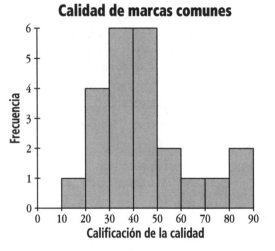

Calidad de marcas comunes

gráfica de frecuencias acumuladas Una representación que muestra la distribución de valores de un conjunto de datos. Una gráfica de frecuencias se construye con el resumen de cinco números del conjunto de datos. La gráfica de frecuencias siguiente representa la distribución de las calificaciones según la calidad de distintas marcas de mantequillas de maní natural.

muestra Un grupo de persona u objetos seleccionados de una población. Puedes estudiar una población grande juntando datos de una muestra. Puedes hacer predicciones o sacar conclusiones sobre la población entera basándote en los datos de la muestra.

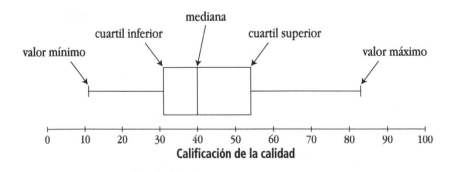

muestra aleatoria Una muestra elegida de una manera que permite que cada miembro de la población tenga la misma posibilidad de ser elegido.

muestra de conveniencia Una muestra seleccionada porque es conveniente. Si entrevistaras a todos los componentes de tu equipo de fútbol que asistan a la práctica esta noche, estarás encuestando una muestra de conveniencia.

muestra de respuestas voluntarias Una muestra que se selecciona a sí misma. Si pones un anuncio en el periódico escolar pidiendo voluntarios para participar en una encuesta, los estudiantes que respondan serán una muestra de respuestas voluntarias.

muestra representativa Una muestra que representa una población con exactitud.

muestra sesgada Una muestra que no representa con exactitud la población. Las muestras sesgadas pueden dar resultados erróneos. Si quisieras predecir cuántos estudiantes de tu escuela reciclan sus latas de refrescos, llevar a cabo una encuesta solamente en el club de ecología daría una muestra sesgada.

muestra sistemática Una muestra seleccionada de una manera metódica. Si entrevistaras a cada décima persona en una lista de nombres ordenados por orden alfabético, estarías encuestando una muestra sistemática.

población Un conjunto entero de persona u objetos en estudio.

resumen de cinco números El valor mínimo, el cuartil inferior, la mediana, el cuartil superior y el valor máximo de un conjunto de datos. Estos cinco valores dan un resumen de la forma de una distribución. El resumen de cinco números para la calificación según la calidad de las marcas de mantequilla de maní común es el siguiente:

valor mínimo = 11
cuartil inferior = 31
mediana = 40
cuartil superior = 54
valor máximo = 83

tabla arborescente Una representación que muestra la distribución de valores en un conjunto de datos. A diferencia de una gráfica de frecuencias acumuladas o un histograma, una tabla arborescente permite que veas los valores individuales de un conjunto de datos. La tabla arborescente siguiente representa la distribución de la calificación según la calidad de las marcas de mantequilla de maní común. En esta tabla, los tallos son una lista vertical de los dígitos de las decenas de las calificaciones. Añadidas a cada tallo están las hojas correspondientes, en este caso, los dígitos de las unidades. Las hojas 3, 3, 6 y 9 al lado del tallo 2 indican que el conjunto de datos incluye los valores 23, 23, 26 y 29.

Calificación por calidad de las marcas comunes

```
0 |
1 | 1
2 | 3 3 6 9
3 | 1 1 3 4 4 5
4 | 0 0 3 5 6 9
5 | 4 4
6 | 0
7 | 6
8 | 3 3
9 |
```

Clave
2 | 6 significa 26.

Index

Index

Index

Sample, 25, 148
  accuracy of, 4, 36f, 41–42, 48f–48h
  biased, 28, 36d, 48b, 147
  convenience, 27–28, 36b–36d, 147
  estimating a population with, 48j, 49–54, 62a–62f
  random, 36f, 37–42, 48a–48h, 148
  representative, 25, 36b, 48b, 148
  selecting, 26–28, 36b–36d, 36f, 38–40, 48a–48e
  size, 4, 36f, 41–42, 48f–48i
  systematic, 27–28, 36b–36d, 148
  voluntary-response, 27–28, 36b–36d, 148
Sampling methods, 1b, 4, 23v, 24–30, 36a–36e
  ACE, 31–35
Sampling plan, 26, 36a–36b
  random, 37, 48a
Scatter plot, 4, 4b, 13–14, 23n–23o
  ACE, 15–22
  displayed on a graphing calculator, 1g–1i
Simulation, 48j, 52–54, 62b–62f
Spinners, 126–127
Statistics, 1a
Statistics Workshop, software, 1f, 23i
Stem-and-leaf plot, 1b, 23c–23e, 32, 148
Survey
  ACE, 15–22, 31–35
  comparing data sets from, 4b, 5–14, 23a–23o
  conducting, 23v, 24–30, 36a–36e
  selecting a sample population, 26–28, 36b–36d
  writing questions for, 4, 29–30, 36d–36e
Systematic sample, 27–28, 36b–36d, 148

Technology, 1d–1l
  box-and-whiskers plot on a graphing calculator,
      1e–1g, 23i–23j
  box-and-whiskers plot with statistics software, 23m
  calculating summary statistics on a graphing
      calculator, 1g, 1l
  entering data on a graphing calculator, 1d–1e
  entering a formula as a list, 1k
  graphing calculator selection, 1d
  histogram on a graphing calculator, 1j
  scatter plot on a graphing calculator, 1g–1i

Transparencies, 103–122

Unit Project, 63–66
  assessment guide for, 86–90
  assigning, 63–66
  Estimating Populations, 65–66
  Safe Water and Life Expectancy, 63–64
  scoring rubric, 90
Upper quartile, 8, 23e–23n

Vocabulary, 1p
Voluntary-response sample, 27–28, 36b–36d, 148